MASTERING MY *messy* LIFE

My journey from chaos to clarity

STEPH PASE

PENGUIN BOOKS

UK | USA | Canada | Ireland | Australia
India | New Zealand | South Africa | China

Penguin Books is part of the Penguin Random House group of companies
whose addresses can be found at global.penguinrandomhouse.com

First published by Penguin Books in 2025

Cover design by Christa Moffitt, Christabella Designs
© Penguin Random House Australia Pty Ltd
Typeset in ITC Berkeley Oldstyle by Midland Typesetters, Australia

Printed and bound in Australia by Griffin Press, an accredited
ISO AS/NZ 14001 Environmental Management Systems printer.

A catalogue record for this
book is available from the
National Library of Australia

ISBN 978 1 76134 925 6

*We at Penguin Random House Australia acknowledge that Aboriginal and Torres Strait Islander
peoples are the Traditional Custodians and the first storytellers of the lands on which we live and work.
We honour Aboriginal and Torres Strait Islander peoples' continuous connection to Country, waters,
skies and communities. We celebrate Aboriginal and Torres Strait Islander stories, traditions and
living cultures; and we pay our respects to Elders past and present.*

For Ady, my greatest teacher.
For Nan, my home in human form.
For Dad, fly high in the mountains.
To Ryan and my girls, my favourite chapters yet.
And to Chris Hemsworth, for simply existing . . .

Contents

Introduction

Steph the Mess

You know that moment at 3 a.m. when the nightclub lights flicker on and all is revealed? Your Maybelline Mousse has melted, and one chicken fillet boob has bailed and is now lounging near the couple making out in the corner. Heels in one hand, dignity in the other, you're praying that whatever's stuck to your foot is just a tiny balloon. Or, best case, that little blue plastic ring from a Coke lid. All you want is a dirty kebab and your bed. You look around and think, *What the hell just happened?*

That's this book.

That's my life.

And that's me – a fucking mess. (Excuse the French but you best get used to it.)

These days, I've upgraded from sticky floors to sticky fingers. (Kids', not mine.) I'm in bed by 8 p.m. – if said kids let me, that is. But hey, that's life, right? Sticky, unpredictable, a little gross, and somehow still filled with the best moments.

I'm Steph Pase. Steph the Mess. Or *Just Another Mummy Blog* if you've followed me online. You might have picked up this book because you know me from social media, or from my stationery brand, Steph Pase Planners. Or maybe you thought, *This chick's gonna fix my life.*

Well, yes and no.

If you've ever felt like everyone else got a life manual and yours came from Temu and smells funny – you're in the right place. I'm not here to hand you a five-step formula or tell you to skol celery juice. (Also, ew.) I *am* going to overshare how I grew up amid chaos, thought my brain was broken and couldn't catch a ball to save my life (or my face for that matter) . . . only to go on to become the CEO of a stationery and lifestyle business that started in my garage and now sells over 40,000 planners a year. And yet, I still forget what day it is. Yes. Dated. The irony isn't lost on me.

It all started about a decade ago when I was a twenty-five-year-old 'newborn adult' holding an actual newborn (mine, by the way). I was drowning in postnatal depression, and desperate for connection. I began creating life hacks that worked for my messy mind and shared them online; even the parts that made my hands shake as I typed confessions into my captions. I wrote about how I felt broken and different, messy and lonely. Little did I know how many women would reply, 'Me too'. I had no idea it would grow into all *this*.

I won't pretend that I made some elaborate five-year plan on a whiteboard. Although that sounds very on-brand now, but no. The truth is I had every reason *not* to be a success story. Like so many of us, I was born into mess. A home where the soundtrack was shouting, tension was part of the furniture, boundaries were myths, and shit was on the walls. Literal shit. Sadly, that's no metaphor. I know it could've been worse. I've *seen* worse. I'm not ungrateful for what I had. But I won't lie and pretend my upbringing was normal – whatever that means.

I spent the next thirty-something years trying to make sense of the mess. I created routines and systems that made life feel lighter – not Pinterest-perfect, but realistic. Somehow it turned into a real business helping real humans. With real hacks that work and real products that people want to buy. I still find it surreal. All of this was built, not in spite of who I am – but *because* of it – even though it'd take decades for me to figure that out and accept it. That's why this book is twenty-odd chapters and not one short essay. Though let's be real, it'd make a great ten-part romantasy series if I added dragons.

This isn't just another influencer or entrepreneur memoir. It's a human one. Tangents guaranteed. You might think you know me from socials, but this book tells the story behind the captions – the mess behind the magic. It's about a girl who always felt the world spun too fast, and who didn't have a voice growing up. How she shared her life online thinking no one would care – only to end up helping hundreds of thousands of people turn their chaos into clarity. All while still managing to lose her phone in the fridge, regularly.

This book is for you if:

- You've always felt like the black sheep.
- You've tried to get your life together, but it lasts three business days (if you're lucky).
- You feel too much – or not enough.
- You secretly believe you could do something amazing . . . if you could just get out of your head and out of your own way.
- You feel like the world spins too fast.
- You're burnt-out from being 'on' all the time.

Mastering My Messy Life is a love letter to anyone who has ever felt like they were too much, or not enough, or somehow both at once. To those scrolling past 'picture-perfect' strangers online, wondering how they seem effortlessly 'together' while you're falling apart. I'm here to show how you can be successful – your own version of success – without cramming yourself into a box. (Or having all your cereal beautifully labelled in storage jars – although that is my version of porn.) But you do you.

This is not a 'how I got my act together' story.

It's a 'how I turned my mess into magic' story.

Writing this book made me face every part of myself I'd shoved behind the shower curtain (this reference will make sense soon – promise). This book is a bit messy – but not accidentally. I didn't wing it. I wrestled with it, cried and had an offensively high Uber Eats bill while writing it. You might find it helpful or even inspiring. More than anything, I hope it makes you feel *seen* to your core. I'm not here to fix you. I'm here to sit next to you, braless, barefaced, elbows deep in the laundry piles of 'shoulds' and 'coulds'. Maybe your mess doesn't look like mine. Or maybe it does. Maybe it's hidden behind a functioning job, a full fridge, a fake smile.

But it's still there. And you're still tired from carrying it.

The good news is the mess was never your weakness.

It was your magic all along.

Steph xx

Chapter 1

Where the chaos began

I'm going to die.

Not today, obviously – I'm in the middle of writing a book – but this was always my overriding thought. The soundtrack of my existence. Not in a dramatic way, just in a 'Hey, don't forget' kinda way. I can't remember life without anxiety. That constant hammering in my chest; carrying around a silent storm no one else could see; the unshakeable feeling that something dreadful was about to happen. To this day, I'm still unsure if it's my brain or body signalling we're about to be eaten by a tiger, not standing in the middle of Kmart agonising over whether to buy the pink or white spatula. Sure, a somewhat stressful situation, but hardly life-threatening. On the bright side, when it comes time to meet my fate, I'll be cool as a cucumber – I'm well-practised.

I was always at war with myself – even before I had the words to describe it. Every thought, doubt and fear lined up like faceless soldiers, ready to fire. It was a battle I was always destined to lose. From the outside, I looked like any other kid: shy, a little messy, but nothing out of the ordinary. But inside the war raged on. I remember being in kindergarten – the first year of school in Australia – and worrying about going into Year 6, the *final year* of primary school. Five-year-old me was stressing about something five years away. Totally normal, right? Consuming my every thought. Just like death. You know . . . regular kid stuff. *I'm just not ready yet*, I'd think, sweaty palms gripping the edges of my kindy desk, the familiar sensation taking over my body like an old friend whom I'd known my whole life, despite my age.

Looking back, Hesitation was my middle name (it's actually Ann, token 90s Aussie middle name). I thought everyone was like me until I realised they weren't. I thought I was 'broken'. Who knows if it was nature or nurture? Probably both.

My mum has struggled with her mental health her whole life. When she was thirteen, my grandfather (her dad) committed suicide in the family home. My mum and grandmother found him. When I was younger, they told me he'd died from 'being sick', but as a teenager, they told me the truth after finding out what I was doing to myself. I'll save that for another chapter; it's only our first date and I need to ease you in gently.

Despite this heartache, my mum's mother – Nan – was a glass-half-full person (actually, she was a grateful-to-have-a-glass-in-the-first-place person). But the trauma had the opposite effect on my mum. She went on to have two children – my brother and then me – but was inconsistent in her love, to say the least. My brother, Adam, or 'Ady', is non-verbal and has Down syndrome and autism. When he was born the doctors didn't think he'd live past the age of two. Then there was Dad, who was wrapped up in the struggle of providing and caring for my brother, so his presence wasn't often felt – for good reason.

In our house, every day meant walking on eggshells. The saving grace was Nan, who'd moved in with my parents before Ady and I were born. She was my mother figure and my home in human form, her bedroom my safe zone; the sheltered harbour in the midst of the storms. Let's just say our household was a *lot*. Situations others would never fathom became our normal (shit on the walls ring a bell?). Now that I'm a mother myself, I can see they were anything but normal. Now when I watch my daughters playing, I often think, *Wow, their greatest worry is whether they can find their sparkly sandal.*

You know how some kids have invisible friends? Well, my friend was named Anxiety. She'd accompanied me everywhere I went ever since I could remember. Playing in the sprinklers on a scorching hot day? There she was hanging by the tap, reminding me that I could drown, slip, fall or, worse, Ady could get hurt.

When Nan and I were alone, another invisible friend would sometimes appear. Her name was Presence. I liked her. When Presence showed up, time would slow and the noise would quieten. I could take a big breath. But her visits were so rare I sometimes wondered if I'd imagined her. Presence was the friend I longed for, but Anxiety was the one who always stayed.

I went to a public school on the South Coast of New South Wales, a couple of hours from Sydney. I had a few real friends who I could be myself with, but I often felt like I existed on the outskirts. *Nobody likes you*, Anxiety would whisper in my ear. *I know*, I'd whisper back. It'd take me decades to learn to hit the mute button on my inner critic. Frankly, I was an arsehole to myself – something we can all be guilty of – but compared to the external voices I grew up with my inner voices were soft. By the time I was five, I'd been called names I can't bring myself to write.

They didn't come from playground bullies. They came from home. From someone who was meant to love me. The worst part? I believed it. I thought it was normal. That's why I hated the sound of the school bell: it meant going home to a house that didn't just hold us – it held the words and actions that scar me to this day.

So what was school like? What was *I* like?

Picture a typical Aussie suburban primary school. Wire fences so hot you could cook Nan's French toast on them (with tomato sauce, obviously – told you I was broken). In the middle of a once-green oval, a soccer game is in full swing. A sun-kissed, six-year-old girl races across the field like the next . . . *insert famous athlete here.* (What? I don't follow sports.) Her slim yet powerful leg kicks the ball into the air towards the 'gravel pit' aka the play-ground (our school didn't have a budget for fun). The ball stops abruptly, thanks to the head of another girl sporting a mousy-brown, home-job bowl cut and a fringe three inches too high above her thick dark brown eyebrows. Who is this beautiful specimen you may ask? Well, that's me. Steph. Or, as Dad liked to call me, 'The Steph' because there's only one like me – thank fuck for that.

Yep. I was one of those kids with zero spatial awareness who always got hit in the head. And the kicker? (Pun intended.) I was never even playing. It was like I had a tattoo on my forehead just under my Lord Farquaad fringe that said, 'Aim here and ask me about my "weird" brother while you're at it'. Mum said she cut my fringe extra short so she wouldn't have to do it all that often. Let's just say it didn't help me fit in with the cool kids.

My friends seemed to move through life so easily, like the world was made for them. I wanted to join them so badly, and on the surface I did. I ran when they ran, laughed when they laughed, and played along just enough to blend in. Separate. I was always separate. It was as though I was acting, wearing a mask. Like I was following a script and playing a character; a role I didn't fully understand.

Except for at home; I knew my lines there.

As you've probably gathered, I wasn't exactly a star athlete. But what about in the classroom? You can't be bad at everything, right? Wrong. I was the exception – I managed to be thoroughly average at *everything*. Unless I really liked something. Then I'd become obsessed, dive in headfirst, become an expert, excel for a while . . . and then ditch it the moment boredom set in. Honestly, not much has changed. I'm typing this next to a Paint By Numbers kit I haven't touched in a year. Think of it as the 'fuck boy approach' to hobbies – intense interest, fleeting commitment. But hey, at least I didn't leave a trail of heartbreak and unread DMs in my wake . . . yet. (That was sarcasm by the way – my first language.) In class, I flew under the radar, unless I was getting in trouble for not listening, which was almost as often as the times I got hit in the head with flying objects. So yeah, a lot.

At home I tried my best to be invisible too – recite my lines, play my part, hide out with Nan and go to bed early. Self-sufficiency was valued there. There were other people who needed more help than me – and I couldn't forget it. I didn't want to be selfish or take up space. Although I tried to fade into the background like a piece of furniture, it didn't stop my invisible friends from rocking up. Hello, Chaos – my second unwanted friend and the unofficial owner of our house. Like Anxiety, Chaos followed me everywhere I went. We were the three amigos: Anxiety, Chaos and I. Lucky me. Chaos wasn't just a visitor – she was the foundation on which our house was built. She seeped through every crack and corner, filled every room, sat at every meal and tagged along to every 'family day', which was often a medical appointment for Ady. We should've had a loyalty card – every five appointments you get a free, sticky magazine a kid's spewed on.

No matter where we went, Chaos came too, and she was always on her absolute worst behaviour. She followed me as I walked out the door, clinging to my skin like an expired perfume. (Britney Spears' Fantasy to be exact.) For a long time, I didn't know how to wash it off, or even if I could. So I stopped trying. That's the thing about chaos – when you're born into it, it's hard to imagine life could ever be any different. They say home is where the heart is. For me it was where the yelling was. Where tension hung like photo frames, and the pantry was always bare – confusing because we weren't exactly poor. If home shapes who you are, then mine sculpted me in chaos, wrapped me in contradictions, and left me with plenty of stories to tell, and plenty I'd rather forget.

Childhood memories? Here's one. It was just another muggy afternoon and I was walking home from school. We lived in a cul-de-sac, Meadow Lane, with nearly thirty other kids – full *Brady Bunch* vibes. There were cricket bats scattered across the lawns, kids running around in dirt-black socks – not glued to phones like they were laced with crack. I loved it – our street that is, not crack. Besides Nan's bedroom, this was my escape. These kids were my unofficial adopted siblings, just like my cousins. They made my childhood, well, childlike. Shockingly, I played cricket here. Yes, my batting stance screamed constipated wizard mid-spell, but hey, I felt comfortable. Whenever the street lights came on, my heart would sink – that was the signal to go home. Kinda like the school bell.

On this particular day, I felt it as soon as I walked in the front door.

Something had happened . . . again.

'Are you happy now?' Mum erupted. 'Your brother drank bleach!' Yes, that wasn't a typo . . . *bleach*. The same stuff you use to clean your husband's skiddies off the toilet. And don't be shocked if you find some in this book (typos, not skiddies, that is). 'He's going to *die!*' The words hit me with a thump, and my heart raced as I tried to make sense of what she was saying. *Shit, is he okay?* I thought, but I just stood there, mute. What was I supposed to say? 'Sorry I wasn't home to stop my brother from drinking cleaning products'?

Our home wasn't small but, in these moments, the walls seemed to close in. And it wasn't unusual for these sorts of storms to erupt. Neighbours would hear and check on me from time to time. But I always covered up the chaos . . .

Adam. Bleach. Dying.

Mum stood in the entryway, one hand gripping the banister like it was the only thing holding her up. 'Are you happy now?' she yelled again, her eyes locked on mine.

My memory of what happened next is a little hazy, but I'll never forget the feelings of guilt and shame. I was just a teenager and didn't understand our family dynamic. I'm an adult now and I *still* don't understand it. Back then all I knew was how to create custom ringtones on my Nokia 3315 and how to be a LimeWire pirate (which always gave our family PC viruses, but, hey, at least I got Xtina's new single). So of course I blamed myself. It didn't matter that Ady was okay in the end. Or that I wasn't even in the house when it happened. *Steph, this is all your fault*, Anxiety told me. I blamed myself not just for that day, but for all of it. My mum needed someone to carry her frustration and I was the easiest target. Adam couldn't. Dad already carried it in his own way and Nan didn't put up with shit. So there was just me.

'You alright, love?' Nan whispered, crouched over my bedside once the incident was over.

I nodded. I always nodded.

'Good girl. Don't listen to it, okay?' she said, stroking my hair like I'd done something brave.

But I did listen. And I quickly learnt the best thing I could do in those situations was to try to be invisible. I saw how much Ady needed, and what happened when Mum needed more than anyone could give. So I decided not to need anything at all. Kept quiet, didn't take up space. Like I was taught. Be a good girl. Be the 'easy one'. Hoping that would be enough to keep the peace. And it did, to an extent. Hers – but not mine. Heartbreakingly ironic, isn't it? How one child couldn't speak and the other wouldn't.

I felt bad for Mum, knowing what I do now as an adult. As a daughter, I forgave her. As a mother, I could never forget. Mum didn't know how to carry the load, so she passed it on. And I took it, clinging to the rare, tender moments that we shared. I basked in them like the sun after a long winter – a version of her I caught a glimpse of now and then. A version I kept chasing, but could never quite catch.

For years, I believed it was my fault. I carried the weight like a second skin, not realising it didn't belong to me. I blamed myself for the conflict, the anxiety and the sadness. I blamed myself for Ady's 'incidents', even when I wasn't even at home to stop them. I blamed myself for feeling anything, when I couldn't cope with the weight that landed on my scrawny, unsteady shoulders. Ady was eighteen months older than me, but in moments like this it never felt that way. His silence made him fragile, and mine to protect.

In case you're wondering, my brother didn't die from drinking bleach that day, but I'm sure it gave him a decent internal clean out. (There's that sarcasm again.)

A SURVIVAL GUIDE FOR YOUNGER ME

1. There are no monsters under the bed, so stop doing long jumps to get into bed. Chill.
2. When Nan's away, stay at a friend's house.
3. Mum never finds out the 'lamp trick'. (Holding the lightbulb to your forehead to fake a fever to skip school and hang with Nan.) Keep doing it. Geography was overrated anyway. We've got Google Maps now.
4. The mean kids at school have shit going on at home. Don't take it personally. Hurt people hurt people.
5. You'll still get hit in the head with the ball when you drop your future kids off at school. Sorry.
6. You're not 'athletic', but one day moving your body will become your medicine and keep Anxiety at bay.
7. It wasn't your fault.

Chapter 2

The R word

I always thought Santa was an arsehole.

Yep, the fat man in the red suit who is meant to bring joy to children all over the world played bloody mind games with me. Before you ask, no, it wasn't some religious thing, and I'm not the Grinch (ask my husband, on whom I force matching PJs every December). My family *did* celebrate Christmas. Dad was always up early with Ady, but Christmas Day – like every day – began and ended with Nan. It started at 6 a.m. and she never turned me away. But after that, I'd be perched on the couch, gazing out the window at my friends playing on their new bikes, PJs still on, already knee-deep in the magic.

Look, I'm not blaming Santa for the fact my Christmas mornings generally sucked balls, but I did have a couple of issues with him. Each year, I'd write asking for one thing and one thing only: *Please let my brother talk.* I didn't wish for toys, a new bike or even a Tamagotchi (and those things were sick). I just wanted Ady to speak. I mean, if this random guy with his sleigh and reindeers could fly around the world, I wasn't asking for much, right?

Maybe my letters got lost. But year after year, every time I blew out my birthday candles . . . there was nothing. Mum even sent my letters to the newspaper where she worked because apparently *they* sent them on to Santa . . . 'cause that makes sense. One year, a journo came to our house. Big cameras flashing and a front-page article about my letter. They gushed over how 'beautiful' it was. Eight-year-old me didn't think it was beautiful. I thought it was heartbreaking.

I didn't want a headline.

I wanted my brother to say my name.

Something even *more* heartbreaking? Ady *used* to say my name. Yep, there was a time he could talk. He called me 'Baba'. As a toddler, my brother spoke, and pretty well apparently, up until about the age of three. But I don't really remember it and still can't bring myself to watch our old family videos. Sometimes I think how different life might've been if Ady didn't have autism. To have had a brother who could look over after a storm and say, 'I know, sis. I know'. Maybe as he got older he could have protected me like Nan did. He would have been my knight in shining armour, but it doesn't change the fact that he is my hero. I was just lonely, I think.

On the bright side, there are two words Ady *can* say: 'chips' and 'Coke'. Honestly, what do you expect? If a non-verbal boy is going to say anything, of course it's going to be something from the McDonald's menu. You may be wondering how I can joke about this. Well, it's how I cope. And sadly, as life went on, the 'funnier' I became.

Everyone in our family went to sign language lessons. I still use it to this day but, to be honest, only the signs for 'toilet', 'drink', 'eat' and 'finished' (Ady's stomach is a bottomless pit and I need to tell him he's been cut off). Oh, and 'thank you', because, well, manners.

Stuff happened every day to remind me our family was different. When we went anywhere, people's heads snapped in our direction, like we were the bloody Kardashians (minus the bank accounts . . . and the butts). As Ady got older, he became a three year old stuck in the body of a teenager. Sometimes when we were out, he would plonk himself in the middle of the road and not move. Cars racing towards us, Dad would use all his might to pull Ady up, sweat dripping down his face.

Another reminder were the locks. Everywhere. On every door, cupboard and drawer. Because besides being a human boulder, Ady had other talents, one being an escape artist. One minute he'd be watching *The Wiggles*, the next, he was in the neighbour's pool after yanking off the gate like it was made of spaghetti. That same neighbour's daughter once stepped out of the bathroom, towel around her, only to find Ady chilling in her hallway like it was his house. Scared the shit out of her. Poor Lauren.

Our Houdini was even more stealthy on holidays. One summer, we were setting up camp at a caravan park when we heard a scream. We turned – and Ady was gone.

'Where's Adam?' Mum shouted, already knowing the answer.

'Shit,' Dad muttered and bolted.

Minutes later, we found him standing in a stranger's kitchen like he lived there, bread in one hand, Ernie in the other. The people didn't seem to mind. I often wondered if Ady didn't *look* like he had a disability, would they have been so understanding? I guess we were lucky. His appearance protected him. Not everyone in Ady's shoes gets the same treatment. And not every moment was dramatic. Sometimes the reminders were quiet, but they still stung.

'Stephhhh, you left your door unlocked again!' My heart skipped a beat as I heard Mum yelling from upstairs.

'Ady, nooooo,' I said, sprinting to the stairs. I was in high school and already struggling. I had stayed up all night to finish an assignment – and had just made it. But in my exhausted state, I'd made a simple but catastrophic error: I'd forgotten to barricade my assignment in. 'No, no, no, nooooo,' I groaned as I entered my room. My homework had been turned into confetti, minus the celebration. Turns out the fall of the Roman Empire happened again – this time in my bedroom. Julius Caesar wasn't the only one betrayed that day. This wasn't the first time that this had happened. Teachers always gave me a hard time about it; apparently 'my brother ate my homework' didn't fly.

'Well, what do you expect?' Mum shook her head. 'How hard is it to lock your room? You're always forgetting things, Steph.'

It's not my fau— I wanted to protest, but I stopped myself. *Shut up. Suck it up.*

Sadly this wasn't the first time Ady decided to 'redecorate with destruction'. When I was fifteen, I saved for *weeks* to buy my first top from Supré. It was black with lace trim – think Paris Hilton from *The Simple Life* era. I raced home, tried it on and for the first time felt . . . decent. Less awkward. Which was a nice change. I planned to wear it that weekend to the movies with some friends.

Two days later, I came home from school and there was my brand-new top – ripped in half on my bedroom floor. I burst into tears. Not because I was angry at Ady, but because I was sad. He wasn't trying to ruin my top: he saw the tag, which he hated, and tried to remove it for me. He was trying to help.

I went down to Nan in tears. 'I swear I locked the door,' I said.

'I know, sweetheart. I believe you.'

I couldn't be angry at Ady, so I turned it inwards. Guilt. Sadness. Shame. And a shitty ripped top. As soon as you laid eyes on my brother's angelic face, you couldn't help forgiving him. After his meltdowns, I would always comfort him – maybe I needed a hug too. I learnt to push the emotions deep inside, and often wondered if one day I might explode. Just like when you're a mum and your kids drive you insane, but you filter your emotions for them. This was something I had learnt from Nan.

Besides Ady being a homework-hating Houdini, he's also a human vacuum. Doctors think he doesn't realise when he's full, meaning he'll eat until he's sick – hence why even our fridge had a lock on it. Ady can skol a beer faster than any frat boy – which is saying something – and was the first person to spew at my eighteenth (food not beer). You're probably reading this thinking, *What about all the locks?* Well, there were five people in our house and it wasn't possible to keep it constantly secure like Gringotts Wizarding Bank. Ady had us all fooled.

So what did my brother do for fun besides escape, eat and destroy people's pool fences (and homework)? He loved the water. Watching him swim is like watching someone arrive back home after being away for months. He seems peaceful and free of whatever restrains his mind and body. Ady lived in our pool. A couple of times Dad tried to get him out for dinner and Ady pulled him in – business suit, shoes and all. Poor Dad, just another Tuesday.

When Ady and I were toddlers we were at a similar stage mentally, so we played together. But as we got older, it became harder. Ady lives in his own world, and depending on his medication, he can drift further away from earth. It often felt like he wasn't on our planet at all, but out in space somewhere, floating around in his own solar system – with Bert and Ernie. All I wanted to do was jump on a spaceship and try to reach him, but I never could.

My brother has his own distinct sounds – like a ghost after a few too many cocktails. Once, when we were kids, we went on a tour of the Jenolan Caves. As we were walking through the darkness with the other tourists, Ady started making his sounds: '*OOOOOOOooooo.*' A bunch of teenage girls started screaming like Freddy Krueger had decided to tag along.

'It's just my brother, Adam!' I shouted, trying to reassure them.

Back home, I'd often find Ady sitting in the lounge room humming as he held Ernie. It was his soundtrack. The sound was comforting, although it sometimes drove me mad – especially at 2 a.m. In hindsight, I wonder if he sensed the chaos in our house and hummed to drown it out. His way of meditating, maybe. Most of the time though, unlike the rest of us, Ady seemed untouched by the storms. I preferred it that way – for his sake.

•

'What do you mean, your brother *can talk*?' I asked Ashleigh, my new preschool friend. I had just met her brother and the crazy fucker was talking. But as soon as the words left my mouth, I knew I'd said something wrong.

'Yes, he can talk,' Ashleigh replied with a confused giggle. 'Why? Can't *your* brother?' Her tone wasn't menacing – it was more curious – but her words felt threatening all the same.

'Well, he just can't . . .' I shrugged my shoulders and put a protective arm around Ady. He went to the same preschool as me – the only time we'd ever get to attend the same school, before he moved to a special needs one. I was four and had just discovered that other people's brothers could, in fact, talk. Mind blown. I thought it was common knowledge that brothers *couldn't* speak. Up till then, I hadn't played with many other children besides Ady and my cousins. I'd seen boys talking at the shops, but I assumed they couldn't possibly be brothers. Brothers didn't talk. As I write this, I know it makes zero sense, but neither does a fat dude with a beard who buys other kids bikes, but never replies to my letters. Rude. As a four year old, a nonverbal big brother was all I knew.

That night I went home not thinking about the painting I did or the lollies I scored, but about my brother – and how much I wished we could be like the other kids. Jealousy was something I typically didn't feel. But I'll never forget sitting cross-legged at my neighbour's house one day, listening to my friend argue with her brother over the TV remote. They were yelling, calling each other names – full sibling chaos. I just sat there watching *The Saddle Club*, but I wasn't taking it in. All I could think was, *I'd give anything to fight with my brother like that.* To be able to yell, have him yell back, say things we didn't mean and roll our eyes at each other. Then share a bowl of hot chips. I wanted that so badly. But it was never going to be us.

On the weekend, Ady often went out with other kids with a disability to give the families a break. I sometimes went too. I liked helping out, especially when they went horse riding. I didn't understand my feelings back then but I felt happy, sad and angry all at once. I loved watching those kids having fun, but I was sad and angry that they had to live their lives this way. You learn a lot being the sibling of a person with a disability, including patience and understanding, but also other stuff you might not expect. For example, I became an expert negotiator. The bribe was always Coke, a swim or food.

Once I got to high school, friends started wanting to come round to our place, and I wanted them to, despite Anxiety and Chaos, but there were two problems. For one, I was rarely allowed friends over. And for two, and I don't know how else to put it, but Ady got naked all the time, which isn't something a teenage girl expects to see when she goes to a friend's house – their brother's dick.

My friends-over disclaimer went something like this: 'Umm, just so you know, my brother likes to get . . . naked, so there *is* a chance that will happen. There might be some yelling too so I'm sorry if that happens. And there's not much food, but Nan will take us to get hot chips. Or maybe you could bring some snacks . . .'

Unsurprisingly, only a handful of friends ever came over. Ninety per cent of the time, they were great with Ads – a bit nervous and awkward at first, which is to be expected when you've never met someone with a disability before – but they acknowledged him, said hello and goodbye, and were friendly and inclusive. But on some occasions, kids acted like he wasn't there, were disrespectful even. Humans can suck when they're outside their comfort zone. One of my teenage 'boyfriends' (we lasted two weeks, hence the quotation marks) didn't bother looking at Ady or saying hi. Major red flag. I broke up with him the next day. I wouldn't stand up for myself, but if anyone messed with my brother this whole other Steph would appear.

While most people accepted Ady, I soon learnt that some kids can be very cruel.

'Say hi to your *retarded* brother for me.'

I had that familiar sick feeling as soon as I heard the 'R word'. I'd just hopped off the school bus at the bottom of Meadow Lane.

Across the street were two boys, laughing like they'd just said something original.

'Don't talk about my brother like that!' I yelled, standing my ground, not knowing if this was the dumbest idea ever. I wish I had the foresight to arm myself with a decent comeback. Something like 'How's your single pube going, arsewipe?' would have done the trick. Brief yet devastating. One I would think of three years later mid-shower – not speaking from experience or anything.

One of the boys walked across the street, smirking. 'Well he *is* a fucking retard.'

'Get lost!' I cried.

The next thing I knew the boy had grabbed my backpack and pushed me to the ground. A sharp pain radiated from my shoulder and the side of my head.

'Stop it!' I screamed.

He kicked me, but then his mate with quarter of a brain said, 'Let's go, we're gonna get in trouble!'

They ran off, leaving me lying on the side of the road, holding my stomach. This wasn't the last time something like this would happen, and it wasn't always physical; words could be just as bad. After what felt like forever, I got up and walked home. By the time I made it through the front door, the sky had already started to darken. I gave Nan a quick hug and headed down the hallway to my room. And there they were, like always: Dad's feet poking out from Ady's doorway. Another night. Same floor. Same routine.

If you're a parent you'll relate to the challenges of raising little people, especially when it comes to sleep. Well, this challenge is amplified tenfold when you have a growing son with the mental development of a three year old. It's a daily battle and an exhausting one at that. Every night for twenty years Dad would be there, lying on Ady's bedroom floor in an attempt to get him to sleep.

'Dad, I'll do it tonight,' I whispered from the doorway, trying not to undo his progress.

'Are you sure, darl?' Dad said. I began offering to help my dad from the age of five.

'Yeah, it's fine, I'll just change the channel on the TV.'

Hauling himself up from the hard lino floor, leaving a cushion from the couch there for me, he gave me a soft kiss on the top of my hand and a pat on the shoulder. 'Thanks, little friend.' He went to the bathroom, his shoulders slumped.

Ady was sitting on his bed, legs crossed like Gandhi, eyes locked on me as he began to make his humming noises. Little bugger.

'Shh, Ady, pop your head on the pillow. It's time to go nigh-nighs.'

He did what I asked, I tucked him in and got down on the floor, grabbing the remote to find something to watch on TV. I repeated that process a dozen times that night before he finally fell asleep. I didn't like seeing Dad do it all the time, and always after a long work day which often included a four-hour train commute. He was so defeated that he went into autopilot after a few years. You could from his eyes that the man he once was had gone.

•

It's a privilege to love a sibling with a disability and to be loved by them in return. I protected Ady like he was made of glass and still do to this day. He still doesn't speak, but we have an unspoken energy that allows us to communicate. He taught me that love needs no words, as clichéd as that sounds. I'm not a woo-woo kinda person (yes, there are crystals on my shelves, and I love a horoscope as much as the next person with a vagina), but love is like energy. Words, although beautiful, are surface level compared to the depths of love. And Ady's love is deeper than Nan's pockets.

Maybe Santa really did grant my wish, after all. But the gift I wanted and the gift I needed were two very different things. Instead of granting my brother speech, Santa gave me a silent angel who taught me endless, invaluable and sometimes hard lessons. Things like seeing the good in everything and everyone, even when some days I had to search a little harder. How to be patient and how to experience a love that I could never describe with words. A lot of life and love can't be expressed with speaking; it's felt. And as heartbreaking as it is, Ady has been speaking all along, in a secret language only I am lucky enough to understand.

TO THE PEOPLE WHO DOWNPLAY THEIR PAIN

I once heard an analogy: two people drowned, one in twenty feet of water, the other in six.

Did the person who drowned in twenty feet of water have it worse? Of course not. They're both dead. (Morbid AF, I know.) Moral is, there are *always* going to be people worse off than you. Just like with Ady. Yes, it could have been even harder – but that doesn't make what he lives with, or what we carry, any less valid. Perspective is powerful but don't let it trick you into downplaying your feelings. Your pain is valid, beautiful.

Chapter 3

A is for anxiety

*Stephanie is a well-mannered, quiet student who shows
enthusiasm for activities that capture her interest. She is kind
and caring towards her peers. However, she often forgets
instructions and struggles to maintain focus during tasks,
becoming easily distracted. Despite this, she shines brightly
in areas she enjoys.*

– Grade 3 report (but let's be honest, it could've been any year)

'Earth to Steph. Earth to Steph.' A deep voice – one I didn't hear
often. Dad. Tall man, invisible emotions. Sadly, with how life
unfolded, he buried his feelings so deep, I don't think he could've
found them even if he tried.

The kitchen slowly materialised like someone turning the focus
on an old camera. I heard a murmur in the background, almost
like an echo. I blinked a few times and realised, *You've done that
thing again, Steph.* When your brain says, 'Hold my beer' and then
ghosts you like a shitty Tinder date. I looked up. Dad stood there
like he'd been watching me for a lifetime. 'Oh, sorry, Dad.'

'Off with the fairies again, little friend?' he said with a chuckle. I loved it when he was silly – or just *there*, really. I often wondered what he was like as a kid. Probably the prankster, the eldest of five boys. 'The trick is to fill them up with rice and potatoes,' Grandma, his mum, always said when we visited her in Melbourne. Smart woman. I hoped Dad had fun back then. Before everything got heavier. Over time, the childlike sparkle faded from his eyes and was replaced by a quiet exhaustion.

I was in primary school smack-bang in the middle of a maths test when it hit me. *My brain is broken.* It truly had a mind of its own. Pun very much intended. What else could I think? All the evidence was stacking up. Unlike my stage-five-clinger friends Anxiety and Chaos, Memory was flaky as hell, showing up late, or not at all. Not ideal in a maths test or, you know, life. Memory was like a dodgy housemate; she'd move things around, make a mess, eat all the food (that we didn't have), then vanish – leaving gaps for me to try to fill, like a puzzle but minus the fun.

My imagination on the other hand was unstoppable – wild and untamed, like Ady at an all-you-can-eat buffet. I was either lost with the fairies or lost in worries; there was no in between, just a constant tug-of-war between magic and mess. Now, you're probably wondering what a five year old has to be worried about. Well, let me introduce you to one of my other hidden talents: overthinking.

I stressed about who I'd sit with at lunchtime and whether I'd forgotten my hat again and would be banned from playing on the oval. I stressed if Nan was going away soon to see her other daughters (my aunties Rosie and Netty, Mum's sisters). I stressed if Adam had eaten my homework again, or if he'd found my favourite teddy, the one I slept with every single night, well into my teenage years. Okay, fine. I was twenty . . . four. And of course I stressed about dying. You know? Typical five year old stuff.

'Is there something more interesting outside, Stephanie?' boomed my teacher. *Shit.*

'No, Miss. Sorry.' I stared down at my desk and the activity I had no idea how to do. *Awesome.* I hated when this happened. I tried so hard to be good at school and felt bad for making my teachers constantly repeat instructions – it wasn't like I was trying to ignore them. Granted, it was boring as batshit, but I wasn't a rude kid. After my brain would take off into outer space, I'd come crashing back down to earth only to realise everyone around me was already working on an activity. Cue the panic because I had no idea what was going on, or what day of the week it was. (Hopefully Wednesday so I could get the cheap icy poles at the canteen with the change Nan gave me that morning.)

What can I say? Life was distracting. The birds chirping outside the window like I was bloody Snow White, pencils grating over paper, kids whispering, feet tapping on the floor, the teacher's chalk scraping across the blackboard . . . Every sound, every whisper, every movement felt too loud, too sharp, too much. It was as though all the unwanted noise overwhelmed my ears and wedged itself deep inside my brain. Maybe I needed to clean the filter inside my head, like our dodgy old robot vacuum. Vac Efron? Or maybe it was Dustin Bieber. Ady often covered his ears. I wasn't sure if he did this to block out the noise or because it was fun. *He must feel like this all the time*, I'd think to myself.

But aside from zoning out in class, I never got in trouble for anything else. As you can see from my school report, I was a kind and considerate student – a people-pleaser in the making – but the teachers always said the same thing: 'You just need to *apply yourself more.*' *How about I apply my foot to your face?*

Most of the time I just felt dumb. Forgetful. Slow to catch on. Especially if the task or conversation was boring. The only activity I felt I had a handle on was creative writing. It was something I'd done ever since I could remember; short stories, poems, soul scribbles in my diary. My little escape hatch. Disappearing into other worlds. Where I could be someone else. Someone smarter, louder, prettier – anyone but me.

Oh, and did I mention I also had a broken heart? And no, not over some boy – Nan taught me better. But my heart did these weird things – it has for as long as I can remember. A sick déjà vu.

'Steph, are you okay?' my kindy best friend, Lee, would ask.

'Yeah! Just thinking,' I'd say with a smile. *Thinking about how I might cark it, right here at my desk.* I'd be sitting in class and off my heart would go – thumping like someone trying to break down the door. My breathing would speed up, like my body was preparing to run a race, which we both knew couldn't possibly be true. I never said anything to my teacher – the last thing I wanted was to get in trouble again. I didn't say anything to my mum, my nan or any of my friends, either. Decades later, I am all too familiar with the symptoms of a panic attack, but at the time it felt like further proof that I was separate, different, not 'normal'. Besides, I had to be the easy one. A good girl.

To make things even more fun, I realised around the age of eight that I was a walking contradiction. Hear me out. I felt anxious without a routine, but when I had one, I felt suffocated. I couldn't concentrate unless I was obsessed, then good luck prying whatever it was from my cold, hyper-focused hands. I couldn't *think* surrounded by mess; but I was also the human equivalent of a junk drawer (minus the junk in my trunk). Seriously, I was the messiest kid alive. Don't believe me?

Some kids had toy boxes. I had a $2 shower curtain. Apparently, my mess was too much for a flimsy box. No, Mum needed an innovative solution in the form of a plastic shower curtain from the Reject Shop, complete with blue dolphins frolicking across it. You know, for distraction (not that I needed any more of that). I will never forget coming home from school to find my bookshelf looking like a motel bathroom. And, much like a motel bathroom, the shower curtain was hiding a crime scene. Except instead of bloodstains, it was books, Pokémon cards and Polly Pockets. Instead of police tape and a body bag, the evidence was camouflaged by marine wildlife. Mum had nailed a rubber cord across the top, threaded the curtain through and . . . Ta-da! Mess? What mess? With one swift yank it was gone like a dodgy magic trick.

That shower curtain stayed up until I was old enough to 'pretend' dolphins weren't lame.

And don't even get me started on cleaning – it overwhelmed me before I'd even begun – except for those rare bursts of energy when I'd suddenly decide to rearrange my entire bedroom and assume a whole new identity. Moving furniture and swapping posters around was pure magic. Fuck yeah. New room, new me. The world was my oyster. It was the same buzz I got from my weird obsession with stationery and planners.

The final contradiction? I was always exhausted, but I hated bedtime – and not for the reason you're probably thinking. At bedtime, my brain was at its messiest, and for some reason my heart decided that 8 p.m. was the perfect time to participate in the Tour de France. Yay. And this was all before I reached puberty.

BEDSIDE BRAIN DUMP FOR THE GIRL WHO CAN'T SWITCH OFF

- Set out your clothes for tomorrow (less for future you to think about).
- Set a ten-minute timer and reset your main living space.
- Get into bed and then journal out these brain unloaders:
  - What did I do well today?
  - What am I worried about that I can't control?
  - What don't I need to solve tonight?
  - What can I hand over to tomorrow me?

Reminder:
Today is done.
Nothing else can be fixed, mended, cleaned or sorted tonight.
Let it go, beautiful. You're safe to stop now.

•

'Mum, I need to tell you something.'

Yep. I was finally coming clean. After a particularly tough day at school, I'd decided to tell her about my broken brain and broken heart. I'd had enough. I must have been about six. Thankfully, Mum was in one of her caring moods.

'It sounds like you have anxiety. I do too, and your Aunty Rosie,' she said gently.

What the hell was anxiety and how do I get rid of it? Maybe antibiotics? 'So I'm not going to die?' I asked.

'No, darling. You'll learn to live with it like the rest of us. You're going to be fine.'

I would never forget that moment. Number one: it was when I found out what was 'wrong' with me. Number two: I felt truly seen by my mum. When I asked for help, she responded with empathy and understanding and, above all, love. I was weirdly grateful that the women in my family had what I had. Of course I wish they didn't have to suffer like me, but I wasn't dismissed or told I was being dramatic.

A couple of weeks later, after Mum took me to our family doctor, I got an assessment from a professional. As we left, I tried to wrap my six-year-old mind around it.

'That's why you get distracted, pumpkin head,' Mum said in the car on the way home. I hated it when she called me that. According to the doctor, I not only had anxiety, but another thing called Attention Deficit Disorder, or ADD. I knew some kids at school who had ADHD. Apparently, I had a version of that. *Great.* Let's add ADD to the long list of unfavourable things about Steph. You would think that having some answers would have made me feel better, but it didn't. To me, it was confirmation that I was different from the other kids. Separate. Always separate. I know Ady was too, but he was beautiful. He was *good.*

'How'd you go, sweetpea?' Nan chirped as I walked into her room and sat down.

'So I have . . . Attention D-Deficit Disorder.'

'But you're still Stephy, love,' she said. 'It's just a word, a label. It doesn't change who you are and what you can do.' Nan reacted exactly as I knew she would. That was one of the many things I loved about her: her predictability. She didn't treat me any differently, either before or after 'the news'.

I exhaled, feeling safe enough to admit my new worries. 'But the kids at school with this are naughty, Nan. I must be naughty too.'

She looked me straight in the eye. 'You listen here, I've told you this before and I will tell you again. *Never* let anyone make you feel any less than. You know what I mean? You block out that noise. Here and at school. It's garbage. You're a beautiful, intelligent girl and a good one at that. You're an angel. You don't listen to them fools, okay? You're going to go far.'

At that time, I didn't know how I would go – I could barely keep up at school and I barely spoke. But I desperately wanted to believe she was right.

'It's just a word,' Nan went on. 'You know in your heart who you are.' She pulled me into a hug. 'Tell them to sit on it and twist. Oh wait, don't say that!' She covered her mouth, giggling. 'Naughty Nanny,' she whispered, giving herself a little smack on her hand.

After the diagnosis, Mum began taking me to a counsellor to help with my anxiety, but we didn't really talk about the ADD, or other stuff that went on at home. Mum was always beside me. I carried my ADD like a shameful secret until I was in my thirties. That little girl who was ashamed of her neurodivergence now shares ADHD-friendly content that helps tens of thousands of people to feel seen. Back then, I was just 'Silly Steph' who forgot things and got distracted easily.

In the 1990s, mental health experts were still learning about how ADHD and ADD presented in girls. Back then, hyperactivity was typically the boy climbing on desks and bouncing off the walls – the kind of energy that couldn't be ignored. But for girls, hyperactivity is often internal; a brain that never slows down, thought after thought pinging around like a malfunctioning browser tab that won't stop refreshing. Sound familiar? Turns out, that's hyperactivity – they just didn't know it yet. Nor did I. It was just more proof that I was broken.

Soon enough someone was about to roll into my life and redefine what it meant to take up space. They would do laps around the labels the world tried to hand us. And for a while, it made all the difference.

HOW TO LIGHTEN YOUR MENTAL LOAD (SO YOU DON'T THROAT-PUNCH SOMEONE)

- **Use a planner:** Yeah, I know, I know. We all start a new year with a fresh AF planner. We tell ourselves it's the year we'll finally get our shit together. Only to get three weeks in, and it gathers dust. But, my dear friend, simply set two 'planner check' alarms on your phone and you'll be the next Jane Ryan in no time. When you have tomorrow or your week planned out your brain doesn't have to hold it all anymore. If you need a good planner brand just ask. *Wink.*

- **Phuck off your phone:** No, you don't need to be filling in a 'What kitchen appliance would I be?' quiz at 2 a.m. If you can see it, you will grab it (the phone that is – dirty bugger). I, like other humans, need to intentionally put my phone away in another room. I charge mine in the bathroom because I can't control myself – stay tuned for the best tech hacks for real people later in the book.

- **Declutter one drawer:** Yep. Forget the whole house. You're not on a Netflix show. Choose one drawer. One bench. One surface that's been screaming at you for a month. Set a timer for five minutes – I bet you smash it.

- **Automate the crap out of your life:** When you have ADHD, our creativity is king but sometimes our memory is not. So AUTOMATE. I'm not just talking alarms, I'm talking subscriptions for toilet paper and online grocery deliveries. I even have lists on my groceries website under 'weekly', 'fortnightly' and 'holidays' where you save items you buy all the time. Have reminders that yell 'TAKE YOUR MEDS' at you. Be dramatic with it. If tech can do it, future you will love you for it.
- **Delegate or explode:** Sadly, most of us believe we can do it all and be it all, all the time. I hate to break it to you but you can't. If you try you'll end up not being able to look after anyone. You have to fit your own oxygen mask first. So ask for help. Stick it on the fridge. Stick a reminder on their forehead if you must.

Chapter 4

PE class

'Faster! Faster!' I yelled, sitting on my friend Jenna's feet as she zoomed us around school during PE. 'Are you sure I'm not hurting you?'

'No, I can't feel my legs, remember!' Jenna cried, laughing.

It must have been a sight. A couple of fourth graders, one in an electric wheelchair and the other sitting on the wheelchair's footstool, zooming around, laughing hysterically. The rest of the class were kicking balls on the oval – it was PE, after all – but Jenna and I were 'excused'. As a nine year old, I didn't ask the name of her condition, but I knew her muscles were too weak for her to walk. Even lifting her arms to eat and drink was a workout. As for me, I was allowed to skip PE because of my asthma. Let's face it, I wagged PE because I sucked at it and wanted to hang out with my best mate instead.

Jenna was in my class for a month or two before we clicked. One day, our teacher plonked me beside her and that was that: best friends by recess. Jenna had a teacher's aide who sometimes helped me too if I needed it and a desk that was higher and had a frame that moved up and down to fit over her wheelchair. I'd sit on the edge while she worked, sometimes reading to her or just talking kid rubbish. Jenna never made me feel like I was too much. Only that I was just right. Like her.

She let me have a go at driving her chair once but I was terrible. I jolted her forward and she bobbed around laughing, while I was shitting myself thinking I'd broken her. Never again. While Jenna's body was confined, her spirit was anything but. And let me tell you – she was dangerous with that joystick. In the best possible way.

Although Jenna had a disability like Ady, she didn't have to go to his 'special school', and for that I was grateful. It broke my heart seeing her a prisoner in her own body, but Jenna saw the fun in everything. She reminded me of Nan, those rare souls who can always find a silver lining. I'm sure there were many times when Jenna's disability would have got to her, but she never showed it and never seemed defeated or frustrated. She had a drive (pun intended) that I had never seen before. Determined Jenna D.

'Why doesn't your mum let you go to high jump districts?' she asked when we were playing marbles one day.

'She said I can't in case my lungs aren't strong enough.'

'Do you want to go? Why don't you just talk to her about it?'

'Maybe,' I muttered, knowing it wasn't going to happen. 'I don't want to worry her. You know what she's like.' When I was seven, Mum told me I might have meningitis and die – I had a cold. When our dog vomited on the carpet one day, she screamed she'd been poisoned. You know, normal stuff like that. Jenna nodded – she'd heard all the stories.

At the time, I took what my mum said as gospel. When she spiralled about sickness, so did I. When she said I shouldn't run, I believed her. Why wouldn't I? There was plenty of evidence of my 'not enoughness' at physical exercise. I mean, sport and I were never exactly best mates. Then there was dancing. I was always shoved at the back in every class. 'It's just because you're tall, pumpkin head,' Mum would say.

Decades later, when everything looked a little different, Dad finally said what we both knew. 'It's not because you were tall, love. It's because you have no spatial awareness.' He laughed when he said it. I did too. I was shithouse. A dancing praying mantis. And no one wants to see that.

But with Jenna, I didn't feel awkward. With her, we just . . . made sense. In my mind, Jenna and I would grow up together. I didn't think about our friendship ending until it did – too fast, too soon. But not for the reason that you might be thinking. Out of the blue, my mum announced that I was changing schools. She wanted me to go to a Catholic primary school, so I stood a better chance of getting a spot at a Catholic high school. At the time, I understood she thought it was the best choice for me. But as a child, I was devastated. I didn't want to leave my friends, Lee and Kathleen, and especially Jenna. But the decision had been made. During those last few months, Jenna became more than just a friend – she became my anchor.

I'll always remember my last day at my old school. We were a small group, but around these girls, I could be myself. Saying goodbye to Jenna was the hardest. I knew playdates weren't likely to happen because of – well, you know. I had no idea when I'd see any of them again. I hugged Jenna as tightly as I dared. Letting go felt like saying goodbye to more than just her – it felt like I was losing another rare 'safe person'.

Jenna died just over a year later. I was in Year 7 and she should have been too. My heart broke into a million pieces when I heard, each with their missing piece that belonged to her. Jenna often spoke of wanting to be a mother. Her eyes lit up every time she talked about the future. But she never got the chance. Since I became a mum, I've thought about Jenna a lot.

This was the first time I had experienced death, outside of my head, that is. When Grandpa, Dad's dad, passed away, I was still too young to feel it. I remember Dad didn't cry. He'd kept his emotions in a vault ever since Adam was born. In fact, the last time Dad cried, according to Mum, was when the doctors told them their son had Down syndrome.

If I wasn't already terrified of dying, I sure as hell was now. Jenna's death was proof of how utterly unfair it all was – how death had no rules, no logic, no mercy for whose time got cut short. I couldn't get my head around it. How was this allowed? How could someone be here one second, and just . . . gone the next?

Dad always said he didn't believe in God – because if there was one, Ady wouldn't have to live the way he did. And I could see his point. I didn't know what I believed anymore. But I had to believe in something, right? Because believing in nothing would mean the entire world was a lie. So yeah, you could say high school didn't get off to a great start. All I could feel was the emptiness. And then came the labels I allowed myself to wear like nametags I never asked for. But Jenna never saw labels – she just saw me. She proved the ones given to her were only as powerful as she let them be. She was all of her, unapologetically. Even after she was gone, that stuck with me.

Maybe I wasn't here to fit a box, any more than Jenna was made to fit her chair. Maybe I was here to take up space in the only way I knew how – fully, and as myself. Just like Jenna, who was a tiny body, massive presence and a spark that filled the room.

Maybe I wasn't broken. Just wired differently. Like her speedy chair. And maybe, just maybe . . . that wasn't something to fix.

WHY WE CLING TO LABELS (EVEN WHEN THEY SUCK)

You might've read that and thought, *No, I don't cling to labels. Being XYZ is just how I am.* But is it? Or was it something that stuck to you years ago – subtle and unwanted, like gum on the bottom of your fave sneakers? Maybe it came from a throwaway comment someone once said – a teacher, friend or parent. Or a fleeting moment that held enough power that not only did you decide to leave it stuck there, but you peeled it off, slapped it across your chest and began to wear it like a badge. A name tag. An identity. Low-key kinda gross, hey? On both counts.

We hold onto labels like a security blanket – even when they're itchy, suffocating, smell like moth balls and are absolutely not our colour. Why? They anchor us. But not in a Jenna kinda way; more in a 'this is who I'm allowed to be' kinda way. They locate us on a map, highlighting our invisible boundaries. They tell us the trails safe to wander and those that are out of bounds. They keep us stuck – static, stagnant and sick of our own self-sabotaging behaviours. And we listen.

Why? Well, if you're 'the distracted one' or 'the dumb one', you know your place. And you shrink to fit the label and call it 'safe'. But it's not safety. It's limitation dressed up as identity.

Here's the problem: Labels don't help us belong. They shape who we think we're allowed to be and pre-set the space we think we're allowed to occupy. And sometimes, that box we squeezed into at age eight . . . well, we're still in it at age thirty-four, wondering why we're not feeling fulfilled. Wondering why we feel stagnant. The reason is you're trying to stuff yourself into a place you don't fit, and never have. So let's peel off that label for good.

Okay, grab some vinegar and a cloth . . . *jokes*.

1. Write down three labels you've worn since you were a kid. You may have to dig deep to uncover ones you didn't even realise you had. To help, mine were: 'I'm bad at maths', 'I'm not athletic' and 'I'm an outsider'.

2. Now ask: Where did that label come from? A parent? A stranger? A moment of embarrassment?

3. Rewrite it. Not only your labels but your story; your beliefs. What's *actually* true and what evidence do I have for this?

Check out these examples to help you:

LABEL:	REWRITE:	EVIDENCE:
'I'm too much.'	I'm creative, passionate and love deeply.	I always have lots of ideas.
'I'm bad with money.'	I'm intelligent and I'm still learning.	I saved for a laptop last year.

Chapter 5

The scales of worth

I can't recall the exact moment I realised it was a woman's lifelong purpose to strive for a certain number on the bathroom scales. But at some point in my early childhood, I learnt this magic number would determine whether you were happy, whether you'd get a boyfriend, whether you'd be successful or whether you'd even be allowed to have a good day. If you didn't hit this magic number, you could forget about all that – or even wearing jeans without hating yourself.

I learnt that you can't be too fat, but you can't be too thin; though the latter was preferable. You can't have cellulite or stretch marks, which Mum said happened when you had kids. But if you didn't have kids, well, there was something wrong with you. You needed to dress up, but not too much or you'd be 'showing off' and no one would like you. If you did a hundred sit-ups a day, you'd get abs, which apparently was *the* goal for all humans. (No idea why. Maybe you get a special card that gives you discounts at Starbucks. Low-calorie beverages only, of course.)

I learnt that carbs are bad. As are fats. Oh, and meat too. But you need to eat lots of protein. Confused yet? Good, so was I.

I learnt the sugar in fruit is bad, but bananas are good for bloating. And if you are bloated, people will think you're pregnant like Paris Hilton when she was spotted leaving Starbucks last week. Spoiler alert: she just needed to poo. Or, you know, maybe she has organs. Same-same, right? It's no bloody wonder Britney Spears shaved her head.

Heroin Chic is in
15 Shocking Beach Bodies
Get Abs Fast!

When I was little, standing in line at the supermarket cash register with Nan, I'd read headlines like these on the covers of the women's magazines. (Let's face it, these magazines still exist, we haven't made that much progress.) As an adult I can see how marketing preyed on women's insecurities and longing for control over the bathroom scales without living off air. There was the boom in 'fat-free' diets and products. Do people realise they don't count as 'low fat' if you eat an entire box in one sitting? Not speaking from experience or anything.

Mum had a pile of these magazines next to the toilet in her ensuite bathroom. My parents had had separate bedrooms since I was very young. I can't even recall them ever sleeping in the same bed for that matter. Dad referred to the magazines as 'garbage', just like reality TV and the Kardashians (sorry Kim). When I used Mum's bathroom, I'd pore over this garbage which always featured women on the front covers, usually in bikinis, or with close-ups of their legs with a big red arrow and the word 'CELLULITE' in capitals next to it. *Why on earth do people care about other people's legs?* I would think to myself.

I wonder now if all these 'adult rules' contributed to my phobia of growing up. It might have been the fact that, with each passing year, I was closer to dying. Every other kid I knew wanted to grow up so they could drive cars, wear makeup and buy a house. (If only they knew what us millennials and Gen Z were in for.) But I wanted to stay the same, even though I hated my home life and dreamt of getting out of there. Growing up – both physically and emotionally – was bloody scary. The adults in my life, aside from Nan, seemed to have so little control. A good example was Mum and her weight, which she was at war with constantly.

'I shouldn't have eaten that. You idiot.'

'I'll just skip dinner.'

'Today I'm going to be good.'

That was the soundtrack I heard every day. A cycle of eating, justifying and then self-loathing. I hated seeing people I loved rip themselves to shreds. It was like watching them fight a battle they couldn't win – all because they dared to eat. I have so many memories of witnessing the women in my life step onto the bathroom scales – that flat, clinical device they seemed to both fear and obsess over. Maybe it was the look of defeat that gave their feelings away, or the swear words that poured from their mouths the moment the number wasn't what they wanted it to be. I'd watch, wide-eyed, as they'd leap off the torture device like it was burning their feet. It never made sense why they kept doing something that made them miserable.

I wondered at what age we are given our 'number'. I prayed that my number would be a 'good one'. Not like Mum's, I think she got a bad number. Years later, in science class, I learnt that bathroom scales basically just measure our relationship with gravity. *So why the hell is everyone so obsessed?* I thought to myself.

However, this discovery wasn't enough to counteract the body-shaming comments that I was absorbing.

'I had such a good figure before I had kids. I was a model, you know,' Mum would say. I still thought she was pretty. She'd bring out her photo albums and show me pictures of herself 'when she was beautiful'. She had big, hopeful eyes, a lovely smile and bouncy light brown hair that framed her face. She was slim, graceful even – everything that the magazines in her bathroom said you needed to be. But now she was . . . a mother. I assumed all women got bigger tummies after they had kids and I wondered how I would look when I became a mum. I wanted a big family, so my future kids could play together.

As Mum leafed through her old photo albums, a small, sorrowful smile would flicker across her face. For a moment, it was like she wanted to step into the photographs and stay there, leaving us behind. I guess it would have been hard watching your face and body change; saying goodbye to a past version of yourself.

I decided then and there that I was definitely not growing up. Fuck that shit.

Nan talked about her weight too, but she didn't say mean things about herself. She'd talk about putting on a few pounds as fact without emotion. Unlike when she watched the footy and got fired up, yelling, 'Come on, you bastards!' It was so cute coming from this little old lady who looked like the Queen. When it came to eating, she'd say, 'I'm just watching my weight, love,' but it never seemed to upset her. She'd tell me stories of the men who used to 'chase her' after her beautiful Charles passed away. Of course, she always swiped left. (Or is it right?)

Spending time with Nan helped ease my fears about growing up. She was beautiful and elegant, but had this youthful energy.

Despite experiencing a tragic childhood, she was just . . . silly. She even put on her red lipstick before going to bed. 'You gotta look good in your dreams!' she'd say, as she popped on her cosy slippers with their two-inch heels. She gave me hope that being a grown-up might be tolerable, fun even. In contrast, the other adults around me seemed to have the weight of the world on their shoulders. And on their bathroom scales.

When I got to high school, the same sorts of conversations about weight popped up in my friendship group. It was the *hot* topic every recess and lunch. Riveting shit, right? Some girls had started to grow boobs. Mine, it seemed, were still on backorder. Some would stuff their Bonds training bras with tissues or socks. I tried it once, but the result was less 'cute cleavage' and more Madonna in her cone-bra era. Clearly, I'd missed boob-stuffing 101.

In those days, 'Dolly Doctor' – the medic who answered readers' questions in the iconic Australian teen magazine *Dolly* – was our guru; our go-to source for all things friends, boys, how to kiss properly, and entertainment. No, seriously, have you read some of the questions in Dolly Doctor? It's some Jerry Springer shit. While researching this book, I googled a bunch of old questions and they didn't disappoint:

> *'I have an irritating itch in my throat after giving my friend's boyfriend a blowjob in the movies. Is there such thing as throat thrush?'*

> *'About a year ago I had pubic lice. I was too scared to tell anyone so I poured a lice control dog wash over the area. I would like to know if the wash harmed me?'*

> *'Is it wrong to be in love with your first cousin?'*

For some reason, I remember the questions more than the answers. But it was comforting to know that people my age were going through their own crises, although mine didn't involve incestual relations or stealing canine bath products. I wondered if the letters were fake – they say no, but if someone wants to come forward who was into their cousin, no judgement here.

Funnily enough, now I'm in my thirties, I wish we had Dolly Doctors for adulting. I would pay big bucks for a Dolly Doctor crash course on life admin or *How to File a Tax Return Without Crying*. But at the time, reading about all the things 'girls my age' were doing – including how sexually active they were – scared the living shit out of me.

Nothing could compare to *The Book*. The one with the diagram of a vagina on the cover. At first glance, I thought it was a picture of a sea urchin sitting next to a butthole. Like some fucked-up children's book. Then Mum sat me down and shattered my world by explaining how babies are made – and worse, where they come out. I just remember thinking, *What the actual fuck? That can't be practical. There has to be a better exit route . . . belly button maybe?* At the age of fifteen, I was *definitely* not ready for any of this. Sure, I thought boys were cute, and I'd had a few crushes, but the only body parts I was comfortable touching were hands as we walked to the video store, thank you very much.

My scrawny, flagpole body certainly didn't do me any favours. My chest was so flat it felt like my pending boobs were more inverted triangles than anything Fergie would call 'lovely lady lumps'. (Millennials, you sang it. I know.) If you couldn't already tell, I wasn't one of the 'cool kids'. Tissue tits and gossip weren't really my thing. I preferred reading *Harry Potter* and, apparently, my body felt the same way. I was one of the last girls in my friendship group to get my period. Honestly? I didn't care that I was 'behind'. I felt like I was living up to my promise of 'not growing up'.

But then doomsday arrived . . .

I was fourteen and the pact I made to myself didn't stand a chance against raging teenage hormones. I woke up like any other morning, hopped out of bed but then felt something weird in my undies. *Nooo.* Sure enough, my undies were covered in blood; my face equally covered in shock and disappointment. It was the beginning of the end.

Shortly after my period began, my boobs that got lost along the way finally showed up. When I say 'showed up', I mean, measly lumps appeared. I was embarrassed and far from happy. I still wanted to be a kid. I tried to hide them, but being the oldest female cousin in the family, I was the 'chosen one' – the one to go through all the 'firsts'. Lucky me. When Mum noticed, she exclaimed, 'Oh, your boobs are coming in! I can see them!' It felt like they were a cruise ship pulling into Sydney Harbour. Mum happily announced it to my aunties when they visited – right in front of me. FML. I wanted to sink into the floor and never come back up.

At school, I felt completely out of sync with my friends. They talked about their boyfriends and wore G-strings under their uniforms like it was the most normal thing in the world. Meanwhile, I couldn't help but wonder, *Wouldn't that be uncomfortable? And do they cut your farts in half?* But soon enough, I bowed to the pressure. When I was at the shops with Nan and Mum one day, I snuck into Best & Less and bought my first training bra and G-string. They were hot pink. I bought them to fit in and because it felt like the 'right' thing to do. I certainly wasn't ready to wear them for another person. It felt like I lived in two worlds. On one hand I'd had to grow up quickly to help look after my brother, but inside I was still a child – and I wasn't ready for the weight that women had to carry (or lose, for that matter).

High school was also where we were introduced to a whole new 'scales of worth': the academic edition. If you're around my age or older and were educated in Australia, you'll remember the University Admissions Index or UAI. Your UAI number ranked all students and determined whether you got into your chosen university or not. Ah, the ol' UAI, aka the 'Unnecessary Anxiety Indicator', crushing dreams, one decimal place at a time. It's now called an Australian Tertiary Admission Rank or ATAR, because the Australian government likes to keep us on our toes.

I'll never forget my Year 10 teacher giving us what was meant to be a 'jolly pep talk' about the importance of the UAI results. 'This is very . . . very . . . *very* important . . .' As I sat on the library steps, the teacher's voice droning on in the background, I pondered these big life choices we were expected to make at age sixteen. My boobs had only just rocked up and now I was supposed to figure out what life uniform to stuff them in? I didn't even know how to operate them yet. It wasn't only our weight we had to watch, it was also this other magic number that measured our intelligence. Thanks to writing and a killer major for Design and Tech where I made clothing for disabled people, I magically scored a decent UAI. It also helped I didn't do maths, otherwise I would have been fucked, divided and left to carry the emotional remainder.

Speaking of scoring, that part of my life was non-existent, even though I'd always enjoyed the platonic company of boys. I found them easier to read. I couldn't understand how girls would say one thing but mean another. Throughout high school most of my friends were male. My parents even let my boy *friends* sleep

over – in my bed – because they were sure I had no sexual intentions. Looking back, those poor guys must have had blue balls.
I'd be in my skimpy pyjamas, thinking nothing of it because I
saw them as 'bros'. The only action they got was listening to my
sleep apnoea. Getting lucky in that situation would be scoring
some ear plugs.

In contrast, most girls scared the living hell out of me.

Natalie updated her MSN name to: NoOnE UnDeRSTaNdS mE

Complete with a sad face emoji and a Green Day lyric in her
status. Could've been Simple Plan. Or Good Charlotte. The holy
trinity of teenage angst.

stephie_bubblegum: hey, are you okay?

nat_4eva: dOnT wOrRy AbOuT It . . .

Classic. Because actually saying what was wrong would be far
too easy.

Then there were the birthday parties and the politics . . .

'Wait, are you still friends with *her*?' I was halfway through my
$2 chicken sticks from the canteen when the interrogation began.

'Um . . . yeah?'

'Well, then you can't come to my party.'

Just like that. Banished.

God forbid you were friends with two girls who were fighting.
All I wanted was the fairy bread and a go at the piñata. Can't
I just be Switzerland? I could barely decide between a red frog or
a Zooper Dooper, let alone decode the cryptic laws of girlhood.
And if you think that's brutal, we were the first generation to use
social media – with our background of street cricket. It was a
whole new world and it was addictive AF, which is saying something. We weren't afforded the privilege of 'scrolling' in bed; we
had to sit in front of a big-arse box computer. Don't even get me

started how frustrating it was when someone had to make a phone call. The *bings* and *beeps* of our dial-up internet connection serve as a nostalgic reminder of a patience humanity once had – but is now long gone. I still recall the day my parents brought the computer home. I was in primary school and too scared to touch it. I thought if I pressed the wrong button, it would explode. I'm not kidding. They'd brought home an alien, and not a cute one like ET.

Once we got the hang of the new space station, it was only a matter of time before MSN and Myspace showed up. Like for so many teenagers then and now, this new-found technology had an immediate effect on my body image. I didn't start my first diet until I was nineteen – long after many of my friends – but the foundations of my unbalanced relationship with my body were set. Suddenly I realised there were a lot more people out there than just those in my street and at my school. Now I had access to hundreds and thousands of teenagers to compare myself to. Yay.

Myspace was cut-throat. If you didn't already know where you stood with someone, you would soon learn. Right there on your profile was the infamous 'Top 10'. Not top ten songs, not top ten photos. No. It was your *Top 10 friends*. Yep, we ranked our friends like judges on *Australian Idol*. And we were as brutal as Dicko. Not only that, it wasn't static. Oh no. Your ranking could and usually would change daily. One minute I was someone's 'number two' and the next I was down to 'number nine'. Don't ask me why – maybe I breathed wrong or forgot to wear pink on Wednesdays. And if you got kicked out of their Top 10 altogether? Well, you were toast. You'd probably come up with some excuse to not go to school that day. You bet everyone remembered your ranking better than we remembered Pythagoras' theorem. (I still stand by my claim; that lesson was useless for me.)

When we weren't being ranked by our friends, we were illegally downloading songs on LimeWire. But it came with a price – some random guy's voice talking halfway through Beyoncé's chorus, or a load of viruses. Often both.

School was a jungle. So you can see where my distrust of females came from. I felt safer with guys because they said what they thought, mostly, and they seemed more loyal (could have been the blue balls but whatevs). They were also more obvious with their social cues, which was one language I could never speak well. But you'd never know it. Remember I was good at masking in primary school? Well, now I had reached an expert level. And while I may not have been able to pick up on social cues, one language I've always been fluent in is energy. I learnt that at home, where I needed it for survival, and from Ady who didn't need words to communicate with me. This was when my people-pleasing really kicked in. If someone in my friendship group was upset, quiet, or even just a bit off, I'd shapeshift without thinking. Even if it meant being the butt of all jokes, I'd do it. One nickname stuck more than others.

'Ah, Steph, you're such a *Crunchy*,' a girl said at lunch one day, laughing. And no, Gen Z, it wasn't a granola-core compliment. Millennials will remember: *Crunchy* meant brunette on the outside, blonde on the inside. In other words . . . dumb.

'She's not dumb,' someone chimed in. 'Just . . . a bit *slow*.'

They had a point. I was always the last one to get the joke. Usually an hour later, in the middle of History class. 'Ohhhh, I get it now!' I'd snort, copping a death stare from the teacher as my friends shook their heads. They knew I was good at some things, like out-of-the-box ideas, English and Design and Tech. But I was gullible and, looking back, naïve – despite having to deal with some very adult shit at home.

So yeah. Growing up in the 2000s was a shitshow. It was a decade where technology grabbed our scooters, skateboards and cricket bats and threw them into cyberspace. Where you no longer left school at school, it now came home with you – along with the bullies and the drama. Where friendship was now gamified and collided with adolescence, creating a perfect storm of dial-up disasters, social media hierarchies, and the unrelenting pressure to keep up and not miss out, all while trying to turn in your assignments on time and stuff your bra accordingly.

Seemingly overnight we went from real life to life online. It was exciting, confusing and downright brutal at times, but it was our normal. We were the guinea pigs of a new digital era that didn't come with a Dolly Doctor. Our 'golden years' became the years our gaze went from the real world to our screens – and never left. Looking back, it's no wonder we came out of it with some glitches. But hey, at least we know the sound of dial-up. Not everyone can say that.

STEPH'S SEALED SECTION: WHAT WE WERE NEVER TOLD ABOUT OUR BODIES

Welcome to what the magazines should've said, but didn't.

- Your body is not a statue and it will change, as will your relationship with gravity; it's supposed to. If it doesn't, then Houston, we have a problem.

- Hunger is not meant to be controlled like a feral cat. It's how your body speaks to you.
- Boobs rock up like a first date to a party – some are late, early, smaller than you thought, bigger than you expected, even lopsided. Sometimes not at all. It's all normal and doesn't make you any less worthy.
- Cellulite and stretch marks are just skin – not a scandal to keep secret.
- Your worth is not reflected in other people's opinion of you.
- No, you don't need to hang onto clothes for 'when you fit into them again'. That's like hanging onto a pair of shoes you wore when you were nine.
- Life is too short to be at war in your head over a fucking muffin – just eat it.

Chapter 6

My anchor

'Amy, where *are* you?' I hissed into the phone, standing at the end of the driveway. 'I've already lied to my parents. I'm already all-in and screwed at this point.'

'Are you sure, Steph? What if you get caught?'

I yanked my gym bag higher on my shoulder. The glass clinking inside made me freeze – bloody raspberry-flavoured Vodka Cruisers practically singing their own theme song, trying to blow my cover. 'We won't get caught. We're saints, remember? I never do anything out of line.' Half of that was true. At seventeen, I was basically Mother Teresa in a Supré top. I hadn't touched drugs and didn't want to, and I never drank, unless you counted New Year's Eve when Mum handed me one pre-approved Cruiser. I'd never been in real trouble – detention only once for wearing my hair out at school. Scandalous. The devil works hard, but Catholic uniform policy works harder.

'You sure your mum didn't hear the bottles?' Amy asked once I finally got into her car. It was sporting fresh red P plates.

'Bloody hope not,' I said with a smile.

I didn't tell Amy how hard my hands shook when I slipped the bottles into my gym bag. Or that I was nervous about drinking for real for the first time. The only thing I'd ever stolen (still to this day) was a bottle of wine from my parents' kitchen. For the record, it was dreadful. I had four sips and gave it to my friend. I even blamed poor Aunty Netty for it going missing. Sorry, but a girl's gotta live.

'Wait. Do we even know who's throwing this party?' I asked.

'Nope,' Amy grinned. 'Isn't that the point?'

And just like that, I was doing something rebellious. Not snort-coke-off-a-toilet-seat rebellious, just . . . teenage-girl rebellious. Breaking character for once. A good Catholic girl with a gym bag full of sugared vodka and a pirate's mouth – inherited from Nan and muted by Mum.

Back to the party. It was at your typical Aussie suburban house – one storey, not far from home, empty beer bottles scattered across the front yard. No cricket bats in sight – I was officially with the big kids now. And I was shit-scared. It felt like a major milestone – almost a rite of passage – stepping into the chaotic world of teenage anarchy. Spoiler alert: I was in bed before midnight. Little did I know, the real milestone that night wasn't the party. It was meeting the person who would change everything.

Four Cruisers deep and fifty-five introductions later, I must have been drunk because every second person's name was Matt. I saw my friend Kara, one of the only other people there I knew, moving through the crowd. And she had someone with her.

'This is Ryan,' she said with a cheeky smile.

And there he stood. In Rip Curl shorts, scuffed skate shoes and a fitted black T-shirt that showed off his broad shoulders. The cutest man-child I had ever seen.

'I'm Steph from St Joeys, I make sandwiches with Kara,' I said. *Smooth, Steph. Really smooth.*

'Nice to meet you Steph from St Joeys who makes sandwiches with Kara,' Ryan said, his eyes never leaving mine. He was a walking contradiction: a baby face with kind eyes but a mischievous grin that made me nervous. *This guy has to be at least twenty,* I thought to myself. Back then people that age were full-blown adults. I now know that in your twenties and even thirties you're basically a newborn adult. Kara dragged me away to finish introducing me to the rest of the Matts. I glanced back at Ryan. 'Nice meeting you!' I yelled across the room. He looked at Kara like she'd stolen his beer. His eyes locked onto mine again and he smiled like we'd shared some sort of inside joke.

A couple of hours later under the twinkling stars, the world melted away as Ryan's lips found mine in a moment of pure passion. Or at least, that's how I'd like to describe our first kiss. The reality? I'd just stumbled back from the bathroom, having spewed up all four Cruisers I'd chugged down. Don't worry, I found some toothpaste and then spent twenty sweaty minutes cleaning up my mess.

Ryan had been all over me like a cute rash all night. (If there even is such a thing.) In the minutes leading up to that first kiss, he found me, grabbed my hand and led me out the front door, weaving us past a sea of drunk teenagers. His hands were rough. Later he told me it was from his job; he'd left high school after Year 10 to do a carpentry apprenticeship. As we got to the front yard, he stopped suddenly, held my shoulders, looked into my slightly bloodshot eyes, and told me I was beautiful. Okay, no, he said I was 'hot'. Which is almost romantic if you squint at it.

And then he kissed me. A kiss that, unbeknown to us at the time, we would one day repeat on our wedding day, minus the part where, mid-kiss, I stepped into someone else's vomit. I can't wait to tell the grandkids that story. So no, it wasn't the dreamy, cinematic first kiss you'd imagine sharing with the love of your life. But honestly, it makes perfect sense. I'm Steph the Mess, after all. It's only fitting that my first kiss with my forever person would come with a side dish of chaos – or spew.

Ryan and I were inseparable the rest of the night. He wasn't shy about his intentions and wouldn't let go of my hand (what can I say, man-child knows what he wants). It gave me a weird sense of calm, even though I was drunk at some random house, holding hands with a boy I didn't know from a bar of soap. But I felt safe when people told me how they felt and what their intentions were – and Ryan was clear as day. I could have read him like a children's book (*not* the one with the sea urchin and butthole).

Sadly, my fairytale was cut short as I had to leave the party at 11 p.m. because one of our mates got into a fight with a street lamp. You know . . . boy things. Before I left, Ryan grabbed my Nokia and saved his number; after some negotiation I gave him mine too.

A whole three minutes into the taxi ride back to Amy's house, my phone started buzzing.

Incoming call: *Ryan Ring Me*

Shit, this guy is keen. Poor bugger, I thought, knowing I wasn't going to see him again. But for some weird reason I answered his call and we chatted the whole way home. He sounded like a forty year old. Honestly, his voice was so deep I half-expected him to start narrating movie trailers. When I went to sleep that night, I remember thinking, *I'm gonna feel like shit in the morning . . . and that guy was . . . different.* Kinda like me. And I liked that.

What's so unusual about meeting a boy at a party? Well, my first encounter with Ryan came as a total surprise. Sure, this guy gave me raspberry-flavoured-vodka-drunk butterflies, but a relationship was the last thing on my mind when I pulled on my sparkly silver dress that night. I was far from being your typical boy-crazed teenager. I dabbled here and there with a couple of boyfriends – if you can even call them that – but we never lasted more than a week or two before I pulled the pin. Looking back, I was pretty harsh. Some of them cried, and I just couldn't understand why. *It's not like we're getting married*, I thought. I even broke up with one guy because he got a bad haircut. I wasn't mean enough to tell him that, but for the record, it was bad. Not mullet bad, but close.

So I was a long way from being the *Playboy* Bunny that ironically graced my bedspread, though I did make my second-ever email address 'stephie_68plus1@hotmail.com' which I thought was hilarious. Truth be told, I was just looking for any excuse to run from a relationship. I'd built walls around my heart, determined not to let anyone else break them. If I was going to have a 'serious' boyfriend, they were going to have to be special and jump through hoops – *Goblet of Fire* style.

I'd inherited my high standards from Nan, who always drilled into me, 'Don't put up with crap, Stephy.' She had a way of delivering advice that wasn't just memorable – it was unshakeable. She said things with such passion you took it as fact. From a young age, Nan set the benchmark I would hold for myself – and others – as I got older. Her favourite advice? 'You make whatever lucky boy you decide to be with work for it.' And sometimes, with a cheeky grin, she'd add, 'You've got to make sure they're handsome, Steph. You'll have to wake up next to them every morning, so they can't be ugly.'

Nan was big on independence and not taking crap from anyone, especially a man. Her message was clear: men should be gentlemen and treat you with the utmost respect, just like her Charles had treated her. He was her forever person. Before she met Charles, Nan had seen enough of the world – and a few men – to know what she didn't want. Those experiences opened her eyes and set in stone the standards she would hold for herself and instil in me. Nan always said that if she hadn't met Charles, she never would have married. That belief shaped her life – and mine – and for that, I'm grateful.

I wish everyone had a 'Nan' in their lives. A voice of reason; someone who set the bar sky-high and didn't let you forget it. She would cup your teary, heartbroken face in her hands, and her words would wash over you like a warm tide until, somehow, you actually started to believe that you were already enough, already whole.

And yes, I'm one of those rare arseholes who met her soulmate at age seventeen. I know how lucky that makes me but, even then, Nan's words rang in my ears: 'You don't need anyone to complete you, Stephy'. It was great advice, but I took it to the extreme. There's a fine line between high standards and cutting yourself off from love. And boy, did Ryan have to work hard to break down my walls.

I often hear how guys like to 'play it cool' and give out mixed signals like Oprah likes to give out free cars. Ryan was the opposite. I knew from day one that he wanted to be my boyfriend. How? Well, somehow, I got dragged along on a double date the very next week. My friend Amy had a crush on Ryan's mate Danga – bogan for Daniel. I went as moral support and guess who was tagging along like an excited puppy? Within hours, Ryan asked me to be his girlfriend, to which I just laughed and replied, 'You could be a serial killer for all I know. I just met you.'

Lucky for our future children, Ryan was as persistent as those creepy men flashing their dicks on *Chat Roulette* (a website we would all rather erase from our memory). Okay, that sentence sounded wrong but you get the picture . . . Wait, don't visualise it. *Gross.* After a few months, I finally agreed. To which he said romantically, 'I need to change my relationship status on Myspace.' What can I say? He has a way with words. Sadly for my friends, everyone was about to move down a rank in my Top 10.

With each brick he removed, the closer he got – not just to me, but to the chaos lurking at Meadow Lane. And worse, I knew that if he kept going, he'd eventually reach the heart of it. He'd see me – all of me – along with the fragile truths and labels I'd worked so hard to bury.

•

'I can't find him in the school album,' Mum said, walking into my bedroom, holding a pile of my school yearbooks in her arms.

Fuck.

'Oh, Ryan was always sick on school photo day,' I replied as casually as possible.

'He was always sick on photo day, eh?'

Some of my guy friends at school had made it clear that Ryan was a derro because of the school he went to and the suburb he lived in. This was probably the only time I saw them show their bitchy side. Sure, we messed with each other, but they were just being shitheads. They hadn't even met Ryan. When they did they loved him. I couldn't understand why people judged schools, locations and others so easily. It was probably because of Ady, but it didn't add up. Nonetheless, their reaction made me nervous, because I hadn't even told my parents I had a boyfriend.

So what did I do? I lied. I said Ryan went to our school, which also would cover my arse for how I met him in the first place. Remember, I'd lied about the party. But I didn't anticipate Mum's journalist nose. My parents didn't judge people because of their status or education, but this was the first time I was introducing them to a 'proper boyfriend'. What can I say? I kinda felt like I was coming out of the closet. With no boyfriend on the horizon for years, I think they suspected I was a lesbian. The fact I wore boys T-shirts from Best & Less probably didn't help.

When I finally introduced Ryan to my family, his confident exterior was nowhere to be seen. He was shy, quiet and very polite. Which surprised me, but also made me realise he was serious. He cared what they thought of him. Nan didn't need any convincing. 'You did good, Steph. He's a lovely chap,' she said. 'Handsome too. Reminds me of my Charles.' Well, no one was ever going to top that. She kept accidentally calling him *Brian* for the first few weeks but Ryan never corrected her.

I didn't tell him about Ady for three months. It wasn't out of shame, but out of fear; fear because I actually liked the guy, and we all know that if he didn't treat Ady the way he deserved to be treated it was goodbye. It was like a personality test or a human decency test. The first time Ryan met Ady he shook his hand and said, 'Hey Ady, how are you going, mate?' Later, he even gave him a hug. A few months into our relationship, Mum convinced Ryan to build a wall in our lounge room. My big brother sat there watching Ryan with more interest than when he watched the Yellow Wiggle singing 'Hot Potato'. At one stage, Ady picked up some sandpaper. I came into the room and saw the most beautiful sight. Ryan standing behind Ads, his hand covering my brother's, helping him sand the wall.

Fuck. I'm a goner.

This was the furthest I'd ever let anyone in. My walls began to crumble, brick by brick. *Surely there's a catch*, I thought. I waited for the red flags; the ones my girlfriends warned me about. But they never appeared. *Maybe that's the red flag!* I told myself. So, six months in, I freaked out and tried to dump him. It didn't work, of course. He just reassured me we could take things slow and do whatever made me comfortable. When everything else felt out of control – the chaos at home, the unpredictability at school, my own spiralling thoughts – Ryan held firm. He became the thing that kept me steady, the thing that made me believe, for the first time, that the storm wouldn't last forever. He became my home in human form. My anchor.

•

Around six months after we met, Ryan said he loved me. It finally hit home that he wasn't going anywhere, like I was expecting him to. I said I loved him too, because I couldn't deny that I did, even though my internal monologue was still trying to convince me otherwise.

A year later, he asked me to move in with him. It felt too good to be real. *Wait, what? I can escape the storm for good?* But then it hit me: it would mean leaving Nan behind. I couldn't do that. The night Ryan asked me, I tossed and turned, unable to sleep. Then I did something smart: I confided in Nan. 'Um, Nan, I have to tell you something.'

'Let it rip,' she said.

'Ryan asked me to move in with him.' I looked at the ground, unable to meet her gaze. Not because I was scared of her reaction, but because it meant our time was coming to an end. We were two peas in a granny flat; a package deal.

'Stephy. What have I always told you? Get out of here!'

'But what about you?'

She pulled me in for a hug. 'I'm tough, you know I can stand up for myself.'

And tough she was.

If it weren't for Nan, I wouldn't be writing this book today. Nan didn't just save me – she gave me the courage to save myself. And while this book is far from over, she was, and always will be, one of the heroes of my story. What I thought would be the happiest day of my life – leaving Meadow Lane – ended up also being one of the hardest. With tears in my eyes, I carried my bags up the driveway and out of there. The guilt I carried was even heavier.

THINGS NOT WORTH BICKERING OVER – A RATING SCALE

A Steph Pase Approved Relationship Irritation Index

- **Socks on the floor: 4/10**

  Mildly annoying. Stick them on his pillow. Passive-aggressive but a satisfyingly smelly revenge.

- **Leaving food out on the kitchen bench: 6/10**

  What are we? A bird house? More like a magnet for flies. Rating starting to get up there, mate. If he does this twice in a day or week (choose one) the score doubles and you ought to roast him like the turkey he also left out.

- **Using your 'show' tea towel: 3/10**
  Okay, I never used to be this person, and honestly can't be arsed to bother with it anymore, but still. The show tea towel is meant to make the kitchen look pretty, not be used to dry dishes. Preposterous.
- **Turning on a shitty action movie and falling asleep three minutes in: 6/10**
  Rating goes to 10/10 if Tom Cruise is in it.
- **Bugging me to get ready and as soon as we're about to leave spends double the time on the toilet: 10/10**
  Bro, I could have spent an extra five minutes at Procrastination Station.

Scale tip: If it's under a 6/10, just give him shit (if you're like us and your love language is roasting each other) and move on. We're not here for mama's boys. Pick up your shit, bro.

Chapter 7

Numb

'We should really get our fridge handle fixed or, I don't know, just get an *actual* fridge handle,' I said, hand on hip, head tilted to one side. I was in the kitchen, leaning against the laminate benchtop in our first-ever rental – a small three-bedroom house which Ryan and I were sharing with another couple. Protruding from the fridge door was a big, black, veiny dildo. You heard me right. You know the saying the kitchen is the heart of the home? For us, it was the *appendage* of the home. Dicks all around. The dildo was the showstopper, doubling as a makeshift handle and a guaranteed icebreaker.

Ever since Ryan and I had moved in together, I'd had one thought running through my head: *I can do and eat whatever I want.* Every time I stared into our new pantry, my eyes lit up (as teenagers on a $80 grocery budget that was saying something). Like many young renters, we had the 'just moved out of home starter pack':

- Mi Goreng and two-minute noodles
- Freezer meals
- A jar of Chicken Tonight
- Nurofen for the hangovers

Coming from Meadow Lane where food was often scarce, it felt like a glorious smorgasbord. This stuff was *ours*, bought with *our* pooled money, and I was free to eat what I wanted, when I wanted. It was a whole new world. Sing it, Princess Jasmine.

The house itself was a fixer-upper. The kitchen featured yellow-stained cabinetry, a sticky laminate benchtop, and a dripping tap. We had a hand-me-down toaster – permanently set to 'incinerate' – and old lino flooring that curled up at the corners. If all that didn't scream 'teenage share house', the fact we had enough alcohol to start our own bottle shop surely would have. Failing that, there was the dildo. A friend had plunged the sex toy into the fridge door during one of our ten or so house-warming parties. Somehow, it stuck. Literally. The suction on that thing was stronger than my will to fix the fridge, though not quite as strong as the messy tendencies from my childhood that had followed me all the way from Meadow Lane.

We stopped noticing the dildo after about a week. I guess I was used to pretending things were normal – like how I'd grown used to sharing my space with my long-time friends, Anxiety and Chaos. The former had moved in, rent-free, and was taking up a room in my mind without so much as offering to cover utilities. Rude. Luckily, I'd left Chaos behind, or so I thought. I was so used to the tension and unpredictability of my childhood home that, despite being a bunch of eighteen year olds stumbling our way through young adulthood, the peace and quiet that echoed through our new rental – well, from Monday to Thursday – felt almost . . . unsettling.

I was in my first year at the University of Wollongong. After graduating high school, I still didn't know what I wanted to do, but I did know I wanted to write, so I went with a Bachelor of Communication and Media Studies majoring in journalism. A fancy way of saying I studied a bit of everything – marketing, PR, media theory (and journalism). A jack-of-all-trades degree.

In many ways, I was thriving living with Ryan. But some days, I felt like an imposter, 'playing house' with my boyfriend. For example, I didn't know how to work the bloody washing machine. Nan had always done my washing. I'd insist she didn't, but she was as stubborn as she was loving. One day, I sat cross-legged on our second-hand couch, surrounded by open notebooks, half-finished to-do lists, and a half-eaten cheese toastie. 'Shit,' I muttered. 'My uni assignment's due next *week*, not next *month*.' I flopped back dramatically. 'Why can't I just be normalllll?'

'Because that would be boring,' Ryan said, watching the footy.

'I just want to be naturally organised. You know, one of those Type A's who are always on time. Not someone who walks into a room and forgets why she's there in the first bloody place.'

He glanced at me. 'You mean someone who actually has a sense of time?'

'Exactly!' I sat up, waving a crumpled page in the air. 'I want to be the kind of person who remembers birthdays without needing them tattooed on her forehead. Someone who doesn't need six alarms just to hand in an assignment. I'm such a goddamn mess.'

He reached over and brushed a crumb from my mouth. 'Yeah, but you're *my* mess.'

Between uni, work, friends and parties every weekend, it was like I was trying to sprint on a treadmill . . . in thongs. Impossible, and not a sight anyone wants to witness. Growing up, our parents' generation seemed to have this 'adulting' thing down pat. We were taught not to question authority, to believe that what our parents said was 100 per cent true, and to never, ever talk back. We then grew into adults, waiting for a switch to click, for life to present a yellow brick road for us to follow – first stop confidence and abilities, second stop a well-paid job, third stop a family – up until you become some eighty-year-old granny swinging her bra that resembled two salad bowls around in the air because she nailed it at life. This pathway seemed to work out for the previous generations, so why did it feel so alien to me? Looking back, I know they were acting in a role too. One they also likely didn't know how to play. They were winging it just as much as we are.

Whenever we had friends over, I played the part of laid-back, easy-going Steph. And in many ways, I *was* that person. Things that seemed to bother others, didn't faze me – like if Bethany said my party sucked, or if it rained on my birthday. But beneath the cool exterior, there was always the storm – the endless cycle of worry and 'what-ifs'. While my mates woke up and got on with their day, I was caught in the undercurrent of everything that could go wrong. Of course, I'm sure my friends had their own anxieties and worries, but they hid them better. I was the same naïve Steph from high school, where stuff often went over my head. Sometimes I'd stare at our dildo-adorned fridge and wonder, *Did it say something about us?* About me? Acting as something I wasn't? Separate. I always felt separate.

Trust me to get all deep and meaningful over a rubber dick.

THE MESSY GIRL'S GUIDE TO KEEPING YOUR HOUSE LIVEABLE

The Catch-All Basket aka This-doesn't-fucking-belong-here tub.

This hack will change your life because unfortunately people can't put their shit away (me included).

Put a basket in the main shared area of the house; we have ours in the lounge room. Throughout the day, chuck in anything that doesn't belong: hair ties, receipts, random toys, socks, fridge dildos. Set an alarm daily to empty it. Or when it's full and starts judging you. In our house we have a basket each so we just grab and put it away ourselves (okay . . . or the mum does it). No stress. No scattered crap. Just one place for the mess to land. A tidy home doesn't need to be perfect – just easier to deal with or disguise.

•

'Number nine, please.'

I was at Noodle Box, my go-to spot, grabbing my new signature late breakfast: Mongolian Beef. Number nine had become my number one choice for the most important meal of the day. Soon after I moved in with Ryan, I started developing little rituals that gave me a sense of control, like my new diet – both solid and liquid. My stomach was thriving, although I couldn't say the same for my wallet. But hey, I was a regular at Noodle Box, which meant that every other visit they threw in a free mixed entrée. That's basically saving money, right? Girl math.

The slippery slope had begun on day one. On our first night, we didn't finish unpacking our stuff – we weren't even close. Instead, I drank half a bottle of vodka, ordered pizza, and passed out at 2 a.m. *Hey, we've just reached a huge milestone*, I told myself. *Of course we're going to celebrate with a few drinks. It's normal.* When I drank, the tight feeling in my chest would ease and the chatter in my head would stop. The only thing that could quiet those million overlapping conversations was booze. When Ryan got home from work, I would innocently ask, 'Do we have any beer?' I knew we had beer. I would never allow us to run out of alcohol, the only 'life admin' task I was all over.

Of course, booze provided only temporary relief. The next day, I'd wake up, my anxiety even stronger. But even so, as I sat up in bed – *our* bed – next to my soulmate, it would take me all of ten minutes to start wondering when I could drink next, so I could make it all go quiet again. Sometimes, I couldn't even work out what the brain chatter was about because it was so loud.

I was in complete denial. All I knew was that I was young, I was free and I deserved a drink because it was a Tuesday and I wrote two paragraphs of my uni assignment. Ryan was a teenager and a tradie and so a few beers after work wasn't unusual. It was easy to do this without questioning it. I was addicted to the feeling of those first few sips oozing through my body, sending a relaxing hum down my arms and legs. My chest felt as though it was having a stretch after it'd been cramped in a confined space for weeks, although it was usually only days (if that) between sessions.

Alcohol became that friend I'd been looking for, the one who doesn't judge, makes you feel like everything is okay, and gives you the confidence to say and do whatever you please. Of course, she leaves you feeling worse than when she found you. She was warm and soothing but her presence was addictive. One thing I couldn't do without her was public speaking. My ritual before every uni presentation was to head to the uni bar, skol a jug of beer, and strut into class with a new-found confidence. While I was speaking, there was Alcohol sitting up the back row, giving me that quiet, false charisma that I needed. With her by my side I could do anything – besides drive.

It was easy to be in denial that my drinking was a problem because we were all doing it. Our house was a drinking den. We drank for games night; we drank on Thursdays if we didn't have to work; we drank when it was a weekday, but it was sunny outside. Then I had my own personal rituals. I drank when I had a rough day, I drank when I had a good day, I drank because I was bored, while I cleaned, and when I needed comfort. Then I started to drink because I was home alone and felt 'grown-up'. Sometimes I even drank out of a water bottle so people didn't think it was weird that I was drinking at 11 a.m. on a Saturday, after we'd been up drinking all the previous night.

I continued to kid myself until alcohol started to affect something sacred: my relationship. It happened slowly at first, but after a while, Alcohol became our third wheel. And while Ryan and I were together physically, mentally I was often somewhere else. My new bestie – let's call her Ally – began to make me paranoid. Was Ryan really my anchor or was he hiding something? Ally would lean in close and whisper in my ear, planting doubts that hadn't been there before. Paranoia wasn't something I typically felt but Ally had a way of making me question everything.

Ryan thinks you're a burden, Ally whispered.

You're broken and he knows it, she snarled.

He's going to eventually tire of you, she sneered.

Most of the time, I could brush her off. I was good at rationalising with myself, knowing which things weren't worth the drama. But sometimes, Ally was *really* good at convincing me that what she was saying was true. Sometimes, when she got into my head, I'd unknowingly start an argument with Ryan about an imaginary problem. This wasn't the person – or the couple – I wanted to be. It was bizarre how much power Ally had over me. And honestly? It scared me. My brain felt like it needed to create drama to get back to a baseline of anxiety – an emotion that felt 'normal' and 'safe'. Happy ever after? Now *that* was scary. Much easier to self-sabotage and create unnecessary drama than to enjoy a peaceful and happy life.

So you could say the first six months – okay, a year – living out of home was not a healthy time. Up until the age of nineteen, I was one of those arseholes who could eat whatever she pleased and not gain a kilo. The one thing that had always been constant in my life – besides Nan and now Ryan – was my weight. But that was changing. One evening, getting ready for a party, I tried pulling on a dress I'd worn just a few months earlier. I hoped Ryan wouldn't walk in and witness what looked like me exiting the birth canal. Let's just say it was snug. But not 'sexy snug'; it was more like trying to put on wet skinny jeans three sizes too small.

'Ryan, I'm going on a health kick,' I announced over breakfast, nursing a hangover and slurping a Diet Coke.

He glanced at the drink in my hand.

'Hey . . . it's *Diet*,' I said. 'I'm going to join the gym. And stop drinking beer. How many calories in a shot of vodka?'

'More than water, put it that way.'

Did my health kick work? What do you reckon? Within eighteen months of leaving home, I stacked on 25 kilograms. I know, right? I was baffled, especially with the intense effort I was putting in.

Who would've thought that switching my choice of alcohol and dabbling in the gym once a fortnight wasn't the secret to a six-pack?

I'd escaped the suffocating chaos of my childhood home. The yelling, the constant tension – it was all gone, no longer clasping me in place with its cruel claws. For a while, I thought that was it. That was the answer. Just leave. Change the scenery and everything will be okay. Here's the thing: changing the environment that made you sick doesn't make you better. Sure, I got away from the person who'd been feeding me poison, but that didn't matter. In years to come, I'd uncover a gut-wrenching truth: I had picked up the spoon myself.

SLUMP SURVIVAL PLAN (FOR WHEN YOU'RE FEELING LIKE A POTATO)

Step 1: Call it what it is (and ask how you got here)
You're in a slump. That doesn't make you lazy, broken, or doomed – it just means your cup is empty. Have you been doing too much of what drains you and too little of what lights you up? Are you burnt-out, overwhelmed, disconnected, or stuck in autopilot? Have you gone weeks without laughing or even feeling like yourself?

Step 2: Ditch the all-or-nothing and pick micro habits
Pick three micro habits that light you up. No shoulds – only wants. This could be a five-minute walk outside (sunlight is therapy), reading a sexy, silly fiction book (hello, mental escape), or journalling whatever the hell's in your head (no pressure, just vibes).

Step 3: Audit your routine (with brutal honesty)

Write out your routine (I mean your *real* routine). Then high-light the habits that are contributing to the slump versus the ones that feel good. For example 'staying up on TikTok until 2 a.m.' is sadly going to be slump.

Step 4: Subtract before you add

Before we even try to add habits, we have to look at what's causing the slump and whatever is weighing us down.

Step 5: Break it down

Reduce overwhelm by breaking tasks into smaller steps and focusing on one thing at a time. Three tasks max – other-wise, it's a setup for failure. Remember: this is not your setback, it's your comeback.

Chapter 8

Cabbage soup, anyone?

Ryan Ring Me: Where are you?

Me: In the toilets.

Ryan Ring Me: You've been gone ages. Did you fall in?

Me: Worse.

Ryan Ring Me: You shit yourself.

Me: . . .

Ryan Ring Me: ????

Me: Well, at least this will be a funny story one day.

Ryan Ring Me: Don't tell me you had those stupid skinny teas before we came to the pub.

Me: . . .

Ryan Ring Me: ????

Me: I was trying to multitask weight loss and socialising. It's called being efficient.

Ryan Ring Me: It's called being silly.

Me: . . .

Ryan Ring Me: And how did being efficient turn out?

Me: Shit. Literally.

I was nineteen when I shit myself at the pub. There's no other way to say it. It happened, and it happened because of so-called 'skinny teas'. I know. You don't need to tell me. I had managed to get through most of my teenage years without officially joining the 'dieting club' – a club where, instead of a welcome shirt, you're handed a pack of those 'Zero Calorie Noodles' – you know the ones that are like chewing on an earthworm. But after my weight climbed, I finally succumbed to the inevitable pressures of viewing my body as an ornament instead of what it actually is – a storage room, housing important shit, so we can, you know . . . live.

Unfortunately for us women, inconvenient things like organs make it rather hard to achieve the stomach of a Victoria's Secret model, post-flu. Ridiculous, right? Clearly, we should be able to swap our pancreas for an extra ab here or there. It's not like it's *important* or anything. Pfft, pancreas, smancreas.

It was the second year of uni, and many of my girlfriends had embarked on the next rite of passage: dieting. Everyone was attempting to commit to the gym longer than their week-long relationships, do shots of fat burners like they were Jager, and only eat things that sucked the joy from our lives, such as rice cakes, soups and celery sticks.

The conversation went from cute boys to carb withdrawals. Turns out both can give you a raging headache and make you feel like shit. It was a collective obsession, like we had all agreed that slimming down was as important as breathing. I, of course, had to get involved. Besides, I had a *proper boyfriend* now that I had to stay 'hot' for. Or so I thought back then. Silly girl. In reality, I could have worn a stained hoodie with a messy bun, odd socks, and a pimple on my chin and Ryan would have looked at me like I was Sydney bloody Sweeney in that rom-com where she's just all hot and shit. He never once commented on my weight, but as soon as I started dieting, he wouldn't stop trying to feed me 'real human food'.

'Steph, look what I have,' he said, waving a plate of pasta in my face like some culinary terrorist.

'I'm fine. I've got my tea,' I muttered. My stomach growled. Traitor.

'That stuff smells like the inside of a compost bin.'

'So do your farts,' I shot back, staring at his plate. 'Can I just . . . smell it?' I asked quietly. But desperate.

'My fart or the pasta?' he grinned, shovelling another forkful into his ungrateful beautiful mouth.

I went back to sipping swamp water and nibbling earthworms, minding my own business like a good girl trying to reach her magic number on the bathroom scales.

It felt like a new fad for me, this dieting thing. Little did I know, the groundwork for how I'd one day view my body had quietly been laid for years. The reality TV shows hummed in the background as I did my homework, soundbites planting seeds in my growing mind, shaping the thoughts that would one day consume it. The magazine headlines; the celebrities shamed as 'fat'; the daily ritual of my mum weighing herself and cringing; and overhearing women talking at lunch about food and their bodies as if they were fragile Tamagotchis that needed constant monitoring and didn't actually belong to them. They didn't. Society made sure they never would. All those lessons were starting to sink in.

Unlike my earlier attempt at 'cleaning up' my diet, this time I was ready and willing to embrace real change to lose those kilos that had rudely decided to not make their way to my boobs. But where do you even start to lose weight or 'be healthy' as I was calling it at the time? I knew as much about diet and exercise as I did about time management, which was precisely *zero*.

So what did I do? Grabbed every 'health' magazine in sight. Looking back, I use the term 'health' *very* loosely and generously here. They were basically a watered-down version of Mum's bathroom magazines. Naturally, my first attempt at 'Mission: Be Worthy' aka 'Stay Hot for Ryan' was to take the laziest, easiest route possible. Meal prep? Eating whole foods? Moving my body? *Ha!* Absolutely not. Enter 'skinny teas', stage left. You may remember the year 2015 when skinny teas became all the rage. While writing this chapter I googled 'skinny teas' and they unfortunately still exist. Speaking from experience, avoid them like the plague.

'I just wish I wasn't always so hungry,' I whined to Kara, my voice laced with frustration. We were on yet another one of our 'diets'. Baby food diet, maybe? We had apparently forgotten our age *and* stopped using our brains.

Suddenly, Kara sat upright on her bed like she'd just discovered sliced bread. *Mmm . . . bread.* 'There's this lady at my work – she's super skinny. She drinks this stuff called skinny tea.'

Perfect. A woman I'd never met became our diet guru. And just like that, I was sold on the tea movement. Next thing I knew I was standing in line at the local health food store that smelled like a wet cat that had been shoved in the microwave. But hey, I had secured the goods and the packaging was green. We all know green means healthy, right?

'Cleanses toxins and reduces bloating. Drink twice a day for best results,' I read aloud to Ryan who was already shaking his head. I optimistically translated this as 'transform you into Xtina from the "Dirrty" music video' – same-same, right? Little did I know you not only lost kilos – but also your dignity. Looking back, the label should have said: 'Drink twice a day for explosive diarrhoea, a ruined pair of Spanx and public humiliation'. In reality, they were just fancy-arse laxatives. Clearly I didn't know this yet.

And guess who's brilliant idea it was to double up on the tea before heading to the pub? The same idiot who was eating baby food. All because I knew that I was about to smash a chicken parma and a shit-ton of booze. Safe to say it was not one of my finest moments. An hour later, there I was, by the pool table, mid-conversation about last night's *Big Brother Uncut* . . . when it hit me. At first, I thought I had a bit of extra gas, but then came the crippling stomach cramps. (I was about to write *TMI*, but I think we're past the pleasantries.) Next came the sweats, melting my carefully painted-on Maybelline Mousse. It never stood a chance. That stuff had the staying power of a Post-it note in the rain. And finally came the terrifying realisation that I had royally fucked up. My insides were a jet about to take off without a pilot. The sticky carpet of the pub – my runway. Trying to play it cool, I casually walked towards the bathroom. Well, as casually as one can while carrying the entire weight of their dignity and livelihood in their tightly clenched butt cheeks. Once in the bathroom, I waddled into the stall like a guilty dog caught chewing the couch again.

I was there for over an hour.

To pass the time I scrolled Facebook.

Skinny teas just updated their status to: 'Here to ruin your digestive system and life'.

I don't need to paint you a picture (no one wants to see that). Let's just say, those teas worked. They worked *too well*. I spent the last twenty minutes trying to figure out how I was going to walk back out there with even a shred of dignity. I texted Ryan for moral support but, as you know, that didn't exactly work out either. The least he could do was bring me a shipping container of toilet paper – I mean, I was doing this for *him*, after all.

That night, I learnt three things. One: Spanx cannot survive a poonami. Two: the pub is no place for a bowel crisis. Three: the dieting world is bullshit. You buy a product that promises to make you skinny and hot, and all you get is the memory of shitting yourself on $10 schnitty night next to the lovely family celebrating their son's thirteenth birthday.

Steph just updated their status to: *PSA: If it's green and it's not a vegetable, run.*

I'd love to say this incident taught me a lesson about 'quick-fix diets' but, dear friend, this is not fiction. Just like Bart Simpson, I need to touch the stove at least ten times before realising that it's in fact hot. In my defence, I was only nineteen. And let's not forget what we women are up against: a system that is designed to make us hate our bodies, so it can then sell us the solution to skinny salvation. On social media, which was heavily Facebook-orientated at the time, my algorithm couldn't wait to serve me up the next 'big thing' in weight loss. The cabbage soup diet had entered the chatroom.

The infamous cabbage soup recipe

Serves: The devil.

Ingredients:

- 1 head of cabbage (because apparently, this is what we're doing with our lives)
- 6 carrots (because a spoonful of *meh* helps the cabbage go down)
- 2 celery stalks (the vegetable equivalent of a wet blanket)
- 1 large onion (so you can taste your tears with every mouthful)

- 1 can of diced tomatoes (if you close your eyes, hold your breath and hit your head on the bench, it tastes vaguely Italian)
- 1 green capsicum (the only green thing I now trust)
- 4 cups of water (because we wouldn't want to overwhelm the cabbage)
- A sprinkle of salt and pepper (don't get crazy now – this is a diet, not a party)

Instructions:
1. Chop all the veggies into tiny pieces, because you obviously haven't suffered enough.
2. Dump them into a giant pot of water and wait for any sign of flavour to evaporate.
3. Simmer for 30 minutes, or until the cabbage reaches its full soggy potential or resembles a foreskin.
4. Season with salt, pepper and leftover tears.
5. Serve yourself a steaming bowl of sadness and question your life choices with every mouthful.

Pro tip: Don't do it.

•

Ah, the good ol' cabbage soup diet. I didn't even last a week on this one. But hey, at least I beat my two-day record on the shit-yourself skinny tea. Did I lose weight? Yes. Did I feel good? Hell no, unless 'good' was code for 'ravenous'. Did the weight stay off? Of course not. As soon as I even looked at solid food it came back. But it did give me something to focus on. A great distraction from my mate Anxiety who at this stage was peaking, as was my insomnia.

I'd always been a dreadful sleeper. According to my brain, I needed to be on high alert, 24/7. And before you start spritzing lavender oil at me, I tried it all:

- **Melatonin:** Cute but useless when your brain thinks over-the-counter sleeping pills are a warm cup of milk.
- **Herbal teas:** Please see my lawyer for further comments.
- **Meditation apps:** Didn't exist yet. But I had one track on my iPod. It seemed that at the time a body scan felt more like a police pat down.
- **No screens before bed:** Hard when your boyfriend loves to watch action movies to pass out. Nothing more soothing than an explosion and Tom Cruise's face that I want to punch.
- **Warm baths before bed:** Pass. Our bath became our unappointed washing basket. Sadly, no shower curtains here . . .
- **Magnesium:** See melatonin.

I just needed someone to hit me in the neck with a horse tranquiliser – problem solved. I'd be good to go.

It's a unique kind of loneliness lying next to someone you love, hearing the soft murmur of voices in the lounge room, each turn of the ceiling fan now as familiar as the back of your hand. The only thing keeping you company is your brain – in all the worst ways.

By this stage, Ryan and I had been together for over a year and, although he had never suffered from anxiety, he tried to understand what I was experiencing.

'Just pretend your old boss rang you the night before work and said he needed to talk to you about something,' I'd explain. Suddenly, a look of recognition reached his eyes and sadness graced his face. This was the closest that he could get to understanding – and it was only the tip of the iceberg. Although he wasn't immune to feeling anxious, he could quite literally raw-dog life: without meds and the need to drink every day. I was one of the lucky ones who found a guy who could carry calm – and carry my storm when I needed him to. I tried to do the same for him. There were nights when he'd come home worn out from a job and a boss who made him feel small and stupid. As he ate dinner on the couch, I'd be in the other room typing out his TAFE assignments, cross-checking notes I didn't understand, so he wouldn't fall behind. I'd done a full day of uni and work but I didn't care. This is what we did.

For years, Mum had been trying to convince me to try anti-depressants. The topic first came up when I was around seventeen, after my parents discovered that I'd been harming myself. If you recall, this is when Nan and Mum finally told me the real reason my grandfather Charles had died. I think they hoped it would give me perspective on what I was doing. I'm not going to go into detail about self-harm. When it comes to that time in my life, I struggle to find the words. Self-harming is no longer a part of the picture. But teenage Steph? She was going *through it*. At the time, it felt like the only thing I had control over. It became an outlet. It happened and it's something too many people experience.

Back to the meds . . . I had my reasons for being hesitant, and no, it wasn't because I was anti-medication. Far from it. It's obvious I didn't live by the motto 'my body is a temple'. But I still had concerns. Growing up, I'd witnessed my mum's journey with mental health medication – the good, the bad and the catastrophic. At the time, back in the early noughties, I didn't know anyone else my age who took antidepressants. I also didn't want more proof that I was 'separate'. I wanted to be like everyone else who didn't need medication to survive. I had a brother who couldn't talk.

Shouldn't I just be grateful to not have a disability? Why couldn't I 'just' be happy? These were the thoughts spinning around in my head whenever I thought about medical intervention.

'Stephanie, the doctor will be ready to see you shortly,' the receptionist called out. If I wasn't already nervous, using my full name was going to do it.

I sat there in the waiting room, the clock on the wall ticking away as I waited to see the doctor that I had been going to since I was two. My leg was bouncing up and down a million miles a minute.

'Steph! How have you been?' the doctor said, greeting me like an old friend.

'I'm . . . okay,' I replied on autopilot. 'Well, actually, I'm a bit of a mess, to be honest.' I stared down at my shoes. I was grateful that my doctor had known me, basically, my entire life. It made talking about this whole anxiety thing a lot less daunting. 'I'm just so sick of feeling like this,' I said, tears filling my eyes. 'I wondered if I could try . . . medication.' I whispered the word as if I was dropping the f-bomb.

He nodded with a kind, thoughtful expression on his face, as though he'd been waiting for this moment for years. He then glanced at his computer screen like it had all the answers. I wondered if I could take a peak and it would tell me the meaning of life. Then he gave me the speech. 'I'm hearing you, Stephanie. We can definitely get started on this, and I really think it will help. But it is important that you understand it can be a bit of a process to find you the right medication. Sometimes you have to try a couple of different ones first. It's also important that you know the common side effects.' And then, like any good doctor, he started listing them:

- Mild headaches
- Nausea
- Possibly growing an extra arm (okay, not really)
- Insomnia
- Oh, and weight gain

And just like that, I was out. Weight gain? Absolutely not. Of course, my mental health wasn't nearly as important as my figure. Obviously. I also wouldn't be able to drink. Hell-to-the-no. Booze was my life raft. Sitting on the worn, grey fabric of the patient's seat, I tried to imagine life without my new roommate Ally. And I couldn't. Without Ally I wouldn't be fun, I wouldn't be confident . . . Then I had the striking realisation: who the hell was I without alcohol? I thanked my doctor for his time and left.

If only I could go back to that Steph and tell her that not only will this journey help us, but it will help so many others. Looking back, I think I was ready to use any excuse not to start the rocky road ahead, from what I had seen first-hand. Fast-forward to today and my posts about anxiety are the same ones flooded with comments from women who finally feel seen. If you're wondering, yes, I did start taking the meds. And yes, they did end up being a lifeline.

So what changed my mind? I'd had enough. Turns out, you can only outrun your own mind for so long. My 'rock bottom' didn't look like a big dramatic moment. It looked like a conversation with Ryan.

•

'Hun, I can't keep doing this,' I whispered to Ryan on the phone, my head cradled in my hands as I sat in a desk cubicle in the uni library.

'What's going on? Are you okay?' His voice was calm.

'I'm just . . . I'm done. Another day of no sleep, sitting through lectures I barely understand because I'm delusional at this point, and now I'm here trying to smash out an assignment I forgot was due.'

'Did you eat lunch?'

'Does four beers at the uni bar count?'

'Hun . . .'

'I know, I know,' I cut him off before he could start. 'I just . . . I can't keep living like this. I'm so tired of feeling this way. I can't focus, I can't sleep, I'm barely keeping my head above water, and honestly? I'm sick of myself. I'm sick of my own shit.'

'Remember, hun, you don't have to do this alone,' he said after a moment. 'Maybe it's time to give the meds a try?' I let his words sink in, the silence between us feeling heavier than usual. I knew he was right.

'I'm scared, you know? What if I lose myself?'

'You won't,' Ryan said. 'You'll still be you – just a version of you that's not fighting so damn hard to survive every day.'

I blinked back tears, nodding. 'Okay, I'll call the doctor tomorrow.'

'Good,' he said softly. 'And Steph?'

'Yeah?'

'I'm proud of you.'

That conversation was the catalyst to stop being passive. Unfortunately, for most of us, the pain of remaining the same has to be great enough in order for us to make a change. And in that very moment, I knew I couldn't keep doing this. I started the pills the very next week. At the same time, I reassessed my 'healthy eating', including the cycle of crash dieting and weight gain. I was slowly becoming aware of my 'all or nothing' personality – a trait I'd come to understand more in the future. Looking back, I can see how my diagnosis played a role in my eating habits and the way I saw my body. The impulsivity, the need for control, the obsession with 'fixing' myself – it was all tangled up with the way my brain works.

The big takeaway is this: being a female is a mind-fuck. Especially when your brain is fighting battles you don't understand. We are such beautifully complex creatures. Where's Dolly Doctor when you need her?

And as for that 'magic number' – the one I thought we'd all get assigned as adults? Remember the holy digits that dictate what we must strive for, starve for and be miserable for? Turns out, it doesn't exist. *We're* the ones who decide what we should weigh, how we should act, what we should do for work, who we should be to feel enough. To feel whole. Because here's the truth: the bathroom scales were never the culprit. It was us all along.

THINGS THE BATHROOM SCALES *CAN'T* MEASURE

- Your kindness when no one's watching.
- How you show up for people you love even when you're struggling too.
- How people out there still remember a time you made their day when they needed it most.
- The amazing, unique, kind energy you bring into a room.
- The hardest days; all of which you've survived.
- Your brilliant brain.

- Your growth even when you won't acknowledge it yourself.
- The feeling you give people when they think of you.
- Your giant heart.
- Your intelligence that no exam or test could ever measure.
- How hard you're trying, even when it doesn't show.
- The days you fought so hard just to get out of bed.
- The love you give freely to others. Now it's time to give it to yourself, beautiful soul.

What the bathroom scales *do* measure
Your relationship with gravity . . . boring!

Chapter 9

Jack of all trades

By the age of six, I had my future careers mapped out. Yes, plural. In primary school, I was already the Editor-in-Chief of my own newspaper, *The Dolphin Daily*. Don't even think about stealing the name – I know it's that good. I'd interview family members and craft front-cover exposés on Dad's favourite breakfast food. Breaking a story like 'Nan's Favourite Animal Finally Revealed' wasn't going to write itself. The people deserved the truth.

I was destined to be an entrepreneur. When I wasn't busy running *The Dolphin Daily*, I was in the laundry, rummaging through Mum's stash of old sheets. To her, they might have been rags, but to me, they were premium materials for my thriving Pokémon toy business, another humble side hustle. My process was flawless. I'd carefully sketch Pikachu, Bulbasaur or another fan fave onto the sheet using textas from the Reject Shop. Then, with surgical precision, I'd place a second layer of Ady's old bed-sheets (aka Pikachu's butt) underneath. After I had cut the outline and sewn around the edges, I would add the stuffing which was the leftover fabric scraps. Voilà! A custom-made Pokémon plush.

You could've called me the real Santa Claus – if I didn't still hold a grudge against him. Armed with an old camp table, a heap of sheet-stuffed 'Pokémon toys' and a big dose of ambition, I'd march up the driveway to set up shop.

'How much for the Nine-Tails?' Alex, the boy next door, asked. Ah, Nine-Tails – she was a masterpiece. Honestly, I almost kept her for myself. Alex didn't know it yet, but he was a lucky man.

'$3 for that one,' I said, my hand reaching to pat the drawn-on, stuffed clump of sheets like it was a loyal family dog.

My creations were in high demand, selling out in record time – five hours flat! Not bad for a kid with a dream, Ady's old bedsheets, a handful of textas and a sewing needle. After a busy day of sales, I'd head back inside and dive straight into managing my bustling newspaper. Regrettably, after many hours of hard work, *The Dolphin Daily* officially closed its doors. Perhaps people weren't ready for aquatic mammal publications – or maybe they just didn't appreciate groundbreaking journalism. A shame, really. But the fire to write, create and make a mark on the world continued to burn.

In high school, it baffled me how other people seemed to know exactly what they wanted to do. Amy: architect. Ash: teacher. Evan: engineer. It was as if they all had a map, with a single trail they simply had to follow. Meanwhile, my map must have come from Temu – twenty trails branching in different directions, chewed up edges, reeking of a boxed fart. Oh, and was that Hogwarts in the back right corner? Maybe I should just go there? Grow up to be a wizard. Knowing my luck I'd end up as Dobby the smelly elf. At least he's kind and somewhat cute, right? But I just never had an 'aha moment' of one thing I wanted to do. I wanted to do it all, be it all. And as a kid, no one told me otherwise.

I thought being multi-passionate was a good trait to have, but as I got older I realised I had to fit into a box. I found my passions exciting – but sometimes overwhelming. Surely we could just have a Sorting Hat that told us what to do. Besides, how could you possibly make a decision about the rest of your life at such a young age? It didn't help that I was indecisive: chicken sticks or sausage roll? *Girlfriend* or *Dolly* magazine? Team Seth or Team Ryan? Obviously Seth. Pretend I'm a lesbian to my parents – or not? Just girl things. At twenty-two, post-uni graduation, I still felt that way. How could I pick just one thing?

I still wanted to be a writer, where I felt safe to spill out my thoughts and make sense of them. I dreamt of working in home decor because I longed to create spaces that felt organised, peaceful, calm and safe – all the things I wasn't. And I'd enrolled in makeup school because, yes, I wanted to be a makeup artist. C'mon, keep up! I loved helping people see the beauty that was already there. Makeup wasn't about changing someone; it was about reminding them of what they already had. Soon, I was working at a M.A.C store. I loved holding up a mirror so a client could see their transformation. Their faces reminded me of Mum looking at her younger self in photos – but without the sadness.

My new antidepressants were helping too. Before them, life felt like a race, but I was tied to a tree at the starting line. Everyone was always 10 yards ahead of me, no matter how hard I tried. But since starting on the meds, I felt clearer. Grounded. I was finally able to *try*. I might not have been the fastest on the track, but at least I could negotiate with the ref. Thanks to years of convincing Ady to get out of the pool, I was good at hustling and negotiation. I'd resisted at first, but now? I wasn't spiralling with every whisper from Anxiety. She still clung to my arm, but her grip was weaker.

Despite graduating with a journalism degree, I knew it wasn't for me. I hated being told what to write. At uni, we were pushed to cover men in politics – a topic that made me want to gauge out my eyeballs. It made bloody cricket look riveting. Lifestyle or mental health stories? Yeah, not so much. Sure, I could hyper-focus when passionate – but if I wasn't interested? Forget it. Marketing and social media were the saving graces of my degree. Where thinking outside the box was mandatory. I enjoyed them, and boy would they help me later on.

I'd already felt the sting of feeling censored. I was fifteen when my writing got me into deep shit. The culprit was one (or five) of my non-fiction pieces that hit too close to home for its starring antagonist: Mum. She didn't appreciate 'finding' my journal under my mattress (I know, I'm baffled she found it too. Talk about maximum security breach). And she wasn't too thrilled to read my reports of a particularly hot-headed argument.

'But Mum—' I tried to protest. 'My counsellor told me to write.'

'Not about this. Not about *us*.' She held my journal in the air, a flash of my private thoughts in my schoolgirl handwriting. To put it mildly, it was like reading the comment section of a heated Facebook thread – minus Margaret's complaints about kids doing knock-and-runs in her street. And then she delivered her final line, 'I'm sending you to boarding school – you can learn some manners there.'

Fan-fucking-tastic. Soon enough there were ten tabs open on her computer screen, each one showcasing a different boarding school. When I became an adult – and I use the term *adult* very loosely here – I learnt all about Mum's parenting philosophy. 'You need to make kids scared of you, so you can control them,' Mum would tell my aunties when their own kids were being, well . . . kids.

Lovely, right? You can just feel the maternal warmth radiating off that nugget of wisdom. Nan told her to go to hell. My hero didn't wear a cape – she wore clip-on earrings and floral blouses from Sussan's. In the end, I wasn't sent to boarding school – for better or worse – but it took me a long time before I could let my thoughts flow freely on paper. Whenever I got pushback later – at uni, in jobs – it made sense why it hit so hard. I hated feeling boxed in. After graduating, I decided to lean into my multi-passionate personality. I could handle it all, right? And what was the harm in trying new things? Unfortunately, I soon realised that dreaming big – or, at least, diverse – can make other people uncomfortable. Shortly after I enrolled in makeup school, I remember having a conversation with an old school friend.

'Wait . . . you just got your journalism degree and now you're doing *makeup*?' he said.

'Umm . . . yeah. Why not?'

'Cool. Well, I got a job from *my* degree.'

Cool, Michael. Why don't you frame your degree and shove it up your arse, I thought, resisting the urge to swan dive into the vodka and Coke I was clutching.

People didn't get why I'd just spent three years of my life at uni, only to veer off in a different direction. To me, though, it felt far stranger to lock yourself into something you hated just because you'd already started. Sunk-cost fallacy, anyone? Better to 'waste' a few years figuring it out than end up like Barbara the secretary, who wanted to be a mime but spent decades buried in spreadsheets. Honestly, Barbara, life's too short – pull on your mime gloves and go make your invisible box already.

I got itchy feet in most jobs after about eighteen months. From my teenage years to my early twenties I held multiple gigs at once, pushing through long days and late nights because I needed the money. Ryan and I were a team – and no amount of alcohol or anxiety would stop that – but no matter how hard I tried, boredom or frustration would always creep in after a while, and I'd find myself craving something new. A major stressor was my bizarre, over-the-top anxiety around authority figures. You know when you're driving and there's a cop behind you? Suddenly, you feel like you've got a dead body and 10 kilos of cocaine stashed in the boot. That was me with every boss, supervisor or manager. Even if I was doing everything right, I'd still catch myself panicking, convinced I'd be hauled in for some imaginary crime or, worse, fired.

In contrast to journalism, I was loving the creative freedom of makeup school. Thanks to the boom in social media, it was an exciting time to be in the makeup world. Initially I taught myself by watching YouTube videos. Unfortunately, it was a tad too late for the concealer lips and glitter eyeliner I slapped on aged eighteen. My childhood friend Liv worked at M.A.C too. She already had a makeup business, and after picking her brain, I started my own: The Lipstick Bandit. The name was inspired by Nan. Whenever we were out at a restaurant and Nan finished eating, she would reach down, grab her black leather handbag and pop it on her lap. She'd then pull out her lipstick case and apply her lippy without looking in the tiny mirror – as though it was a reflex. Then came the signature move: she would grab a napkin, fold it in half and press her lips onto it. 'The lipstick bandit has struck again,' she'd say with a giggle, placing the napkin down to reveal a lipstick-shaped kiss.

I had never run a business before, but thankfully Ryan showed me the ropes of bookkeeping and all that boring but necessary stuff. Surprisingly, getting clients came easily thanks to some of the marketing I'd learnt at uni. I created Facebook ads (which at the time a monkey could do), and had stalls at wedding expos. I was carting yet another camping table up our driveway to set up shop, except this time my gear included banners, signs and a bulky 20-kilo makeup kit. I loved meeting excited brides-to-be and it wasn't long before I was booked out a year in advance. There were downsides, sure: the 3 a.m. wakeups and weekends gone. But it was mine. And I loved helping people see how beautiful they naturally were – with or without makeup.

'All finished! You look absolutely stunning,' I said, placing my eyeshadow brush into my brush belt – like a builder's belt except, instead of hammers and drills, it held an array of different-sized brushes. My client, Tracy, was the mother of the bride and I was doing a 'trial'. She was in her forties, and I could tell by the way she nervously fiddled with the hem of her shirt and kept saying 'sorry' for basically having a face, that she was extremely hard on herself and self-conscious. These were my favourite clients, not because I wanted them to feel that way – but because I was about to change that.

I passed the handheld mirror to her and she said . . . nothing. Perfect. Mission accomplished.

'How did you do that?' she said finally, staring into the mirror. It was as though instead of her reflection, Chris Hemsworth was staring back at her. Mate, if he was, I would have been licking that mirror like a dog. Sorry Ryan, love you.

'I didn't do anything,' I said. 'I just highlighted what is already there. It is all you. Your beauty. Nothing to do with me.' One of the best feelings in the world was when I could make people feel beautiful. All I had to do was show them what was already there. A stroke of eyeliner to bring out their jade green eyes, a pat of blush to show off their beautiful skin tone. It was all them.

I also got a job at the local gym. If you're confused, I don't blame you. The same girl who used to inhale takeaway like it was a sport and still couldn't catch anything besides a cold was now working at a gym. I'll explain in the next chapter, pinky promise. One day, Dad caught me handing out flyers on the street outside. At that point, I hadn't told my parents exactly what this new job entailed.

'What are you doing, Steph?' he asked.

'Ah, hey, Dad! Want a flyer?' I was joking, but he wasn't laughing.

We made small talk for a while, and then he gave me a hug. A pause. 'You know, you're better than this, Steph.'

Ouch. I knew he wanted the best for me, but it hit a nerve, one I pretended that wasn't there. Don't get me wrong, Mum and Dad always wanted me to be happy, but I know my constant career pivots gave them whiplash. Once they saw my business taking off, though, my trail of multi-passionate chaos didn't look so messy anymore. Funny how success can make even the biggest mess look intentional.

Dad wasn't the only person who was concerned about my career choices. I was flaky. Indecisive. Unable to commit. I knew that's what people thought, because my overly honest friends told me so. Always with a laugh, like it was an insider joke, not realising how much it hurt. 'Jack of all trades,' they'd say. And then the pause. The one where they're thinking 'master of none'. And then there were the comparisons to Ryan. Some said it as if it were a matter of fact. Apparently, Ryan was 'carrying the team' because . . . builder boyfriend = real job. Go sit on the pointy end of a hammer.

No one warns you that when you meet your future husband young, you grow up together. And people start comparing you like siblings. It's weird, right? Full-blown sibling rivalry with a side of incest vibes. Who's achieving more? Who's more sorted?

But inside our relationship, there was no scoreboard. In real life, Ryan and I weren't keeping score because we were both batting for the same team. Unless it was *Mario Kart* or bowling, then it was game on like *Donkey Kong*. But the big stuff? There was no jealousy, no resentment. We are teammates and want each other to win – because if one of us does, we both win. We combined our finances from early on. I mean, why have $5 when you can pool your cash and make it $10? It was a lifesaver for teenagers trying to scrape through life – or just a Tuesday – while praying there was enough cash left for heat-up pies for dinner.

Although Ryan is neurotypical, he's as driven and passionate as me. He also likes taking risks and doing things differently. He backed me every single time I wanted to switch gears, gently placing his warm, familiar hand over mine as I shakily got ready to engage the clutch. Glancing over at him seated in the passenger seat of my life, a small but encouraging smile would appear on his face; a smile that said 'you got this'. He gave me that extra push I needed, my fumbling hand, now steady. The familiar click echoed and suddenly, the path ahead didn't seem so uncertain – even if neither of us knew exactly where it would lead.

●

'I'm a complete failure,' I wailed one day. 'What am I doing, Ryan?'

I had met a friend for lunch and a few beers in, she'd made a comment about my *rollercoaster* career. As always, it was Ryan who reassured me. 'Don't listen to them, Steph,' he said. 'You don't have to do shit you don't want to do – even if it's written on your uni certificate.'

'But people think I'm just the girl with the wasted degree playing with blush and hanging out at the gym,' I sniffed, feeling sorry for myself.

'Who cares? People told me not to leave school after Year 10. They said if you don't make it to Year 12, you're stupid. And now look at us – we're killing it.' Ryan wasn't just on my team; he was simultaneously on the sidelines, pom-poms in hand, cheering me on – thankfully minus the short skirt and crop top. No one wants to catch a glimpse of a snail trail mid-cheer.

He wasn't my only cheerleader – I also had Nan. Whenever I felt doubtful, I heard her voice in my head and the speech she'd been giving me since I was a toddler:

'You can be anything you put your mind to.'

'You're going to do great things one day, Stephy.'

'The sky's the limit.'

So I stuck with my careers, despite my doubts – and the doubters. And soon I had evidence that showed I was making 'good' choices – at least in a financial sense. When you tell people you're a makeup artist, they picture you playing with glitter and pretty colours all day. The reality? I made more money doing a single wedding than I did in a week at the gym. I was working hard and I was on a curly, swirly career path – it just wasn't traditional. When I was younger, I seemed flighty and scattered. I won't lie – there was an undercurrent of wanting to feel 'good enough' in my career detours. We all learn that we *are* enough in our own time. Hence why most founders of successful businesses are often well into their forties when they decide to truly go for it.

From the outside my path did have a whiff of desperation about it, but really I was far from feeling lost – I was just trying things on for size. My passion always led me, even if it didn't make sense to others. I figured why stick with something you hate? I was finding my own way. I felt as if I had a bird's-eye view, zoomed out on all the paths, detours and hidden tracks I could take. Other people were zooming in on one path. They seemed laser-focused on what they needed to do to be successful. But what about happiness? I would rather sit in a stinking hot car and suffer through a game of cricket on the radio than narrow my dreams – because, let's be real, the only thing worse than watching cricket is *listening* to it. But then something changed: a conversation with Ryan convinced me to do the unthinkable.

I had just got home from another long day at the gym. No idea if it was the completely unfiltered look I wore or the fact he just knew I wasn't feeling fulfilled there anymore, but he *knew*. 'Steph, why don't you just quit?' he said.

'I can't. I need to make enough so we can afford a deposit for a house.' I was shocked he'd even asked the question.

'You make enough from one wedding. Imagine if you spent the extra energy juggling a full-time job at the gym on your business instead?'

Crazy fucker. Like that talking boy in preschool.

'Think about it,' he went on. 'You could spend the days doing bookkeeping and getting yourself out there even more than you do now. You'll be booked out for years.' He wrapped his arms around me, like he had already seen it play out.

'But what if I stop getting bookings? We won't have enough money,' I said, trying to pick his idea apart.

'But why would you?' he said in his logical, matter-of-fact tone. 'You just need to back yourself.'

Apparently I was dating Gandhi.

Looking back, was all this scattering of myself just another form of self-sabotage? Maybe the reason I gave myself so many 'options' and spread myself so thin was because I wasn't ready to truly bet on myself. That deep down, I didn't believe I could be successful at just one thing. People had always said I was flaky, indecisive, unable to commit. And somewhere along the way, I started to believe them. But Ryan never bought into that. He saw right through it – through me, the masks, the jokes, the endless distractions I piled on to avoid facing the truth. He believed in me even when I didn't believe in myself.

As children you're told you can do and be anything, but as you grow older, that message becomes more confusing. Oh, you can do anything as long as it's the one thing with a title we accept. You can be anything other than yourself. It felt like the world wanted to reduce my fire to a single flickering flame. All my passions were still there sizzling beneath the surface just waiting for that one pivotal, life-changing decision that was yet to take place.

Do you know what's surreal? I'm writing this book in my third warehouse, surrounded by a team of fifteen incredible staff members. Today, I'm the main breadwinner, providing for Ryan and our family. But in saying that, all my experiences led me here, bread crumb by bread crumb. Even in the moments when I felt lost, I kept moving – sometimes forwards, sometimes sideways – but I was always moving, even when the steps seemed so small they were barely noticeable. But they all add up. All you have to do is zoom out, and not be afraid to get messy.

Handing out flyers outside the gym? Not glamorous, but it helped me push past the shyness that made me avoid eye contact with the check-out chick at Coles. Working at the gym taught me more about marketing than my degree ever did. Managing wedding makeup bookings? A crash course in connection and organisation – two things I thought I sucked at . . . until I realised they were just fancy ways of saying 'care a lot and write it down'. Both essential for running a business.

I'm still a multi-passionate mess – and I never want that to change – but there's a season for juggling it all, and it comes at a cost. I wasn't just chasing my many passions, I was also running from stillness. Stillness wasn't safe growing up, and felt like failure at the time, and so the goalposts continued to move. But every single job was a stepping stone towards my future, and I wouldn't be where I am without any of them.

Maybe Jack had it right all along.

SEVEN THINGS TO REMEMBER AS A MULTI-PASSIONATE GIRL WHO'S SICK OF CHOOSING

1. **You're allowed to love more than one thing.** You are your 'one thing'.
2. **You're not flaky.** You're curious, creative and your brain craves newness and that's a *strength*.
3. **Not every idea needs to be monetised.** Some things are allowed to just be hobbies and make you happy.
4. **Burnout can happen when you try to do it all at once.** Rotate your passions, or if it's a hobby that relaxes you then go for it! But the big ones? Don't juggle them.
5. **Your path will look different because you pave the way yourself and that is bad-ass.** That doesn't make it wrong – it makes it yours.

6. **Fuck timelines.** You're not behind. Remember direction is more important than speed.
7. **Start before you think you're ready.** You don't need to be the best to begin. You just need to begin. Trust me.

Chapter 10

The photo that changed it all

What's worse than a stranger calling you a fat pig in the middle of a bustling Sydney pub? The photo that confirms it. It's wild how a single moment can change everything. Not in a dramatic, thunderclap kinda way, but more like a slow dust that settles over your body but stings deep in your chest. A feeling you can't shake. A moment you didn't ask for, but one you'll never forget.

During our makeup school lunchbreak, I'd recruited three of my girlfriends to join me for schnitzel and, more importantly, a schooner of beer. My latest attempt at being 'healthy' had failed miserably, so in true Steph style, I didn't just give up, I sprinted in the opposite direction. Straight to the pub. What can I say? I don't do things by halves. We were at my second favourite pub – my first being the one with 12 p.m. happy hour – down the hill near the train station. It was packed with tourists, retired couples ignoring each other and corporate workers on a break after firing someone for not being passive-aggressive enough. There was also group of loud twenty year olds getting drunk. I was mid-conversation with my friend Georgia, inhaling a chicken parma with mash and veg, when a voice sliced through the noise.

'YOU FAT PIG!'

Silence. I froze mid-bite. My eyes darted around the pub. *Who said that? Poor bugger, whoever that was directed at . . . bloody brutal.* And then I saw it. A finger pointing at me.

Fuck. My. Life.

The man stood half-in, half-out of the doorway. Dishevelled grey-brown hair clung to his head, a stained white shirt hung off him like a flag of surrender and jeans far too big gathered at his ankles. His eyes were wild, angry and locked on mine like he knew me. And hated me. But he didn't know me. He didn't need to. That's the thing about being a woman – your body is on public display, open for review like you're some faulty product someone wants to return. Later, when I was pregnant for the first time I'd understand this better than ever.

Out of *everyone* in that noisy pub, this bloke chose me. And now everyone else was staring too, probably thinking what I was thinking a mere five seconds ago: *Poor thing. How embarrassing.* I'd never liked being the centre of attention. It made me feel unsafe. But here I was, centre stage, with an audience I never asked for and a wakeup call I definitely didn't want. And worst of all? I didn't even get to finish my beer. This little piggy wanted to go *wee, wee, wee* all the way home. If I'd had Harry Potter's invisibility cloak, I would've vanished right then – but not before kicking my new mate in the balls. After what felt like hours, he turned and stormed off to ruin someone else's day. Or beverage. My friends jumped in with comforting words – kind but clumsy. I joined in, obviously. If I could crack a joke, I wouldn't be the joke. Old habits die hard.

'Don't listen to him,' Claire said. 'He's probably high on something.'

'Yeah, Steph,' Georgia added. 'Don't let some random guy ruin your day.'

Sweet. But I knew. I knew there was truth in it – not in *what* he said, but in what it represented. I didn't look like I used to. I hadn't weighed myself in months, but I could see it. Feel it. I wasn't totally out of touch. He was clearly having a rough day – maybe hungry, maybe unwell. Maybe me shovelling food into my face triggered him. But no amount of awareness stopped the insult from stinging. *Well, it was fun while it lasted*, I thought. It was time to quit makeup school and never show my face in Sydney again.

You'd think being abused by a stranger would be enough to make a change, but no. The only change I made was going to a different pub for lunch. Apparently, I needed something more tangible, more concrete.

•

At makeup school, we were learning about 'historical makeup' and the day's focus was the Victorian era. You know, rice powder for foundation, crushed fruit for blush. At least they were resourceful. The Mecca tweenagers on TikTok would have a heart attack knowing Drunk Elephant didn't exist back then. Speaking of, these Victorian women also had a (medium) rare skincare routine: placing a slice of raw meat on their face and *sleeping* with it. Apparently it kept their skin looking supple, and honestly, it's cheaper than retinol. But imagine waking up to your wife with a full T-bone slapped across her face. Talk about counting sheep – or veal. I'll stick to my expensive vegan retinol any day, thanks.

After we completed the makeup, we finished it off by dressing up in costumes and taking photos. It was fun playing dress-ups as full-grown adults. It always turned our class of twenty- and thirty-something year olds into a bunch of giggling highschoolers. Our teacher, Carmen, would stick the best photos on the classroom wall. There were never enough costumes for our class of twenty-eight, but Carmen always chose who got to dress up. This particular day, she sent me to the storage room. It was my time to shine.

The place looked like a clown's fart: colours, glitter and frills everywhere. I headed for the Victorian section and grabbed a puffball of a dress with balloon sleeves. Giggling, I went into the change room. 'One size fits all' apparently didn't include Steph. The dress clung tighter than expected, but I shrugged it off. *The girls will help me zip it up*, I thought. I came out and turned to Georgia. She tugged. The zip moved 2 cm . . . and froze. 'Shitty zipper,' she offered. 'You can't even tell from the front.' Beautiful liar. Mortified but committed, I got in line. Carmen was waiting, camera in hand. It was finally my turn.

Click. Click.

After removing our costumes and makeup, I plonked down at the table, grateful to finally be sitting down after standing for hours. I grabbed my phone and started scrolling, completely unaware of what Carmen had just stuck to the wall.

'Look Steph! You got a spot on the wall,' Mitch called.

I looked up.

At first, I didn't recognise the woman in the photo. The words spilt from my mouth before I even had time to think them through, 'Who. The fuck. Is that?' Except I knew *exactly* who it was – and that made it worse. The girl in the picture looked like me – same facial features and the same hair colour – but her body was definitely not mine. Fuck. *How did I let this happen?* Sure, being tall helps disguise weight gain. I'm 171 cm and, for a while, that gave me cover. Things spread out more evenly. My boobs looked bigger, which felt like a win. My eyebrows were even growing back after a long-term battle with the 2000s. But even so . . . when you gain 20 kilos, no amount of height can hide it. At that moment, a switch clicked in my brain. *This is it. Enough is enough.* Scales of worth aside, I had been thinking for a while how terrible I had been feeling. Lethargy. Chronic headaches. Rising anxiety. My medication didn't feel like it was working anymore. Not to mention, I had reached a point where my daily attire now featured Band-Aids, slapped on the insides of my thighs, so I could walk without copping twenty fresh new blisters. The truth? I was sick and tired of feeling sick and tired.

I wish I could say my only motive was health, but it wasn't. I was fresh out of the teenage years – and I wanted to look good. I missed fitting into my old clothes, which had slowly begun to move from my wardrobe to a box labelled *Someday*. While I knew my body had changed, I didn't realise how much. Maybe I was in denial, or drunk. Probably both. The change was gradual. Like a roll of toilet paper, but instead of subtracting layers and the roll slowly shrinking – I was adding layers instead. Speaking of toilets, I wasn't going to rely on skinny teas and cabbage soup this time. I was going to lose weight the smart girl way – working *with* my changing body instead of *against* it.

'The women in our family gain weight easily, Steph,' my mum had always told me. 'You need to watch what you eat. I used to be like you too, but it doesn't last forever.'

At the time I thought I was never going to have to worry about calorie counting or buying an Ab Coaster 3000. My parents had one in our garage. I still remember when I caught Dad using it; sweat dripping down his face, his whole body sliding back and forth like a human pendulum. It was quite the sight. This was just my metabolism now. My life now. I accepted that. No more getting away with eating shit. Well, it was fun while it lasted.

At the time, I was very hard on myself. I beat myself up for 'letting myself' get this way. Just like the first time you ever called yourself 'fat'. Now you just want to punch the younger version of yourself in her smooth, beautiful, youthful damn face.

Dewy skinned dumbass.

The reality? Everyone's bodies evolve through different seasons of their life. Writing this now as a mother I have a different perspective: why would you want to stay exactly the same? Women's bodies are fucking insane. Imagine looking back at the best years of your life, the years where your body was the most 'able', and all you cared about was looking like the bloody fifteen-year-old version of yourself. Cute granny Steph would click her tongue, shaking her head before she said, 'Fucking twit'. There has to be a better way to motivate healthy habits than judging and punishing yourself – and I was determined to find it. I wasn't going to go all in and fail yet another attempt. So on the train ride home after seeing *the photo*, I began plotting my action plan – and it all started with a list in my journal:

TEN REASONS EVERY DIET AND FITNESS PLAN I'VE EVER TRIED HAS FAILED

1. I misjudged discipline as punishment and thought success meant suffering.

2. I convinced myself that carbs were the devil, only to realise that a life without pasta is a life half-lived (and carbs fuel our brain, vital organs and shit, so they're kinda important).

3. I valued speed over direction.

4. I relied on motivation, when in reality, it's fleeting and unpredictable like that guy you met on MSN who turned out to be a mama's boy who wears way too much Lynx Africa and is emotionally attached to his video games. Ew.

5. I made consistency and perfection synonyms, when they are, in fact, not even frenemies.

6. The second I labelled a food 'bad' or a 'cheat meal' it became the most delicious, tempting thing on the planet.

7. The plan worked perfectly until life happened. Some days I'm a machine. Others? I'm just a human-shaped pile of laundry.

8. I built a routine for who I thought I wanted to be, rather than how I want to feel. What it takes to have abs doesn't equal having a great time.

9. Every time I tried to overhaul my entire life at once, I forgot that big change happens in tiny, boring, unsexy steps.

10. I assumed that not doing it 100 per cent all the time equalled failure. When really, progress looks like my handwriting: a messy squiggly line.

Then came the epiphany – the lesson I would one day share with not only my friends but thousands of women: *You can't fall off the bandwagon because there is no bandwagon. There's just life.* We built the goddamn wagon. Unknowingly, but we did it. We've been brainwashed to believe that to be 'fit and healthy' there's this moving vehicle of success we must constantly chase, sprinting to catch up, leaping on board, and fighting to stay there. The wagon speeds up. The wheels rattle. The screws begin to loosen. The hours of cardio stretch longer. The food portions shrink. The scales don't budge for a moment and so the wagon picks up speed. Soon, it becomes impossible to hold on. You tumble off. Flat on your arse. Knees scraped and weeping. And instead of realising the wagon was just moving too damn fast, you blame yourself for not being able to keep up. You hate yourself for not being able to hold on. For being *hungry*. For being *tired.* For *failing* – again. And so the cycle continues. Until one day, we decide: *I can't do this anymore.* And so we give up, not only on the idea of feeling healthier – but we give up on ourselves.

But here's the truth no one told us: our lives, just like the dirt road beneath us, are bumpy. Uneven. There are detours, potholes, chunks missing. Some days, the wagon will *need* to slow down. You'll get sick. You'll be stressed. You'll be sad. Life will throw in birthday parties, weddings, hormones, late nights with friends. The moments you don't want to miss. And when the road gets too rough, the wagon simply cannot maintain its speed. It breaks. You fall off. Or worse – you wave it goodbye and convince yourself that *you* failed. Again. But the problem was never *the road*. It was *the wagon*.

This was beginning to hit me on my train ride home even though it would take another decade for me to truly live through it in order to teach it. For now, I was at least ready to shake off the crippling level of pressure I had placed on myself to be the kind of person who was 'effortlessly healthy'. The type of person who didn't even *think* about their weight because it naturally hovered within an acceptable range at all times, as if by divine intervention. I was going to have to do 'the work', but I also wanted to find a way to do it that was sustainable. If I was going to change my habits, I had to start with acceptance – not shrink my way towards it. At the time, I despised running; I had a deep hatred for cabbage, a stance I still maintain, unless it's disguised as coleslaw in a burger; and my idea of balance was having fries with water instead of beer. I was done pretending otherwise.

I don't know when we collectively decided that life was a six-week challenge, but it is a *terrible* idea. We don't need to treat ourselves like soldiers in the military when, really, we're just a bunch of hungry girls in spin class, obsessing over all the food and fun we *can't* have, clutching onto every calorie, like Gollum with his Precious. No wonder we struggle to change. We set ourselves up for failure before we even begin. And then? We create the narrative that becomes our identity. Think about how often people, yourself included, say:

'I'm just not a fitness/gym person.'

'I can't be healthy – it's too hard.'

That was the label I had been wearing ever since I gave up trying to lose weight by sucking on boiled leaves. Of course I wasn't going to be a fit or healthy person, because I had already decided I wasn't. I had accepted it as fact. And in turn, that became my truth. It became fact. When we tell ourselves we are something – or that we are not something – it becomes our reality. Because we have already made up our minds. *We essentially become our own cockblockers.* And then we spend our lives beating ourselves up for not being something we never even allowed ourselves to be in the first place. It's a profound mindfuck, isn't it?

I had been walking around for years wearing the label: *I'm just not a fitness person.* I had told myself so many times that I stopped questioning it. It became a fact, just like 'I have brown hair' or 'I can't wear white without spilling something on myself'. It didn't matter that it wasn't technically true. Well, actually the latter is 100 per cent true. It didn't matter that I *could* love movement or that I *could* make better food choices. I had decided this about myself, so it had become reality. My words had transformed me. Then there was Ady who never allowed a lack of words to hold him back.

If you say you are something – it's true.

If you say you aren't something – it's also true.

If you say you can or you can't do something – guess what? That's true, too.

The way you view yourself is your truth. And because it's your truth, it becomes your reality. You become the narrative you decide on. It dictates your habits, your actions and ultimately, the rest of your life. And that's when I decided, I was going to *fire* my narrator. You know that voice in your head? Mine was a condescending, judgemental, snarky little bitch who I named Jessica. She'd been running the show for years. (Apologies to all the Jessicas out there, I'm sure you're lovely.) But this Jessica? She was out. Done. Redundant. Sacked. Effective immediately. Why let that person continue to narrate my life when it clearly wasn't working?

It was time to bring in a new narrator – one who would remind me that being healthy is a lifestyle, not a six-week challenge. That I am a work in progress. That any small change is better than no change at all. That there is no end goal with health – you don't just get fit and then stay that way – it's the consistent habits and daily efforts that ultimately make up your life. I had to find a way to live without obsession or extremes. Then maybe I wouldn't spiral straight into the Macca's drive-thru. My 'healthy hustler' era had officially begun.

EIGHT JOURNAL PROMPTS FOR BODY LOVE

Okay, enough with shit-talking your body like you're watching a reality TV show. I know there are days you just feel a bit *meh*. Well, I got you! Here are your go-to prompts for those days:

1. What has my body carried me through that I haven't thanked her/it for? (Spoiler: a lot more than you realise.)
2. What would I say to my daughter if she said or thought these things about her body?
3. When do I feel most at home in my body?
4. What parts of life – and happiness – have I missed by waiting for my body to change?
5. What would it look like to treat my body with kindness this week? (A nap counts. So does pasta.)
6. What does my body do that I take for granted?
7. One simple habit I can change that makes me *feel* good.
8. Your body is the love of your life, so start treating her like it.

Chapter 11

The healthy hustle

'Please don't tell me you're going to drink that tea and shit yourself again,' Ryan said, clearly pleased with himself. Apparently, he wasn't just a carpenter anymore, but also a comedian.

'Yeah, hun, because that was absolutely my favourite pastime,' I shot back. One of our love languages is sarcasm, a close second being terrible dad jokes – the cringier, the better. I gave him a playful but stern side-eye, but I was fighting a losing battle. The laughter was bubbling up. I am terrible at being mad with him. His one-way ticket out of the doghouse? A well-timed joke or one-liner. He knew I am a child at heart. No matter how deeply I *want* to stay mad, I have the emotional resilience of a wet paper towel the second something funny happens.

We were deep into our usual post-dinner routine, catching up after a long day while watching *MTV Cribs* in bed. Nothing like a bit of light-hearted distraction and the occasional jaw-drop over a rapper's bathtub – complete with in-built fish tank. I swear the thing was bigger than my shitty Suzuki Swift Cino. If I was *really* lucky, we'd land on the Crime Channel – because nothing soothes the soul quite like a touch of homicide. Mid-banter and mid-*Pimp My Ride* reveal, something inside me made me sit up. I pulled out my favourite notebook and wrote down a list.

THE 'CUT THE CRAP CRITERIA', AKA THE 'COMMON SENSE CHECK'

Three questions to check if you're dedicated or delusional:
1. Can I picture myself doing this forever?
2. Is this adding to my life, or does it feel like a punishment?
3. What's the laziest version of this I can still commit to? (e.g. Can I adapt it easily when life gets rocky?)

Over the next few weeks, this list became my filter, whether it was around exercise or healthy eating. Food? My rule was simple: no takeaway or eating out unless it was for special occasions. Workouts? Three times a week felt do-able.

What did I have to lose? I'd already lost my dignity after the skinny tea shitshow. But it wasn't going to be easy. Apparently, when you cut out takeaway and stop eating crap it's far from gentle. And let me tell you, those first three days of my 'lifestyle change' were utter hell. Throbbing headaches like my skull was going to explode. Brain fog so thick I didn't know what was up or down. I could barely function. They say your body is 80 per cent water, well it turns out mine was 80 per cent Passion Pop. Despite the discomfort, I was determined to make slow and steady progress. The next step was to join a gym. (Yes, the one I would go on to work at – keep up, it's only a rollercoaster.)

Throughout high school, whenever I'd start going to a new gym, I always felt that everyone was looking at me, or talking about that tiny pocket of fat that everyone has near their armpit (aka your third and fourth boob). I was sure people could sense that I didn't belong. When I decided to go back to the gym as an adult, I got the same vibe. Hello, gym anxiety. This time I walked in armed with my gym towel, an old plastic water bottle, and a whole lot of I've-got-nothing-to-lose attitude.

You are here for you, not them. Remember?

Roger that, Captain.

There I was in the weights session blankly staring at contraptions that looked more like medieval torture devices – or something I'd seen in a true crime doco. Ginormous mirrors lined the walls, designed to make you question *everything* about yourself. The gym mirror is the equivalent of your friend's photos on a digital camera from a night out – the ones taken from the worst angle imaginable; sweaty upper lip, double chin, rogue fake lash on your cheek. The ones she kindly uploaded to Facebook – in their own album. Luckily I was about to meet my saviour – or my knight-in-Puma-tights.

'Lock your core in, and pull your shoulders back,' said a confident but friendly voice. I looked up to see a fit-as-fuck tanned pocket rocket approaching.

'Oh, thank you! Sorry, I have no idea what I'm doing.' I tried to sound casual but instead sounded like someone who *absolutely* had no idea what they were doing.

'Don't be sorry! Totally normal,' the woman said. 'I'm Lena, I'm a personal trainer. Let me show you.'

I stepped aside as she hopped on, effortlessly demonstrating how to use the machine without looking like she was going to pop a disc or give herself a hernia. I nodded along like I'd be able to retain this info beyond the next thirty seconds.

'Alright, now you try.'

I got back on, adjusted myself to replicate what Lena had just done, and gave it another go. 'Oh shit. Yep. I feel that *now*,' I laughed, suddenly realising that whatever I had been doing before wasn't *actual* exercise – it was just me flapping my arms about like some kind of interpretive dance performance: awkward pigeon edition. It made the exercise piss-easy – and *entirely* defeated the purpose.

Lena grinned. 'I offer three free training sessions to new members. If you're keen, I can book you in.'

What did I have to lose? I didn't have the knowledge to do this alone and, with my new makeup business going well, I could afford to invest in myself. When I went for my first session, I was shocked by how unfit I had become. This isn't me being hard on myself. I was struggling, big time – as in struggling to breathe. For our first workout Lena announced we were doing something called HIIT, which apparently stands for High-Intensity Interval Training, but roughly translates as: Help, I'm In Trouble.

I thought my good mate Anxiety had my heart-rate covered, but it turns out she didn't hold a candle to 'the step' – which brought illegal Indonesian fireworks and a flamethrower. The step itself was *laughable* – one of those little plastic platforms they use in group fitness classes where you add extra layers from the bottom up to make it higher. Yeah well, I was just using the top part. As in the actual step – the *bare minimum*. When I walked in, I immediately clocked a group of grannies absolutely *dominating* a step class. Their steps were *four times* the height of mine. No need to show off, Beatrice.

I stepped back up onto the tiny platform for what felt like the twentieth time, gasping for air. Super fun. But I was doing it.

And for once, I wasn't embarrassed about how hard I was finding it. It helped that Lena was so . . . *nice*. At the start of our session, she had weighed me, taken my height, and logged a few other stats. She did it casually, like she was noting the weather – no judgement, no lingering looks, no dramatic sighs. Lena meant business but in a way that made me feel like I was actually capable of doing this. She gave the impression that this wasn't such a big deal; I was just making some changes. If you really looked at it, it was true, but it felt like a revelation to me.

When I'd signed up for those three free sessions, I'd secretly assumed that I would 'fail' and not continue. But when the sessions ended, instead of ghosting Lena like a bad Tinder date, I decided to keep going. My new plan? We would meet once a week and, in between, I would follow a program she created for me. I was no longer wandering around the gym like a suspicious dealer smuggling chocolate into the free weights section. I finally had direction. And that was all I needed.

I started enjoying this new life. I was feeling good and the weight was coming off, all while I maintained a social life. And bonus points: I wasn't miserable. I managed to turn multiple setbacks into comebacks. So much so that I began posting about my journey on Facebook. (Sorry Tom, Myspace was long gone now.) My new status was: 'Motivation is what gets you started. But it's habits that keep you going.'

I'd post about my goals for the day, motivation and even some of the lightbulb moments I was having. This was the first time I'd actually broadcast what I was doing. I didn't want praise or acknowledgement; I just wanted to help. I could recall years of conversations with my friends, all feeling defeated for thinking we had fallen short when it was never us: it was that bloody bandwagon. I knew many of my friends struggled too. I wanted to help. I knew I could help. I realised how easy it really was, not the work itself – but the mindset for the work. How we approached being healthy was all wrong. I wanted to share what I was learning. Then my friends could begin their own journey if they wanted to.

Unfortunately, but fortunately for them, I wasn't preaching some fad diet, or a drink that makes you shit yourself. The look on their faces when I revealed that my 'secret' was exercising three times a week, not eating shit, and drinking 2 litres of water a day was underwhelming to say the least. No hacks, no diets, just the basics of healthy living. Boring as bat shit, right? Their responses went something like this:

'Is that *it*?'

'How about fat burners?'

'Are you at least counting calories?'

'What about your steps?'

'Do you eat after 5 p.m.?'

These sorts of comments made me realise how society has programmed us to over-complicate *everything*. Because as the old saying goes, 'nothing worth having comes easy', right? My friends and I are mostly millennials. We don't know any better. From childhood, our mindsets became a copy-paste of the woman next to us, each one learning the same unspoken rule: your worth is directly linked to the number on a scale. And then social media rocked up unannounced and poured petrol on the fire – endless 'before and after' shots, every transformation claiming that some drink/pill/detox/insane level of self-punishment had *changed their life*.

We were taught this *huge, complicated lie* from the moment we could walk. From the moment we could read. From the moment we heard our own mothers sigh at their reflection, pinch their stomach and say, 'I just want to get back to how I looked before'. Before what? Before hormones, growth and life graced us with the evidence that we had lived in the first place? We learnt that we had to look this way. That we *needed* to look this way. And it had to be miserable. Painful. Complicated. It had to be hard. Until we *finally* realised it didn't – *if* we ever realise it at all.

Because when we're eighty years old, we won't give a fuck about whether or not we lost those pesky last 3 kilos. You know the ones that you have to go that extra 10 miles to lose? So you miss out on that little after-dinner treat you love so much; you stop heading out for that weekly coffee with your friend, scared you will 'cave' and order lunch; and you stop seeing the people you love and doing and eating the things you enjoy. All for 3 kilos that – I'm sorry to say – people don't even notice you've lost. So you live your life half-empty, restricted and missing out, purely because that's what you *thought* you had to do. We'll regret the way we ran our lives like a military boot camp. The way we missed out on our most physically able years, sacrificing joy, experiences, actual living, just to fit into a pair of jeans that were designed too small in the first place.

So naturally, when I revealed my 'big secret' – that all I was doing was eating real food and moving my body three times a week – friends looked at me like I was withholding something. Like I was keeping the *real* secret from them. And I guess I was. Because the *real* secret – the one no one wants to admit – is that our lives are worth so much more than our relationship with gravity.

Over time, my posts had a ripple effect. A few friends reached out to say they'd decided to join a gym or rethink their eating habits. This drove me to keep learning and I began to even play around with recipes to make my fave foods healthy. This was something new – handing out advice rather than jello shots at a random's party. 'Today's goal is 2L water!' was a bit different from 'I got drunk in a field last night'. But not everyone was a fan.

'Why are you posting that stuff?' asked my friend Kate one Thursday afternoon. We were sitting on my couch, scrolling socials – being socially anti-social. Amusement and even a hint of second-hand embarrassment had spread across her face.

'I dunno, I just like to share.'

'It's kind of . . . lame,' she laughed.

My heart sank but Kate's comment wasn't going to stop me. I wasn't sharing life-changing wisdom, just how a twenty year old was making changes for her health. Maybe that's why they didn't accept it? But this was a new season for me – going from the butt of jokes to not being afraid to use my voice for once. One day I would go on to share my fitness journey on a much larger scale – including my challenges and setbacks. Speaking of setbacks . . . Despite my fitness goals, I was still drinking. One night, six or seven vodka and sodas deep, I decided to show off my ability to run in heels on a dodgy, uneven city street. Because that's a good idea. Two doctor's appointments and an MRI later, it was time to find out exactly what level of self-inflicted stupidity I was dealing with.

'Honestly, you'd have been better off if you'd just broken your ankle,' the doctor said. Torn ligaments are a bitch to heal. Sweet.

In the middle of my lifestyle change, I found myself confined to a sweaty, stuffy moon boot for three long months. It was a velcro-strapped nightmare. This would have typically been the moment where my health and fitness journey ended. Even the most seasoned gym-goer would take time off. But this is where I was grateful for the 'Cut the Crap Criteria'. I had made a commitment to long-term habits, knowing that I was allowed to adapt them if needed – and adapt them I did. Soon I was doing sit-ups in my moon boot, a little puddle of sweat pooling inside. Delicious, right? This injury wasn't going to stop me. With Lena's support, I found ways to work out while wearing it.

Things are always going to pop up in life – sickness, work, moon boots. But here's the thing. We can *choose* how we respond. We can decide whether the bumps in the road derail us or not; whether it's a setback or a comeback. For the first time in my adult life I wasn't a yoyo dieter, I wasn't skipping the gym – dare I say I'd even begun to enjoy it. And the biggest plot twist of all was that somehow, along the way, I was motivated by something other than weight loss. Every time I increased the weights, or died *less* on the treadmill, a spark rippled through me. I could feel change happening, physically and emotionally. And on the days I worked out, ol' mate Anxiety wasn't as feisty.

I had cracked another simple code: your 'why' has to be deep enough to get you up on the not-so-good days. In reality, weight loss wasn't a big enough why for me. But now I had found a why that *really* made a difference. It also felt good to make Lena proud. After work, when all I wanted to do was crawl into bed and morph into a sloth, I knew Lena would be at the gym, setting up for our session. So, I *showed up*. And on the days I trained alone, she'd spot me across the gym and give me that proud mum look – the kind usually reserved for kids who don't coat-hanger their siblings.

Like most things in life, my health journey wasn't linear. There were weeks where I missed a gym session. But this wasn't a challenge – it was a change – and so I picked it right back up again.

For the first time, I wasn't forcing it or obsessing over it. I was just letting it happen as a quiet side effect of actually treating myself well. This wildly simple approach would help me in the next season of life – moving in with Ryan's parents. We were saving to buy our first home and although we had some money and good credit history, the banks were making it hard to get a mortgage – I guess they didn't trust a couple of twenty-one year olds. Crazy, huh?

In the meantime, our 'new' bedroom was smack-bang across the hall from Ryan's parents' bedroom. Prime real estate for zero action. The last thing my future in-laws wanted to hear was their son getting off while they tried to watch *Australia's Got Talent*. Cockblocking aside (sorry Tom and Carol #awkward), there was another challenge to living with the in-laws – they make good food. A *lot* of good food. It turns out Ryan is half-Italian – a detail I only learnt months into our relationship. His dad, Tom, was born in northern Italy in a small town called Treviso. Tom's family came to Australia when he was just a one year old, and he spent his early years speaking only Italian. Before long, he decided he needed to learn English and get Nonna to stop packing rolls of salami for lunch if he wanted to fit in. His real name is Attilio Luigi Pase. A real-life Mario brother. He decided to embrace Aussie culture and *bogan-fy* himself and change his name to Tom – you know, like your first friend on Myspace.

When I met Ryan, I was initially worried his family wouldn't accept me. But boy was I wrong. The first time I met Nonna she covered my face in beautiful, loud and passionate kisses. 'Oh Stefania, you're so beautiful! Bella! Bella! Good job, Ryan!'

I'll never forget my first dinner at Ryan's parents' house. I was the first girl he had ever brought home – I know, bloody Ryan, always being cute and shit.

'Are other people coming?' I whispered to him as his mum, Carol, placed the *fourth* plate of food on the table. Spaghetti – real spaghetti. Oh, and fresh bread with thick slabs of butter. A roast chicken. Crispy potatoes. And a salad the size of my head, drizzled in olive oil and topped with feta; not just sad, dry lettuce posing as a meal. I glanced at Ryan, wide-eyed, as if to say, *Are we feeding a football team – a fancy football team – or is this just a typical dinner at the Pase house?* 'What's all this for?' I whispered.

'Um. For . . . dinner?' Ryan replied, like it was the most obvious thing in the world.

'Just for us—' My eyes darted around the table, mentally counting the lucky Pase family, '*Five?*' My eyes bulged as Ryan's dad and brother, Chris, grabbed the tongs and started loading up their plates. *They got to choose what they wanted. And there was more. You know, for seconds. And shit.* This felt so foreign to me. Growing up, Nan would secretly take me to get potato scallops on the way home from school, an attempt to feed me before we got home to scarcity. But this felt like Christmas lunch – but on a Wednesday. Insane. Delicious. *Amazing.* Sign me up. I should have just proposed to Ryan then and there. Naturally, it didn't take long for my metabolism to no longer be able to keep up with not only my partying days, but also my new salami-loving family.

I loved going to Ryan's parents' for lunch – an excuse to over-indulge – but living with them full-time during my new fitness kick was . . . way too tempting. There was no food scarcity in this house. And as a people-pleaser, I didn't want to be the one who said, 'Oh, I'll just have a tiny plate' after Nonna has just spent six hours hand-rolling gnocchi. Choosing to not fill up my plate is the Italian equivalent of the rude finger.

Shifting gears when you live with other people is its own kind of challenge. When we decide to make a positive change, it's never smooth sailing, especially when there are others on board. Life rarely rolls out the red carpet when you have a new goal. In fact, it's usually the opposite. A big deadline at work; an injury; kids get sick; a change in your schedule – it can feel like the universe is trying to act against you. Now in my thirties, I've had so many conversations with friends who, mothers or not, try to make healthy changes in their households, but end up struggling because it's not what their family want to eat. Usually it just ends in arguments and deep breaths in the pantry. But here are a few things I learnt.

HOW TO 'SOFT LAUNCH' HEALTHY EATING HABITS TO YOUR FAMILY

1. **Show don't tell.** You'd be surprised how much more powerful it is to lead by example, rather than force. Instead of announcing to the household that everything is about to change (cue the outrage and hysteria), just start making small, consistent swaps. People start *naturally* gravitating towards the healthier option when it's already there.
2. **Make slight modifications, not separate meals.** If your family loves pasta, don't force yourself to eat a dry chicken breast while they tuck into a bowl of carbonara. Make small swaps – like adding more protein, extra veggies, or using a healthier sauce alternative. The goal is to make it work for you, without feeling like you're missing out.

3. **Give them choices, but you do you.** As they say, pick your battles. If they want their usual meals, sweet – but that doesn't mean you have to cave just to keep the peace. It's okay to say, 'I'm gonna have this tonight, but I'll make extra if you want to try it.' No pressure, no passive-aggressive side-eyes – just options.
4. **Find your 'why' and stick to it.** At the end of the day, it's your health, your body and your life. People might not always understand at first, but the more consistent you are, the less they'll question it. Eventually they might even join in.

If I could get through a moon boot and not overload on mountains of delicious pizza and pasta every night, I can do anything!

Chapter 12

The sad bikini model

Over the previous six months, since starting my new health kick, I'd been feeling the best I'd ever felt. In fact, I was loving this new, healthy lifestyle so much that I kept moving the goalposts. *If I can get even fitter and healthier then maybe I'll feel even better?* These were my exact thoughts right before a training session with Lena.

'Steph, you don't understand how good you're looking!' she exclaimed. 'You should compete.'

'Compete in what?' I asked, puzzled. *Maybe an eating competition?*

'In a bodybuilding competition. You'd be in the bikini division. I was saying to the guys at the supp' store that you have a lot of potential.'

'Wait, you're talking about the girls who wear bikinis and walk on stage in front of a crowd of people in stripper heels?'

'Yes! But there's more to it than that; you train hard, follow a meal plan and look the best you ever have. People say it's an awesome experience.'

Yeah, they definitely aren't downing fifty apple pies for a plastic trophy. I wanted to take my health and fitness to the next level, but getting up on stage half-naked? C'mon. Back at uni I needed two schooners before I'd even open my mouth in class.

'There's no way,' I told Lena. 'Absolutely no way. Not for me.'

But when I went home that night, I couldn't get the idea out of my head. I'd already pushed myself out of my comfort zone to share my fitness journey online. Did I dare take it further? Cue hyper-fixation. After a weekend of intense research, I was hooked and, before I knew it, five months out from my first bodybuilding competition.

I'd like to report I made balanced, sustainable changes but I didn't; I was still Bart Simpson with third-degree burns. The preparation was intense, to say the least. If you've ever wondered what it takes to go from Zinger Boxes at 3 a.m. to white fish at 10 a.m., allow me to introduce you to my new obsession, ahem, hobby.

A day in the life
of an aspiring bodybuilder

TIME	SCHEDULE
4:45am	Alarm. Snooze. Contemplate how much I actually need abs.
5am	Supps and fasted cardio
6am	Breakfast: Protein shake, oats mixed in. (Feels like when you take a swig out of a water bottle & your mouth is assaulted by floaties your kid left behind).
7am	Gym shift. Sell memberships while resisting the urge to nap under the dumbell rack.
10am	White fish & beans. Riveting. Try not to offend co-workers with the smell.
1pm	Lunch: Chicken breast, beans & sweet potato so small, it's a garnish.
3pm	Snack: Cottage cheese and sugar-free maple syrup. Call it 'dessert' to feel something
7:30pm	Leg workout day. Pray for my grandma arse.
9pm	Dinner: Chicken and green beans, and the hope that one day I'll love this.
10pm	Collapse into bed, too tired to dream. Wonder if I really have lost my goddamn mind.

Something for me:
- Beach walk with our dog, Lily.
  (and Ryan if I bribe him with post-walk snacks)
- Survive the week without smacking someone who asks, 'Why don't you just eat 'normal' food?'
  (Though, they might have a point.)
- Smell Ryan's food and convince myself it's nearly as good as eating it.

Notes:
Sunday - 'Rest day' (a.k.a fasted beach walk and posing practice). Because nothing says relaxation like power-walking while starving, then standing under fluorescent lights in a bikini, learning how to make my non-existent abs pop without looking constipated...

Don't forget:
Convince Ryan this whole thing is 'fun' for both of us...

TO-DO LIST

1. Survive leg day
2. Text Ryan - remind him I still exist ✓
3. Write down 1 non gym-related thought to prove I still have personality

Find new way to make cottage cheese exciting (fail)
Buy more gum
Pack tomorrow's meals (meal plan is etched into my soul)

Wash gym hair (3rd time this week)
Measure every gram of food like my life depends on it (it does) ✓
Cry... I'm out of sugar-free syrup ✓

Movement
- 45 mins fasted cardio
- 1 hr strength training (leg day, RIP me)

I am grateful for
- Ryan's patience - sugar-free syrup
- Chicken breast on - Lily, who doesn't care how sale at Woolies shredded I am
- sweet potatoes

Water: ✓ ✓ ✓ ✓ ✓ ✓

BREAKFAST
Protein shake + oats mixed in

LUNCH
chicken breast, beans and sweet potato

DINNER
chicken & green beans

SNACKS	
white fish & beans "	cottage cheese & sugar-free syrup

Daily habits
1. 3-litres water (not tears)
2. 10,000 steps ✓
3. Avoid googling 'how to stop protein farts smelling like eggs'.

•

Yep. Welcome to the world of bodybuilding – the good, the bad and the hungry. I had somehow turned into the Australian version of *Jersey Shore* 'gym, tan, laundry'. In my case, 'tan' was a shade of dehydrated tandoori paste and 'laundry' was washing ten loads of sweaty Kmart activewear a week. If I was going to stand on stage in a bikini that cost more than my first car, I needed help – and probably a psych evaluation too. Just like Lena had given me a crash course in exercising, I needed someone to show me how to sculpt my body into exactly what the judges wanted. So I did what any Kardashian would do if they wanted to shave 1 millimetre off their big toe: I got surgery . . . I mean a coach. And when I say 'coach' I don't mean some gym bro throwing out unsolicited tips between mirror flexes. No, this was a whole new world. Macros, meal plans, training schedules – every detail of my life was mapped out in a spreadsheet so granular it could have been classified government data.

I'll never forget when Coach handed over my first meal plan. My hands shook with nerves and excitement, only to discover it was about as thrilling as an unseasoned chicken breast – because that's *exactly* what it was. Chicken. Fish. Green beans. Eat. Train. Repeat. What did I expect? It's not like I signed up for *MasterChef: Bodybuilding Edition*. I'd gone from a walking contradiction to a walking Excel sheet. And honestly? I *loved* it. No thinking, just following the plan. If my former gym anxiety had stemmed from not knowing what to do, I now took comfort in the rigid structure.

I trained six days a week, sometimes twice a day. Leg days where I could barely walk afterwards? Success. Hunger pangs? Discipline. Exhausted? Good. That meant I was pushing. This is where I should add a disclaimer: I'm sure there are a lot of healthy bodybuilders with sensible and sustainable exercise and eating plans. I'm just here to share with you what I did. For some competitors this sort of regime works. They love the intensity and still manage to achieve balance. They have a social life, keep up at work and jump on stage looking like Arnie. And that's why bodybuilding is such a respected sport. But my messy mind wasn't built for it. Sadly, it would take years – yes, years – for me to figure that out.

A surprising side effect was that I was now sober. You may be wondering WTF. Well, if there's anything stronger than my dependence on alcohol, it's my whatever-current-hyper-fixation. So can you guess what my new obsession was? That's right – competing. I was swapping shots for soda water and clubbing for cardio. And just like that, my reliance on alcohol became as obvious as my fake tan on white sheets. I had spent years convincing myself I was just *fun*, but now I could see it for what it was – social anxiety disguised as an overpriced cocktail.

'You never come out anymore,' Kate said. We were at a mate's twenty-first birthday, something I couldn't bail on. I felt a new kind of war begin in my mind. Except I was now a lot older. My old friend Anxiety whispered in my ear, *You're boring now. They don't like you anymore.* But if I drank? Then Coach would hate me. Either way I'd lose and/or disappoint someone.

Some friends weren't on board with the idea of me competing, not just for the fact 'Fun Steph' was now boring; they worried it was too intense. But unless you were in this new world, it was hard to understand. Once you were in, *you were in.* The outside world ceased to exist. I hoped when they saw me thriving and feeling even better they would understand.

•

'I need to get rid of this bit of cellulite here,' I said to Ryan one day, studying my legs like I was dissecting a frog in science class.

'Steph, you literally have *nothing* there.'

'No, that's what I was told – I have to be *perfect* for the judges.' Anxiety was shaking through my voice as I looked away from the mirror, self-hatred starting to brew. Long gone was the appreciation for my body that was getting stronger. I was no longer focusing on the small wins like not eating takeaway that day. Instead I was obsessing about whether I got my chicken breast to exactly 180 grams . . . or did I go over?

'You were beautiful before you even began this whole lifestyle change,' Ryan said. 'Don't pick yourself apart.'

It's not like anyone was forcing me. I *chose* this. I wanted to prove I could be athletic. That I was more than just a bowl cut ball-magnet. I wanted to finally show the world that I could be dedicated to something for once. The problem was, dedication and self-destruction look eerily similar.

My bodybuilding regime wasn't just difficult to swallow, it also proved to be a challenge for my business and work. I had officially become *that* person. You know the one who meal preps and microwaves their smelly pre-prepared protein pulp in communal spaces. I did have the decency to carry gum. As a makeup artist, smelling like the Little Mermaid isn't exactly key to getting a five-star review. Despite my jam-packed workout schedule, I was still taking on makeup gigs, as well as working at the M.A.C store and later picking up shifts at the gym. Luckily for me, most of my makeup clients were on the weekend, so I had plenty of time for my new passion.

I couldn't say the same for my actual relationship . . .

Unluckily for Ryan, the treadmill was getting more action than him. I was either at the gym or thinking about the gym. Which meant when I was with Ryan in the evenings, after we got home, I may have been there physically, but I wasn't there mentally. All I talked about was food, training and my dramatically changing body. Luckily for me, Ryan was the ultimate golden retriever boyfriend – loyal and happy to go along with whatever made me happy. The man deserves a medal, or at least a free T-shirt that says, 'My girlfriend has ADD and I'm tired'.

When I first started training for the bodybuilding comp, he loved seeing the positive changes. He assumed, like me, if anything I would get even healthier and therefore feel even more amazing. But looking back, bodybuilding was creating a rift in our relationship, not that either of us spoke about it. It can be a double-edged sword when you're in a relationship with someone who is as laid-back as you – you both let things slide. When neither of you makes a fuss, you both assume everything's fine because no one is actively *not fine*. Weeks can go by before you realise you haven't actually spoken . . . in weeks. Not properly. Not beyond 'How was your day?' and 'What's for dinner?' and 'Did you put the bins out?'

There was no tension, no fights, no slamming doors. But there was little connection or deep conversations or growth. We were just existing, together but separately. We had finally moved into our own place – just the two of us – but a slow drift was happening beneath our very noses. For someone who prides herself on being pretty self-aware, I had *zero* self-awareness at this time. It wasn't like I ignored Ryan – I loved it when I could drag him to the gym. That counts as quality time, right? But one thing that somehow stayed during this time was that consistent love. That unwavering knowledge that we'd be just fine, and neither of us was going anywhere.

Sundays were my 'fasted cardio' day. (Translation: fast walking while starving.) This meant a long beach walk with our dog, Lily. And in those moments, I was present. There was something about being outside that always pulled me back to reality, even if just for an hour. It reminded me of when I was young, wandering up into the back paddocks near Meadow Lane, escaping into the open air, away from the chaos that awaited me back home. But aside from our weekly walk, Ryan and I spent little quality time together. And if we did, it was on my schedule (or my gym schedule). Looking back, it reminds me of young Steph, living at Meadow Lane. I was there, but not really there; so hyper-focused on whatever had caught my attention at the time that I didn't notice what I was missing. Love and presence aren't things you can pause while you chase something else. Time doesn't wait for you to figure things out before it starts taking things away.

•

The one thing that I didn't expect to gain from this experience was becoming part of something bigger than myself. Technically, in bodybuilding, you compete as an individual, so I assumed it was going to be a fairly lonely pursuit. But it was the exact opposite. We were a team, working under Coach, and striving (and starving) for the same goals. We were each other's support network. On the days you were hungry, had no energy, or felt like you were going backwards, we were there, cheering each other on. It was a beautiful thing to witness and be a part of.

Picture *Miss Congeniality: Bodybuilder Edition*, but instead of beauty contestants lining up to prance around on stage, it's aspiring bodybuilders learning how to walk in what they call 'comp heels' (aka stripper heels). Half the class, let's call them 'Team Miss Universe', glided in them effortlessly, like they popped out of the birth canal sporting six-inch platforms. Then there was the rest of us, 'Team Sandra Bullock' *before* the makeover, wobbling about like newborn giraffes. It's kinda important to keep your teeth for your stage smile.

Every Sunday at 10 a.m. we took a class called 'posing practice'. Coach was a pro and we'd watch her eagerly, our puppy dog eyes glued to her every move as she demonstrated what she wanted us to do. Men and women posed differently, and the men were lucky because they got to go barefoot. Why do they always have it so easy? Comp heels put the shoes that landed me in a moon boot to shame. Surprisingly, they weren't too bad to walk in, with a clear platform base resembling 50 Cent's bathtub fish tank, and a matching clear strap across the top, securing your foot in place. I had splurged on a pair with diamantes sprinkled across the toes, like icing on top of a no-calorie, tasteless cake. If stripper heels could be beautiful, these were it. The day they arrived in the mail, it felt like Christmas.

I'm not sure if I was more in awe of the shoes, or the fact that I was actually doing this. Something big. Something loud. Something athletic. The heels represented so many things I once thought were unattainable: discipline, confidence . . . the ability to walk in heels and not resemble the gravitationally challenged human that I was. Friends and family were amazed I'd made it this far. Honestly? Me too. In the lead-up to my first comp, which was to be in Melbourne, I was dedicated, determined and, despite being terrified, definitely going through with it. I was too far gone to back out now.

My parents, Ryan's parents and Nan were planning to come to the next comp, which would be held closer to home. 'We'll come and cheer you on then; just make sure your bikini bottoms don't ride up into your butt crack!' said Nan, giggling. She had a point – but there's butt glue for that. No. Seriously.

'You're gonna love it,' I told her. 'All those bodybuilding guys in their budgy smugglers.' It was great giving Nan a new life experience. Come watch your granddaughter prance around in a bikini and be judged by a panel of strangers. What's not to love?

A few weeks before that first comp, I got a phone call that would turn my world upside down.

'Your mum's on the phone, Steph,' Ben, my boss at the gym said, gesturing me into his office.

'Hi Mum.' I barely finished the words before she cut in.

'Nan has Alzheimer's. She should still live a while, but I just thought you should know.'

No words formed.

'She'll start to forget more and more things, pumpkin head. Even people.'

People.

For some, hearing that a grandparent is sick isn't a big deal – they're old, right? It happens. But this was my surrogate mother, my home in human form. I'm not exaggerating when I say I found the news devastating. At that moment, I wasn't thinking about my upcoming bodybuilding competition. I wasn't thinking about how many kilos I could lift or how many calories I'd eat for lunch. One of the reasons I threw myself into my hobbies was to escape Meadow Lane. But now all I wanted to do was go back there.

HOW TO BE PASSIONATE WITHOUT LOSING THE PLOT

1. **Is this energising me or exhausting me?** Sometimes passions can be exhausting (exhibit A over here) but if it's constant then there's something deeper going on.
2. **If no one clapped, would I still be doing this?** Yes, a hit to the ego. No likes, no recognition, no external validation. Would you still be chasing this thing if the only person to pat you on the back was you?
3. **Is this adding to my life, or is it *becoming* my life?** When your passion seeps into every part of your life, your relationships, every thought, moment, who you are – it's time to take a step back. You can love something but it should not become you.

Chapter 13

Do judge me

Today was the day – the one that had lived rent-free in my head for months – and I couldn't stop nervously pooping. And yes, I'm sadly aware how many times I've written 'poop' in this book already. So when I said earlier I was scared I'd shit myself on stage? Turns out, it was less of a metaphor and more of a legitimate concern.

Fantastic.

Ryan and I made the eight-hour drive to Melbourne instead of flying as it was easier to stick to my meal plan, and harder for me to pretend this wasn't taking over my life. I had a huge hot-pink Eski-looking bag that could fit all six containers of my meals. Side pockets held diuretics that I was now taking to rid my body of any remaining fluid. Don't do this at home, kids. Much to Ryan's dismay, we had to stop at a servo every three hours.

'Can I use your microwave?' I asked, too hungry to care.

The guy behind the counter blinked. 'Are you . . . buying something?'

'Oh. No. Sorry.' With a goofy grin I held up my container of white fish. 'Just to warm this up.' Parked outside was a very patient

Ryan, shaking his head. Usually doing something like this would embarrass me too, but I had bigger fish to fry, or rather eat.

I wasn't sleeping well. How could I, when I was soon to walk on stage in dental floss – in front of strangers . . . and people I actually knew? The big day started with the alarm at 4 a.m. I kicked things off with dinner pretending to be breakfast: egg whites and a tiny steak. Nice and light. Give the tastebuds a chance to wake up before the shitshow. It was hard to chew with a mouth that dry. We were completely stripped of fluid – all in the hope that *maybe* one extra ab would show up. My mouth was so tacky, my lips were sticking to my teeth. I learnt to smear Vaseline on my teeth before stepping on stage to stop looking like I was trying to smile while constipated. But it was too late to back out now – Ryan had already shaved my back. I never thought I'd say these words, unless menopause turns out to be a real doozy.

'Do you want me to do your beard too?' he asked.

'Shut up, you little shit,' I giggled, handing him the razor. Why did I need to be shaved? Apparently, so that my fake tan would be even. The first step was you had to shave your entire body – and I mean your *entire* body. When Ryan agreed to help, we laughed . . . until we didn't. The moment he asked me to hunch over so he could work the razor around my spine, it stopped being funny. His eyes locked on mine in the mirror.

Fuck.

I knew what he was seeing: my rib cage. Every bump, line and crevice on every individual bone on display. For the first time I started to wonder, *Have I gone too far?* But, like I said, it was too late to back out now. I was in too deep.

Three layers of tan down, I was feeling like a hairless cat. A hungry one. On the positive side, one perk of being a professional makeup artist is that I didn't have to pay someone to do my hair or makeup. I soon regretted doing it myself though as my hands shook as I went to apply some eyeliner. Once I was ready (on the outside), I packed my bag with my bikini, heels, jar of peanut butter, lipstick, and our team's T-shirt, which we all wore along with our branded robes.

Backstage was filled with meal prep bags like mine, people still applying blush, and coaches helping competitors 'pump up' – when you do some exercises to make your muscles show as much as possible. Girls in bikinis and heels doing push-ups was a sight I didn't think I'd ever see. One girl was smashing a jar of oats like it was her last meal on earth. As our stage time grew near I was even allowed to have some lollies. If heaven has a taste that was it. After months of nothing but chicken and fish, beans and broccoli with zero oil or sauces, the feeling when the gummy snakes hit my tongue was better than sex. Sorry, Ryan. Like a lot of the other first-timers, I was not after a trophy or even set on placing in the top ten. We just wanted to do our best and not completely humiliate ourselves.

'You got this!' Kara said.

'Smash it!' Ryan whispered in my ear as he hugged me.

It was nearly my turn. *This is really happening, I'm actually doing this.* As I began walking towards my fate, my teammates cheered me on. The moment I had been waiting for, and working so hard for, was mere minutes away. As I took my place in the lineup, the nerves backstage were contagious. Girls biting their fake nails, letting out deep exhales between quick pep talks – some for themselves, some for each other. I took comfort in that they were just as nervous as I was. They were real people. Nice ones too.

'Steph from the South Coast!' the announcer called. Taking my first steps onto the stage, I walked to the centre, replicating the poses I knew so well, except this time there was no mirror. A huge fake smile was plastered across my face, trying to hide the fact I was absolutely petrified. There they were. The judges. Seated behind a table directly in front of the stage, deciding if my body was good enough, rating every inch of me. Behind the judges was a sea of people, watching and judging all the same. It was like I was back in high school, but with fewer clothes on. My time on stage felt like it went by in two seconds. Before I knew it, the 'activewear round' (outfit: a tiny crop top and shorts) and 'evening wear' (a beautiful blue dress with ab-showing cut outs) were also over. As I left the stage for the last time, Ryan, Kara and the team were all clapping. I wasn't sure if they were just being nice, but I didn't care. I couldn't stop real-smiling. I fucking did it. And how did I do? Somehow, I placed twelfth out of more than thirty girls. Wild.

•

'Ryan, hurry up! I need to poop!' I yelled through the hotel room door. After a huge day of fake smiling, posing, and stuffing my mouth with whatever my tandoori-coloured hands could find, I needed to get to the bathroom . . . asap. The taxi had barely stopped before Ryan had claimed 'shotgun' on the toilet. So there I was, desperately trying to get into our room, Kara beside me, totally unfazed by the fact that I was about to shit myself on the nicely carpeted hotel hallway.

After what felt like an eternity, Ryan finally opened the door.

'Thank you,' I huffed. 'I was going to burst.' I was still mid-panic when the air shifted. Everything was still. Too still. The room was dark. That was weird. Flickering light lit the walls as I walked towards the bedroom. There were tealight candles scattered everywhere. My ears pricked up at the sound of soft background music. Suddenly, my 'situation' wasn't so important. For the first time without vodka, my mind was utterly blank.

What is this?

The hotel bed was covered with rose petals. And there beside it, down on one knee, was Ryan. His usually steady hands trembled as he pulled out a small jewellery box. 'Steph, I've loved you ever since I met you.' His eyes searched mine. 'Will you do me the honour of being my wife?' His voice cracked; a sound I had never heard before.

My feet stayed planted. Here I was thinking I could read this guy like a book – that he couldn't get much past me, but this . . . Grasping his forearms, I got down on my knees so my face could meet his.

I didn't say yes.

I just kissed him.

'Ouch! Shit. Sorry, guys!' Kara half-whispered from behind the curtain. I forgot she was even there. Judging by the phone in her hand, she had been documenting the whole thing. Legend. Her words snatched me from the fairytale. I blinked, wondering if the sugar had gone to my head. My eyes dropped to the ring, needing confirmation. The cool metal pressed against my skin, imprinting this moment into my brain. I looked up – and there he was. Like always. Present. Anchored. Proving he wasn't going anywhere. My home in human form. But this time, it was forever.

You may be thinking twenty-one is pretty young to get engaged. Looking back, I agree. These days, when I meet people that age, I genuinely think they're still a foetus. But by this point we had been together for five years and it felt right. Both of our families were over the moon and Ryan being the gentleman he is, had asked Dad's permission. Dad said, 'Sure, good luck.' Way to boost a bloke's confidence. Behind his joke, Dad was stoked too.

This proposal didn't come after a picture-perfect patch in our relationship. But maybe that's why it meant so much. Because he stayed through it all. Every phase. Every tired, hangry, delusional version of me – and still wanted forever. He loved me when I didn't even like myself. And that kind of love? You don't walk away from it. You marry it.

I said yes to Ryan Pase – but sadly, I continued to say no to myself.

I went on to compete in three more bodybuilding comps that season, placing eighth at the nationals and even becoming 'Miss December' in a fitness model calendar. Just call me the next Gigi Hadid – Wish version.

•

Instagram message: Hey Steph. We'd love chat to you about being an ambassador!

Brands started reaching out as I continued to share my journey on Instagram. I finally felt worthy of something, not because of the free samples (which were cool) but because I had done something I said I would, and didn't completely suck. People said I had potential. And for once, I believed in myself too. Maybe this Jack could amount to something, after all.

Despite this progress, my body was about to send me signs that this new 'lifestyle' wasn't sustainable. Duh, Fred. For starters, my period stopped some time before that first competition in Melbourne. Naturally I freaked out. So I went and asked the other girls who didn't even flinch. A good sign. 'It happens,' I was told. 'A lot of the pros don't get theirs in season either. It'll come back after comp.' *Obviously just part of the process*, I thought. When my period didn't come back after comp, it didn't occur to me that my body wasn't just getting 'stage lean' – it was shutting down functions it no longer considered necessary. It was waving a white flag, and I was giving it a round of applause.

What was even harder than squeezing into the dental floss that we called a bikini was trying to control myself after each comp day. I began binge-eating like a stray cat – wild, insatiable and probably shouldn't be left alone on the couch. The team plus our partners all went out for dinner after each show, and we were allowed to eat whatever we wanted. But this one 'treat meal' soon turned into multiple days. I loved being able to indulge at the time but my body, not used to a 'normal' amount of calories, couldn't handle it. On countless occasions, I'd end up throwing up. Again, I dismissed it. My new normal was getting harder to justify.

My anxiety rose because I knew I was doing something 'wrong' and felt guilty. *Why the fuck did you eat that, Steph?* The thrill of having competed in my first competition soon wore off and was replaced with self-loathing as I picked apart everything 'bad' about my body. This is when I began to abuse laxatives. Comp after comp, bikini after bikini, binge after binge, I kept pushing through. This went on for, I hate to say it, nearly two years. To the outside world, especially those in the bodybuilding community, I was thriving. The medals, praise and new opportunities were increasing all while my mental health was taking a dive. And how could it not when my whole life revolved around an unhealthy obsession and essentially hating myself?

A couple weeks later, on a visit home, I made a beeline for Nan's room. As soon as she saw me, her face dropped.

'Stephy, sweetheart, there's nothing left of you!' She put her face into her hands, shaking her head.

'I'm eating six meals a day, Nanna, and so many vegetables, I promise.' I sat beside her, stroking her back, trying to reassure her.

'It's not good for you darlin',' she said, 'you looked perfect the way you were.' Her eyes grew bigger when she was sad or concerned. I felt terrible for making her so worried. She was getting more forgetful these days, which crushed my heart. I had this conversation with her a few times like it was the first.

I didn't try to deny what everyone was saying, but when I looked in the mirror I saw something very different. I saw skin that needed to be tighter, arms that should've been more defined, and a fat pocket under my butt that refused to budge. I saw a girl who never saw anything through. Who'd never amount to anything. Flaky. Distracted. A Jack. Desperate to finally do something extraordinary – just to be enough.

At my lowest, I fainted during a shift at M.A.C. By this point, I was used to being lightheaded, but this was the first time I'd fainted, and it earnt me a trip to hospital. I remember feeling mortified as the ambulance took me away. I'd forever be referred to as 'that girl who passed out applying blush'.

'So your blood pressure and blood sugar levels are low,' confirmed the paramedic as she released the strap from my bicep. 'Have you eaten today?'

'Yes, I had breakfast and I've been drinking heaps of water. But I've been on a strict meal plan for a few months now.' My face blushed bright red.

'Alright, well you're gonna need to eat these.' She opened up a storage cupboard and pulled out a mini pack of jelly beans. As soon as I recognised what they were, my heart started racing. Every fibre of my being was yelling, *No! It's not on the meal plan, this will wreck all your hard work!* Ultimately my manners and the very little common sense I had won and I took the pack from the woman's hand. As I ate them, while lying on a stretcher in an ambulance, I was already calculating that night's cardio. A single jelly bean was the difference between success and failure; being worthy or not worthy.

I resigned from M.A.C shortly after the fainting episode – not just because I was an idiot sandwich – but because, as I mentioned, Ryan had convinced me to go 'all in' on my makeup business. But really? I thought *the job* was the issue. I told myself it was the standing for hours that was making things worse. I didn't want to admit that maybe my *hobby* was the problem. It's wild how something that starts with good intentions – like wanting to get healthy – can spiral when you're missing one crucial thing. Balance. Or a brain. Or at least a version of balance that works for *you* and *your* brain. At this point, I wasn't even close.

•

Who knew a measly toothbrush would be the last straw? It was 6 p.m. on a Sunday and I was in the bathroom getting ready for bed. I was going to sleep earlier and earlier, as my body that was meant to be getting stronger was feeling weaker and weaker. I stared in the mirror, something I now did often, and saw sunken eyes, a hollow face and a stomach that felt just as empty. Every ounce of energy was drained. It was a week out from the first comp of my second season. My entire identity revolved around gym, tanning, food and self-loathing. I held my toothbrush, the bristles lined with toothpaste ready to go. But my arm felt as though it weighed a tonne as I tried to raise it to my mouth. After a couple of brushes, I dropped the toothbrush in the sink and sunk to the floor. I had abused and betrayed my body for years. Shit food, alcohol, partying and now deprivation. It was finally showing me that we couldn't do it anymore.

I'm sad to say it took not having the energy to brush my teeth to quit bodybuilding and not all the other warning signs that came before; my period stopping, binge-eating, disordered eating, protruding ribs, fainting at work and depression. The universe will send us subtle nudges but if we ignore them it will serve you with a spiritual uppercut that stops you in your tracks; it could be an injury, an illness or something so huge it makes you wake up to yourself. Although a toothbrush is hardly earth-shattering, as I sat there, tears rolling down my face, I realised the shackles I had placed on myself needed to come off.

It was time.

I walked into our bedroom. Ryan was lying on the bed patting Lily while he watched TV. 'I can't even brush my teeth, Ryan, I have nothing left. I'm done.' I stared at the floor, feeling like I had failed yet again.

He looked at me . . . relief on his face. 'Thank god,' he said.

'Aren't you disappointed in me?'

'Steph. I've wanted you to stop this shit for so long now, you know that. You're not healthy. *This* isn't healthy.' He gestured to my frail frame. Then he got up and held me.

'I'm scared to tell the others,' I said, already picturing their reactions. Maybe they would try to talk me into continuing.

'I'm not letting you do it, Steph, even if you change your mind again. This is it. No more.' My shoulders softened with relief that he was making the decision for me. I knew I couldn't trust myself anymore. I didn't want be a Jack. But at least Jack could brush her teeth.

A week later, I did go to the competition – but only in support and to do makeup for the other girls. Did I wish I was on stage? Nope. In fact, I'd never felt so sure of anything. As I cheered my teammates on, I felt lighter; grateful even, to be on the outside looking in. I was no longer caged in a gym, tied to the scales, saying no to everything that actually *was* my life. In reality I was newly engaged to an absolute legend, planning a wedding. I had a thriving makeup business. I had so much to focus on and be thankful for. So why did I keep piling things on top? Layers of expectations that were mine, but I believed were 'theirs'? That was a question I'd keep asking for years. Quitting competitive body-building felt like I was removing a layer. But I had no idea who I was without it *all*. I went back to being just . . . Steph.

And just when I thought I'd run out of chances to believe in myself – I got a message that changed everything.

HOW TO KNOW WHEN TO QUIT (BEFORE YOUR PERIOD DOES)

The idea of quitting gets such a bad rap. We associate it with failure, or giving up. But what if walking away is actually the most *self-respecting* thing you can do? Why force yourself to stay in something that's no longer working? It's like being served your favourite meal . . . but it's off. And you eat it anyway. Why? To make other people comfortable?

Walking away from bodybuilding, heels in hand, was one of the best decisions I ever made. If you're wondering whether it's time for *you* to walk away too, here are the questions that helped me:

- Are you staying for the right reasons – or because stopping feels scarier?
- What is this costing you mentally, emotionally and physically?
- Are you sticking with it because you're scared of what other people will say if you quit?
- Would walking away feel like failure? Or freedom?
- If tomorrow the 'thing' was suddenly no more, how would you feel?

Chapter 14

The man on the phone

It all started with an Instagram DM.

> *Andrew: Hello Steph, I hope you have been well. You might remember me, I'm the photographer for your bodybuilding federation. I'm reaching out because I had an exciting opportunity come across my desk. And I thought of you right away. It could really open some serious doors for you. If you're interested, could I please grab your number? I'll need to call a landline – just standard agency policy for confidentiality on these types of projects.*

My heart fluttered, nerves bubbling up in my stomach as I stared at the message. What could this be about? My mind started to wander, imagining all the possibilities – a little mental holiday from scanning gym memberships and dodging conversations with juiced-up blokes who believed their back acne was just part of 'the gains'.

Since I stopped competing, I'd been feeling a bit lost. Eating regular food again was nice, but my brain was still playing catch up. My body dysmorphia hadn't clocked out, nor had the bad habits I'd picked up during prep: the guilt, the obsessing, the binge-eating. Ryan and I were in a good place and had decided to hold off on the wedding until we could afford it. Like me, he hated asking for help. Our engagement party was nothing fancy – just a bunch of us at the pub, laughing, eating and drinking – our kind of perfect. It was a nice contrast to the last couple of years, which had felt like a full-time performance. In spite of the progress I'd made, I was still lacking purpose.

Now, thanks to this random DM, here it was. Maybe. A new path began forming on my tattered, defective map. But I didn't want to get ahead of myself. I took a beat. The journalist in me was still alive somewhere, except now, instead of hard-hitting investigative pieces like Nan's favourite breakfast food (still my finest work), I took a look into this Andrew guy. I scrolled his Instagram page, checking out old posts of his work – polished shots of models, fashion, and lifestyle spreads. He seemed legit. After a few messages back and forth, I gave him the gym's phone number. It was dead quiet and I was working solo, so it seemed harmless enough. I felt another flutter deep in my belly and there it was: hope.

'There are some huge campaigns I think you'd be perfect for, Steph,' Andrew said. 'I've got tonnes of shoots lined up with brands looking for a young, fit ambassador with the right look, and I really think that's you. They're going to love you.'

I swallowed. 'Brands? Like . . . what kind of brands?'

'We're talking high-end fitness labels, activewear companies, even fashion.' His voice didn't waver.

I let out a breathy laugh. Right. Me. The girl who still didn't know how to take a selfie without a rogue thumb appearance.

I couldn't believe what I was hearing. The more we talked, the more this felt real. I had already proved to myself, and to others, that I could do the unthinkable. If I could get up on stage in a bodybuilding comp, I could dip my toe into modelling, surely? Of course, I'd have to keep my weight in check, but I figured the modelling world wouldn't want me to look like a dehydrated prune with a six-pack.

And just like that, my imagination was running wild.

At this point you may be thinking, *Steph, you just stopped doing bodybuilding comps and now you're throwing yourself into something else? Haven't you learnt your lesson?* From the outside, it must have seemed as if I was bouncing between identities like a woman three wines deep, spiralling into a side-bangs rabbit hole on Pinterest. But this felt different. This had come to me out of the blue – I didn't chase it. At the time, I was still the old Steph who said yes to everything. Not the one who currently throws her keyboard the second she gets another 'just a quick thing' email.

When I got home, I barged through the front door, tripping over my feet in the process. I couldn't wait to tell Ryan. Maybe this opportunity could help pay for our wedding. 'Hun, you're not going to believe what just happened!' I called, throwing my bags down like I had just come home from school. Ryan looked up from the couch, his face a mix of intrigue and concern. Rightly so, the man had been through enough of my big ideas to know that excitement arrives first, logic later – or never. 'So the photographer from comp messaged me today,' I blurted. 'You know, the guy with the camera. He reckons I could model. This could be an *actual* career, Ryan.' I grabbed his hand. 'He's already spoken to an agency about me. He even mentioned some huge brands. Can you believe it? I can't believe it. This is *insane!*'

Ryan looked at me, carefully and purposefully. 'Why is it insane?'

'Hun, it's *me*.' I gave him the look. You know the one. The *duh* face.

'Steph, it's *not* insane. What's insane is that you go out and achieve all these things and still, somehow, manage to put yourself down.' And then he delivered one of his perfect Ryan speeches. 'Of course you can do this. Number one: you're beautiful. Number two: you've already proved that when you set your mind to something, you don't just do it, you *smash* it.' He grabbed my shoulders. 'You're not insane, you're *Steph the Unstoppable*.'

Rather than making a joke or dismissing what he'd said, I let his words sink in. Maybe Ryan was right. Unlike competing, this wasn't something I had to force myself into. I didn't have to carve it out from sheer discipline and hunger. This wasn't me chasing validation – it was someone else saying, *Hey, you could do this. We want you. We choose you.*

And that felt good.

•

Over the next few weeks, Andrew and I continued to discuss my new modelling career over the phone. As the photographer for the bodybuilding federation, he knew everything about the comps I'd been in – the judges, the process, even the tiny behind-the-scenes details. While he was professional and knew a lot about the modelling industry too, he was also patient and happy to explain the ins and outs. He even spoke to Ryan and my mum and dad on the phone who were also stoked.

So you can imagine our excitement when Andrew called with some news: a big Australian department store wanted to fly me to

Western Australia for a photoshoot for their next campaign! They had arranged flights and accommodation and the tickets would be waiting for me at the airport. I couldn't believe it: my first gig was going to be with a big retail name and I was being flown across the country. Shitballs. The best-case scenario would be I'd quit my gym job but continue to run the makeup business on the side. I wouldn't have to be such a Jack of all trades anymore. My new modelling career would fill the empty gaps inside me, and finally I'd be enough.

•

A couple of days before I was due to leave for Western Australia, Andrew called me on the landline at my parents' house. By this stage, we had got to know each other pretty well. He knew all my hobbies and my favourite foods; he even knew that our family dog was named Goldie after our beloved pet goldfish. He made me feel comfortable, seen and valued.

'Steph, I'm just looking at this photo of you from your last comp,' he said. 'Can you hop online? It's the third photo I took of you.' When I pulled up the photo on my laptop, Andrew began to explain that he needed my measurements, so that my wardrobe for the campaign could be tailored to fit me. He asked me to go and grab a tape measure and then explained how to measure myself 'correctly'. Then his voice seemed to change. His tone was different. He asked me to stay on the phone and rub myself 'down there' and then give him the new measurement. He also asked me to rub my breasts among other things I can't bring myself to write.

My stomach dropped. Andrew suddenly looked very differ-ent. The whole *situation* looked very different. Although I was only twenty-two and could be naïve at times, it didn't take longer than a millisecond to realise what was happening; what had been happening all along.

In a voice that barely sounded like mine I said, 'Um, I have to go,' and hung up before he could respond. I didn't want to admit it to myself. I barely made it to the bathroom before I threw up. And in that moment, not only did the contents of my stomach leave my body, but so did my self-worth. All I could think was, *You stupid idiot.*

The phone began to ring.

And again.

It kept ringing.

I sat dead still, like if I moved an inch Andrew would somehow step through the phone and into the room. Fumbling the hem of my jumper, my mind started working overtime, piecing it all together. There was nobody at my parents' house but me, which I was grateful for at the time. And I didn't want to tell Ryan, because I was so embarrassed.

Why did Andrew always insist on calling the landline?

Was that even *really* Andrew?

I went from doubting *him* to doubting the whole *modelling industry.*

What if this was just how the industry worked?

What if models really did have to 'comply' to make it?

It wouldn't have been the first time. But I knew one thing – I wasn't going to find out and I sure as hell wasn't going to let a man play me for a fool. 'Don't put up with shit!' Nan's voice rang in my head. So I decided to go full-blown detective on Andrew's arse. If he was the real photographer for the bodybuilding federation, they needed to know what kind of man they had working for them. And if he *wasn't*? Well, then I had an even bigger problem. I grabbed my phone and went straight to Instagram, searching for his page. *Nothing.* Gone. Vanished. Like he had never existed.

The federation was just as speechless as I was. I explained everything, my voice shaking but firm, skipping over the details of what he had said. I just told them it was *sexual* and *inappropriate*. That was enough. They were horrified, apologetic, and said they would get the real Andrew to call me as soon as they got hold of him. As I sat there waiting for his call – the one that would confirm everything, the one that would make this entire thing crystal clear – it felt like I was waiting a lifetime.

My phone rang. Finally. And it was the real Andrew. At this point I didn't know what was worse – this all being fake or Andrew being fake. I put the phone to my ear, as if it were a grenade.

'Hello?' said the real Andrew in a voice that was *nothing* like the one I had been speaking to. The real Andrew was mortified and offered to help, including speaking with the police. That was all I needed; confirmation that Steph was not only a fool but had just given her personal information to a complete stranger. Hanging up, I began replaying in my mind all the phone calls, interactions and false promises. All of the red flags I had ignored suddenly became glaringly obvious. His clever banter and confidence had been so convincing, and I'd allowed myself to believe. As if I had all the puzzle pieces but refused to put them together because I wanted it so badly to be real.

At the time I felt guilty and ashamed; and Ryan felt like he should have protected me and seen through the act. My parents were just as shocked as we were. But that's the problem with arse-holes: they're good at what they do. They're convincing. They do their research and lay the groundwork. I had no idea who fake

Andrew was. He could have been anyone. But he knew all about me. He even knew where I lived. Suddenly, I no longer felt safe in my own home. It was time to call the police.

The following day, Ryan and I sat in our lounge room with two officers standing across from us. One pulled a notepad from her pocket, the other leant against the kitchen bench, arms crossed. I suddenly felt ridiculous, like I had wasted their time. *Was it really that bad?* I thought, my brain already beginning its gaslighting campaign. The police explained that fake Andrew always called on a landline because it made it harder to trace his number. 'Just be careful,' one of the officers said. 'We don't know who this guy is. He could be in another state, maybe even another country. But just . . . be smart.' They were trying to be supportive, but those words stuck. Smart. *That* was the one thing missing from this whole equation. I hadn't been smart enough to see through him. I hadn't been *smarter* than fake Andrew.

•

Weeks passed and I heard nothing. No updates from the police. No new information. Fake Andrew was a ghost. No traceable number. No face. No real name. All I had was a voice. That voice. The voice of deception. Every sound outside made me flinch. Every passing car, every shadow cast by the streetlights, suddenly felt like a threat. I kept peeking out the windows like a bloody caged rabbit, scanning for something . . . or *someone*. It felt like I had been dropped into the middle of a true crime show. Except I was the main character, and I really, *really* didn't want to know how the episode ended.

I still wonder what would have happened if I had got on that plane. What was waiting for me in Western Australia?

Walking through the grocery store became an exercise in hypervigilance. Flighty glances over my shoulder. *Every* man was a suspect. The guy behind me in the checkout line. The bloke passing on the street. The creep at the gym who *always* stared too long. My brain had turned them all into blurry faces on the evidence board in my mind.

On the days Ryan worked late, I'd stay back at work or drive to my parents' house, where at least I could sit with Nan – just like old times. She was as ropeable as Ryan when I told her what had happened. 'That bloody bastard!' she fumed, shaking her fist. 'How dare he do that to you!' I didn't tell her – or my parents – the details. I just told them enough. Enough for them to be furious.

The worst part was telling my co-workers and friends. Their reactions were the same – shock, sympathy, *pity.* I hated pity the most. Deep down, I was sure they were thinking the same thing I was. *Of course it wasn't real. How could that have happened . . . to you.* Reading this, you can see that past Steph was an absolute arsehole to herself. Writing this chapter cracked open stuff I haven't touched in years. It's been a trip, dragging myself back into that headspace – stepping into the mindset of someone who constantly second-guessed her worth, chased validation, and picked herself apart at every turn. She was brutal. She attached her self-worth to external labels and achievements. Like a good girl. How we are taught.

What surprised me the most was that as much as it hurt, it also showed me how far I've come. I don't speak to myself like that anymore. I trust my gut – and back myself without needing Ryan to say it first. It didn't happen all at once, but somewhere along the way, I started choosing me. The real me – even the messy parts I used to hide behind the shower curtain. Back then, I didn't realise I was standing at a crossroads: I could keep tearing myself down, or finally figure out how to have my own back. Turns out, I was building something – even in the mess. And at this point I wasn't asking for directions anymore.

As I sit here in bed, laptop resting on my legs, dragging it all up, I have one wish. I wish I could walk through the front door of our first home, march right up to twenty-two-year-old me and grab her shoulders. I would tell her she was changing the narrative that had been etched into her soul before she was born. I would take her hands – hands that, in the not-too-distant future, would hold her own children, stroke their hair, and then rewrite her own story – and tell her that she was becoming all the parts of Nan she had always admired, and that one day, all this pain and all these hard lessons wouldn't be for nothing. I would cup her face, meet those blue eyes full of shame and tell her – *that look?* That look is meant for someone else.

If I could go back to twenty-two-year-old Steph, I wouldn't just tell her that she's strong; I'd tell her that one day she will be standing on the other side of this moment, not just surviving, but thriving – unmasked. That her strength isn't in how much she can endure – it's in how she will rise. I'd tell her she chose to keep showing up in a world that tried to make her into something she wasn't. And I'd tell her it's okay if this left some scars along with the others. Two things can be true at once. You can be healing from a past hurt and you can still be unstoppable. You can learn to protect yourself without putting up walls. It's not all or nothing.

To anyone reading this who has ever felt that shame, that sense of being tricked, used, or taken for granted – I need you to hear this: *You are not the fool.* You are not the problem. You are not weak for having trusted, for having dreams. The only people who should feel shame are the ones who prey on good hearts. And they *do* feel it. Deep down, they know exactly what they are, and what they *don't* have. So they take what they can, hoping to steal a little bit of your light. But the thing about light? It doesn't run out. It shines through even the tiniest crack, illuminating the darkest of spaces. And your light – they can't bottle that. That's yours to keep.

At the time I didn't know I would go on to collaborate with countless brands and photographers through my blog and my business. Being photographed would become part of my job. I would get better at reading people, and doing my own version of a background check. I would still feel vulnerable and scared sometimes, but I wouldn't let it stop me. I've replied to many DMs in the years since that have turned into incredible, empowering, valuable partnerships. I didn't let what happened with fake Andrew keep me down – but I did let it teach me about boundaries and trusting your gut. Even today, I ask Ryan to come to meetings about new ventures. On some level, I'm still scared of being 'out there' alone, and I get frightened driving in places I don't know. But I do it because I'm worth it and I won't let Anxiety and scars that arseholes left tell me otherwise. Although the scars from this event have faded, I still live with the repercussions to this day. I can't sleep at home alone ever, even with the kids. I won't stay at a hotel alone, unless it's in a room on a high-level floor. I can't drive anywhere in the dark alone, unless I'm meeting someone and it's a super familiar place. Like many women, and people, I do have a level of fear. But I don't beat myself up about it.

Now in my thirties, I don't blame myself anymore, and I certainly don't think I was stupid. I wasn't foolish for believing that amazing things could happen. The real shame isn't in hoping – it's in how quickly we shut ourselves down. How often we tell ourselves we can't, shouldn't or aren't enough. How quickly we let one person take away our power because *they* fucked up.

In recent years, we've seen many actresses, singers and women from all walks of life step forward, sharing their stories of harassment, manipulation and abuse. Famous or not, abuse does not discriminate. And worst of all, it can take years – sometimes a lifetime – to feel okay to speak out. Not because we did anything wrong, but because, somehow, we're made to feel as though we did.

Should I have known better?

Should I have said less?

Should I have been smaller, quieter, safer?

Maybe that would have 'saved' me. But what kind of life is that? If we let fear take away the best parts of us – our trusting hearts, our hope – then what are we left with? A world where no one dares believe in anything, let alone themselves. And that's a life far sadder than any betrayal. Most of us have a version of 'the man on the phone', and many of us have never spoken about it. I hope you read this and at the very least know that you're not alone.

And to Fake Andrew, whoever you are, wherever you are, I hope you managed to heal the parts of yourself that were crying out to be healed. I hope you didn't go on to hurt anyone else. I hope you know you didn't stop me and that although I carry this memory, I no longer carry the shame, the guilt or the embarrassment for what *you* did to me.

P.S. You're a douche canoe. What? I can't be all 'woke', can I now?

A LOVE LETTER TO ANYONE
WHO CARRIES SHAME

Your embarrassment and disgust do *not* belong to you. They are not yours to carry. That weight is for the people who take, the people who destroy, the ones who cannot create, dream, or build anything of their own. Next time you look in the mirror and see judgement staring back at you, I need you to remember: *You are merely carrying the overflow of someone else's shame and lack that they feel for themselves. And it is time to put it down.*

Chapter 15

Handing over the reins

'I can't say I've ever seen a bride do her own makeup, set up the reception and memorise her speech all at the same time,' said our wedding venue coordinator. I spun around, eyeshadow brush between my teeth, leather brush belt strapped on, juggling five bottles of baby's breath.

I was a bride on a mission.

Of course I'd do everything myself instead of bothering the people that, you know, actually did this for a living. Handmade decor in one hand, blending blush with the other; I don't do things by halves. And yet I was calm – as in Ryan Pase calm, my soon-to-be golden retriever husband. Weddings? Pfft. Piece of cake. Booking a doctor's appointment? Pure terror.

I'm the type of person who will experience crippling anxiety and lose three weeks' sleep over something that takes exactly two minutes. But when it comes to the *big* stuff? The life-altering, once-in-a-lifetime stuff? I suddenly became organised. Our wedding was the first time ever that I was fully prepped and ready *six weeks ahead of time*. Six. Weeks. I wish I could say that about literally anything else I do. Wedding prep was completed during shifts at the gym (sorry, Ben, you really should've fired me).

When I have everything I *can* control under wraps, my friend Anxiety doesn't have such a grip on my imaginary nuts. As Nan always said, 'If you can't change it, don't worry about it.' So that's exactly what I did. I prepped the hell out of our wedding day, even creating a wedding planner from scratch because I couldn't find one that worked with my brain. I felt like maybe for once I had my shit together. I couldn't be sure if Anxiety would show up, but there was one guest I really hoped would; my long-lost friend, Presence. I wanted her front and centre, no distractions, no scattered thoughts and worries – just me, Ryan and this moment.

Mid-setup, I stopped. Turned around. Took in the devastatingly beautiful scene in front of me. Rustic glass vases filled with pastel peonies, brass candle holders centred upon the soft white linen. Perfect rows of white garden chairs framing the grassy spot where, in a few short hours, I would stand and say 'I do'. Today was the day I'd marry my home in human form – Mr Ryan Pase.

This contradiction was ready to walk on down the aisle.

But not everything was perfect. I'd woken with a cold sore brewing, running off two hours' sleep. But there were no cold feet here. I was Steph the Unstoppable now. The unstoppable mess marrying her teenage sweetheart. We had decided to send each other gifts first. I untied the white ribbon and lifted the lid – and immediately burst into a snort-laugh. Inside was a tennis ball with 'Dolphins Rule' scrawled across it in permanent marker, and a tiny Hulk figurine. Apparently I make similar sounds when I'm angry or hungry – which, thankfully, I wasn't today. It was silly, specific, and full of love. And in that moment it hit me; maybe this was the inside joke Ryan had always seemed to know, even back when we first met. That quiet smile like he already saw the whole story unfolding. Maybe I was finally in on it too.

Ady wore a T-shirt that looked like a suit, because an actual one wouldn't have lasted a second, and we really didn't want naked Houdini making a cameo appearance. I'd asked Ady's carer-turned-family friend Julie to join us – not just to help, but as a guest. Nan's pride never wavered. Dad's childlike grin was there – a rare sight – and for the first time in years, I felt it: his pride. I'd be his only child to get married and have children. And of course Mum was there too. This wasn't just my day. It was all of ours.

The arch of flowers came into view, my hand tightened around Dad's forearm, both for nerves and balance. 'Are you nervous?' I said, exhaling hard and glancing at Dad, searching for the reassurance that Ryan would normally give me.

'No, darl. It's going to be fine,' he said with a knowing smile, as though he had lived this day before.

The walk down the aisle was as graceful as the time I landed in a moon boot – tulle flailing, heart hammering. Our eighty-five guests came into view. Nan front row.

And then, there he was. Ryan. My anchor.

His eyes found mine, and instantly his shoulders dropped.

The beginning of our forever.

As much as I ached to reach Ryan, I savoured the moment – just Dad and me. Alone time with him was rare. He was always Adam's carer first, Mum's right hand second, my dad last. But now it was just us. No distractions. A father walking his daughter down the aisle. I didn't know it yet, but this was a moment I'd one day replay endlessly, trying to remember the way his eyes crinkled when he smiled, the warmth of his hand on mine, his quiet pride. He may have been a man of few words, but in this moment his love was loud. As he squeezed my hand one last time, I felt it – everything he couldn't say.

Naturally, Ryan and I giggled like seventeen year olds during the ceremony. And if you couldn't already tell we were millennials, you would have, based on our reception; everyone slut-dropping, belting out 'Get Low' – a vision of classy, I know. Laughter filled the marquee.

Ryan's speech had everyone in stitches. 'Steph's into fitness now. Which I love, because she carries me into the bedroom.'

I was out of the bodybuilding phase and could look back on that period with amazement. I'd spent months 'reverse dieting', slowly reintroducing calories to avoid the rebound others faced – rapid weight gain, hormone issues, even fertility problems. It scared me more than I cared to admit.

•

'Kids are cool,' Ryan said one night.

'Um yeah. I guess.' I glanced over at him, waiting for his point. We were halfway through some awful Tom Cruise movie. *Maybe being married really does turn conversations to shit? Is it downhill from here?* But before I had a chance to call the marriage counsellor he added, 'What do you reckon?'

I'm shocked I didn't jump his bones right then and there. Nothing says 'put a baby in me' like a lukewarm discussion on the couch watching a crappy Tom Cruise movie. Meanwhile, my hormones were giving me the cold shoulder. Physically, I'd escaped comp prep mostly unscathed – but my skin? Not so lucky. Adult acne, right before the wedding. My face resembled my new Italian family's homemade pizzas. Thank god for acne cream that's as strong as Ady's drinking bleach. Too far? As for my cycle? All over the place. Sometimes three times in a month. Sometimes nothing.

Until now, the thought of kids was miles off. I could barely manage myself, let alone a tiny human. Sure, growing up, I played with *Baby born*, but I wasn't allowed to feed it that powder that made it poop. A travesty, I know. I thought I'd be closer to thirty, but at twenty-three, we were both feeling it. Our friends were partying, breaking up post-hen's night. Meanwhile, we were dreaming of a family. Of building the kind of connected, loving home I always wanted as a kid. If that was possible.

So we decided: let's do it. But one thing first.

'What do you think they'll say?' Ryan asked as we walked up my parents' driveway. Kinda weird, when you think about it – telling your family you're planning on having more sex. But Ryan was excited. Especially about the *trying* part. Men.

Nan opened the door. 'Stephy, love!' Her face lit up as she hugged me. She fit perfectly in my arms, just like when I was a kid. But I hated how old she was getting. Some nights, I'd lie awake haunted by thoughts of losing her. But another part of me couldn't imagine it. She felt eternal.

'We're going to start trying for a baby!' we announced, as I shifted my weight between my feet.

Nan cheered like she'd won the lottery. Mum beamed. And then there was Dad. I turned to him, expecting a hug, a joke, a grin. Instead, his face was unreadable.

'What do you think, Dad? Poppy suits you.'

He looked at me and said, 'Steph, are you sure? You're so young. It's too early to throw your life away.'

For a second I was stunned; but then I got it. Dad had lived wild and free – until Adam's diagnosis. His world became work, doctors' appointments, physio, exhaustion. He didn't have much support. This was thirty years ago, with stigma and scarce resources. Parenting was lonely, even with all of us around. I knew many joyful, fulfilled parents raising kids with a disability. But Dad's experience was different. And his fear came from love, not judgement.

We tried not to let it overshadow things. After the announcement, we booked a trip to Bali; one last hurrah before parenthood. Cheap flights, Bintangs – the works.

But Dad's words lingered.

I knew the stats: all three types of Down syndrome are genetic conditions, but only one per cent of cases have a hereditary component passed from parent to child. Still, I was anxious – not just about that, but any condition. Not that I'd change Ady for the world, but I wouldn't realise how deep that fear ran until I saw two red lines on a pregnancy test.

And that day was coming soon.

The week before we were set to fly out for our final piss-up in Bali, Ryan, again, the pinnacle of seduction, turned to me and said, 'Wanna try?' Translation: he just wanted to get lucky and, shocker, it worked. I'd started tracking my cycle so I knew I was in a fertile window, but still, what were the chances?

Cue Sponge Bob narrator: Two weeks later . . . (Don't lie, I know you read it in the voice.)

During the first week of our holiday, I had been feeling rough so I snuck off to a chemist and bought a very suspicious-looking Indonesian pregnancy test. Ryan was sitting by the pool drinking his fifth Bintang, blissfully oblivious to how our lives were about to change.

'What's up? Why are you looking at me like that?' he asked, mid-sip.

'Oh, nothing. How's that beer taste?' I smirked, holding myself back.

'Like freedom,' he grinned, raising it in a toast.

Not for long, sweetheart.

Casually pulling out the pregnancy test from my bag, I said, 'Well, either I'm pregnant or I've just taken my temperature with a dodgy Balinese thermometer.' His face began to cycle through the emotions. 'We're about to have the most expensive souvenir ever,' I laughed.

'Wait . . . so that means—' he said, arms stretched towards me.

'Yep. Hold onto your Bintangs, Ryan. We're having a baby!'

TO THE ONES IN THE WAITING ROOM

I want to pause here because I know that for some of you this chapter might be difficult reading. I know that for many women, the journey to motherhood isn't as simple as deciding and then two weeks later seeing two little lines on a pregnancy test.

Some of my closest friends have spent years trying, hoping and grieving the dream of a baby. I couldn't imagine the silent pain behind the well-meaning questions, the emotional rollercoaster of treatments, the ache of yet another negative result. And if that's been your reality – if you've known the waiting, the hoping, the heartbreak – I just want to say, you are not forgotten. I really appreciate you reading this, but feel free to skip the rest of this chapter and the next if you need – whatever feels right for you.

•

I've never had to break life-changing news over dodgy Bali wi-fi before, but here we were, pixelated and frozen on the most unflattering of faces, telling my Nan she was going to be a great-grandmother, and my parents they were going to be grandparents. We waited until we got home to tell Ady and my new in-laws; Ady for obvious reasons and Ryan's parents because they were already worried about us travelling so we didn't want them to worry more.

It's funny how much you learn about yourself – your beliefs, your fears – when you reach new milestones. Up until this point, I hadn't fully realised the mark that growing up with Ady had left on me. I was already terrified of anything health-related, and now I was (hopefully) going to be responsible for bringing a human into the world. We may have just found out I was pregnant – or, you know, that I had a fever – but either way, the thought that there was possibly a baby inside me was exhilarating and terrifying all at once. Suddenly, I wasn't just scared of having a baby – I was scared of losing it.

So naturally, I did what I always do when I don't understand something: I researched the absolute shit out of it. Books, articles, forums . . . I basically became a midwife overnight with the amount I learnt about conception, pregnancy and childbirth. I wasn't just pregnant, I was starring in my own reality show, *Pregnant and Panicked: Every Breath Could Harm Your Baby*. The plot? Me, spending all hours of the night obsessively googling things like 'What happens if I accidentally eat a prawn?' Spoiler alert: the prawn was fine and so was the baby, but that didn't stop me from spiralling every time I glanced over at a slice of soft cheese. Delicious but dangerous. It was like comp prep except this time I felt like my food fears were warranted, and there were no abs to be seen. Then there was the stress that came with stressing about the above, which I read wasn't good for the baby. So I stressed about the stress that was stressing me . . . This wasn't just careful parenting – it was a level of overthinking that could only come after a lifetime of training.

Growing up with Ady and a mum who could turn a sniffle into a full-blown medical emergency, I learnt early on that health was largely luck of the draw. I was wired to see danger everywhere. Most mothers worry about their baby's health – it's natural – but for me, those worries became an all-consuming spiral, driven by the need to do everything perfectly and the fear that one misstep would spell disaster. I figured if it could happen to my parents, surely it would happen to me too.

Health, anxiety and fear of deli meats aside, Ryan and I were excited to be starting a family. Now it was just a nine-month waiting game – and I was extremely impatient. Between my tenth and thirteenth week I could pay for a genetic 'harmony' test to see if our baby showed signs of a chromosomal disorder, but at this point I only had a few weeks on the clock. The test was pricey, but Ryan was all for it. He understood this was big for me.

'Why would you spend $400 on some test? The baby will be fine,' my friend Kate said, like I was splurging on a handbag instead of trying to ease my worries over my unborn child.

'I just . . . want to make sure everything's okay. With Ady and everything . . .' I suddenly felt stupid for even trying to explain.

I hated feeling this way. Like I was being overdramatic. I wished I could be like everyone else, trusting that everything would be fine. But my brain didn't work like that. It made me wonder if all mothers felt like this. I'd heard about 'mother's intuition', how we're supposedly wired to protect our kids at all costs. But was this level of worry normal? How do you tell the difference between intrusive thoughts and regular first-time mum nerves? Mate, this kid was already exhausting. God help me when it was actually outside of my body – crawling, climbing, eventually running straight into danger like a drunk Steph on a mission. Fuckballs. Pass me the retinol and a Valium.

Speaking of drugs, I decided to come off my antidepressants. You're probably thinking, *You idiot*, or, *You know you can take most of them while pregnant, right?* or maybe even, *Honestly? I get it.* That's the thing, we all think we know what we'll do until we're actually in the moment. And in that moment, with my health anxiety in full force, Mum spamming me with articles (as per usual) and Dr Google whispering worst-case scenarios into my already over-active brain, I wasn't willing to take the risk. With my doctor's support, the plan was to get through pregnancy, then go back on the meds. Surprisingly, going off them wasn't what I expected – I actually seemed to survive okay. And of course, I wasn't drinking anymore.

As the date of the harmony screening test grew closer, I couldn't help thinking back to my own parents and the day their world was rocked by Ady's diagnosis. The doctors didn't think he'd live past two years. I had always felt for my parents but now, with my own baby on the way, it was hitting me differently. I couldn't imagine what it must have been like for them. No wonder it was the only time anyone had seen Dad cry. And now I was about to find out if history would repeat itself . . .

I was alone in the kitchen when I decided to phone the doctor. I couldn't wait any longer, not even until Ryan came home from work. He understood and told me to call. One hand grasped our laminate kitchen bench, the other clutched my phone. The phone rang once. When the clinic answered, the woman's voice was calm, like she wasn't holding the fate of my entire world in her hands.

'Hello, um, it's Stephanie.' My voice came out high-pitched. 'I . . . I don't need to know the gender yet. Just if you could please tell me . . . just tell me if everything else is okay.'

A pause. The sound of clicking keys. 'All right, so no gender. Let me just pull up your results.'

I couldn't care less if the gender was dinosaur, as long as it was healthy dinosaur. I exhaled sharply, pacing the floor, my now free hand gripping my stomach. The same stomach that held our tiny future. The same stomach that had been through years of anxiety when I opened the door home from school. Gut punches from the people I loved. Of neglect. Of discipline disguised as control. I had spent my entire life terrified of what my body was capable of – or incapable of. *Please, please, let my baby be healthy and I will love it, and my body, forever.*

The sound of typing stopped.

'You can pop in tomorrow to collect the gender results on paper if you'd rather—'

'That's fine! If I could please just know if everything is okay?' My voice began to crack.

Her voice was steady: 'The results for your harmony test are all good.'

I stopped breathing. 'I'm sorry?'

I heard her smile through the phone. 'Your baby is completely healthy. No concerns here. Congratulations.'

My knees buckled. I hit the floor. Hard. The phone nearly slipped from my grip as I muttered what I thought was a 'thank you' and hung up. A deep sob erupted before I could stop it as I folded over my knees, releasing the weight I had been carrying for years – a weight I had prepared myself to never be free from – I finally let go. Tears came fast, like a dam breaking. The cold tiles grounded me as my shoulders shook with relief. It was *okay*. Our baby was okay.

Sitting on the floor, I let it *all* come out – the relief, the grief, the guilt. I was surprised by this reaction. Just because you carry it well, it doesn't mean it isn't heavy. Then I felt it. Grief for Ady. For my parents. For every mother who didn't get to drop to their knees in relief like I just had. I didn't know if I was worthy of this moment or this mercy, but I took it. I wiped my face and fumbled to dial Ryan's number. It barely rang before he answered. 'The baby's healthy, Ryan!' My voice was part sob, part shout. The sound of winning the lottery. At that moment, I knew I would never take this for granted. I would never stop being grateful. Thank you, Ady, my teacher, for this lesson, the most important one: gratitude.

THINGS I ASKED DR GOOGLE: THE GREATEST HITS

- Can you die from eating ham?
- What does this mole mean? (Yes, I tried to attach a photo.)
- Does stress cause early ageing or is this just my face now?
- What happens if you accidentally inhale dry shampoo?
- How long can a kid survive on just chicken nuggets and air?
- Is it normal to google symptoms every day or do I need therapy?

What's helped my health anxiety more than any search result

- Set a ten-minute spiral timer for Dr Google, then shut it down.
- Confide in your doctor and be honest about your health anxiety.
- Ask: am I seeking facts, or trying to calm fear?
- Therapy (game-changer) – understand where your anxiety stems from and how to manage it.
- Movement – it will quieten the noise in your head.
- Look at symptoms for what they are – your headache likely isn't a tumour, it's probably dehydration and stress.

Remember: uncertainty is uncomfortable . . . not unsafe.
P.S. Put the phone down. It doesn't help.

Chapter 16

The seven-hour pump shift

The cold maternity ward floor pressed into my hands and knees as I crawled across the room, tears streaming down my face. The off-white walls felt like they were closing in on me; it was more like a cage than a place where mothers met their babies for the first time. 'Please, please – can my husband come back?' I sobbed, looking up at the midwife.

In just hours, I was supposed to become a mum, but right now I was that scared little girl again, back at Meadow Lane, trapped in a ward too cold, too bright, too empty. Strangers in medical coats wandered in and out, but the one person I needed wasn't here. I had never felt smaller. What the hell happened?

Earlier that day, we arrived at the hospital, baby bag neatly stacked in one hand, a perfectly printed birth plan in the other. I walked in like Elle Woods strutting into Harvard Law School for the first time. Full of false confidence. Prepared. Delusional. My medical team had decided it was best if I was induced for a number of reasons, including the fact I'd been diagnosed with gestational diabetes during pregnancy. We had made it to 39.5 weeks before

it was officially time to kick baby out of the *Big Brother* house –
and mate, it felt like a sweet victory. I learnt a lot about the female
body while I was busy making a foot. Turns out, your cervix is
basically a hidden storage cupboard and my 'Do Not Disturb'
sign meant jack-shit. I used to wonder how women built up the
courage for birth, until I had another human growing inside me.
Suddenly, it wasn't about courage. It was about *comfort* – or, more
accurately, the complete lack of it. Our daughter, whose legs were
apparently in the ninety-ninth percentile (giving *major* Daddy
Long Legs vibes), wasn't just growing – she was trying to break
out. I was dreaming of the day I could lie on my stomach again
without getting a high-kick to the fanny. Little did we know, our
picture-perfect vision of birth would soon come crumbling down.
The only thing that was about to bend-and-snap was my sense of
control – and, eventually, my pelvic floor.

Of course I knew childbirth was going to be a whole other
level of pain. What I *didn't* expect was to be stuck in a relentless
cycle of excruciating contractions with zero actual progress – like
a shitty gym program from a TikTok influencer who swears by
'glute activation' but secretly has butt implants. This leads us to
the obvious question: where the fuck was Ryan?

Well, after a couple of hours of contractions, he'd been sent
home. There were no labour ward rooms available, so I was put
in the maternity ward – which didn't allow visitors after a certain
time. I also wasn't considered to be in 'active labour', which didn't
help my case. Apparently, having a baby wasn't reason enough to
let someone stay with you. I didn't want to cause a scene, so after
politely asking if Ryan could 'pretty please' stay – and being told
no – he reluctantly left.

I spent that night on the bathroom floor, under the flickering clinical lights, phone glued to my ear as though it was a lifeline, sobbing to Ryan. I was so excited to finally meet our baby girl – I wanted to do this. Just not alone. On the other side of the curtain in the shared room, a mother and her newborn were sleeping. Every few hours, a midwife would come in, check my cervix, and deliver the same news: *no progress*. My uterus was contracting like it was going for gold, but my cervix? All talk, no action – like Craig from MSN.

Finally, around 5 a.m. my body did . . . something. I stood up and a gush of warm liquid soaked through my underwear. I stared at the puddle and felt relief. My waters had broken. At last. Progress. But then the midwife turned and raised an eyebrow. 'Are you sure you didn't just pee yourself?' she asked, deadpan.

I know I didn't have the strongest pelvic floor at that point, but I was twenty-five – and pretty damn sure I could tell the difference between amniotic fluid and a rogue wee.

'Oh, no – it was definitely my waters. Sorry for the mess,' I said, trying to stay polite. Nan always taught me to kill them with kindness, even when they're implying you've pissed yourself. At this stage in my life, I was still a full-blown people-pleaser – something that would soon have to change.

Moments later, the rest of my waters gushed all over the bed. Sucker.

And just like that, Mr Pase was on his way. It was time to have a baby. The pain felt bigger than my body, but I was surprisingly quiet. Ryan, who had never seen me like this, looked genuinely concerned. When I'm in pain I go inwards – a coping mechanism I learnt as a kid. Don't take up space. Be a good girl. By this stage I was in 'active labour' but the contractions were different. I actually found them easier to deal with than the ones the induction gel had caused. But after a couple of hours, the contractions still weren't frequent enough, so the midwives decided to start a Syntocinon drip to speed things up. And *then* things really kicked off.

The next few hours were a blur of my entire body feeling like it was being ripped in half, *needing* to be in the shower to ease the relentless contractions, and switching between *front* and *back* labour (because apparently, having labour pains in just one location wasn't enough). I was about to throw my fictional birth plan out the window.

'Ryan, blast my workout playlist,' I huffed between contractions. If I was going to push this kid out, it was going to be to the sound of Blink-182, not the shitty relaxing birth playlist I made. There was no fucking way I was summoning the energy to push to the sound of birds chirping.

Fifteen minutes and nine pushes later, she was here.

We had a daughter.

Harper Rose. Fair hair, 3.3 kgs, 51 cm long. Our sweet girl.

'Why . . . why isn't she crying?'

'Just give it a . . .'

And then a small but mighty wail filled the room. That precious wail. Instantly, all the pain, exhaustion and fear evaporated. A sweet, beautiful amnesia. A new room was added to our home in human form. As she was placed on my chest, I glanced at Ryan. 'Steph, you're incredible,' he said, his voice thick with emotion. And for the first time, maybe ever, I believed it. A week earlier, I'd told Ryan about this thing called 'skin-to-skin' – no, not some woo-woo full-moon ritual, just lying your baby on your bare chest to bond. 'I'm not taking my shirt off in front of the nurses,' he'd laughed, like I'd asked him to do the *Full Monty* at smoko. But the second Harper was born, he didn't hesitate. Before I could finish suggesting it, his shirt was already off and he was lying back on the bed, arms out, reaching for her. 'Put her on me,' he asked. And just like that, I got to watch him become a dad. He was made for it.

•

'She can call me whatever the hell she wants,' Dad exclaimed a few hours later when he got to the hospital. His walls crumbled as soon as he saw her. Those same crinkles around his eyes from my wedding day grew deeper as he beamed at Harper. I felt all of the weight he had been carrying for me lift. A healthy baby.

'Oh Stephy, she's so beautiful.' Nan's face when she looked at her great-granddaughter transported me right back to my own childhood – evenings filled with magical lands she created with her stories.

As Mum approached the bassinet, a maternal energy emerged that I had never seen before. When she held Harper, it was like second nature. So why did it seem so foreign? I was watching her dote on my little girl in the way I had always longed to be loved by her. I basked in the version of Mum that surfaced now and then. I prayed that becoming a grandmother would be healing for her. That maybe it would be the beginning of something different between us. And for a brief time, it was. Sadly, it never stayed that way.

I had stuffed my birth trauma into neat little squares, told myself it wasn't that bad, locked it up and threw away the key. Even after the harmony test, I still carried doubts and, partly, I was waiting for the worst-case scenario. The deep relief that history wasn't repeating itself hung thick in the air, unspoken but felt by us all. Harper was healthy and I couldn't wait for her to meet Uncle Ady, who would become her greatest teacher, just as he had been mine.

If you asked me to name one of the happiest, proudest, most content moments of my life – a time when my old mate Presence actually decided to stick around – I wouldn't even hesitate. It was the day after Harper was born. I'll never forget walking through the hospital, gently holding onto the cool metal of Harper's bassinet. I may have had a second degree tear (RIP vagina), but I strutted those halls in a way that would have put my stage walk to shame. I wish I could bottle that feeling. It was more than just the high of new motherhood; it was a shift, a quiet but undeniable meta-morphosis. The kind that sneaks up on you, rearranges something deep inside, and leaves you forever changed.

For the first week, I floated.

Breastfeeding? We were nailing it. Harper fed like a trooper – latched easily, fed even easier, then passed out for hours. Like father, like daughter – just swap a Tooheys for a nipple. It felt too good to be true. And of course it was. The mantra drilled into my brain was 'breast is best'. It should have been printed on everyone's shirts. Apart from the pressure I put on myself, it was flying in from every direction – minus Ryan and family, of course. I quickly learnt that when it comes to babies, parenting and breastfeeding, every man and his guinea pig has an opinion.

And it was tolerable . . . until my milk dried up. This wasn't part of the 'perfect' motherhood plan. The culprit? A retained placenta, although I didn't realise this at the time. It's basically when part of the placenta stays in your uterus after your baby is born. It's not common and, for most people, it's discovered right after they give birth. Of course, I was one of the exceptions. Again, I don't do things by halves. I discovered it ten days later during our newborn photoshoot. Lights, camera, action . . . and suddenly blood gushing everywhere. After a trip to the hospital in an ambulance, the medical team explained what had happened, and also the possible side effects: pelvic pain, feeling fluey, a reduction of milk supply. Ah, that makes sense. What followed was a blur of doctors' appointments and feeling worse and worse. Eventually, I had to have surgery. It was the first time I'd left Harper's side. And just when you thought having a newborn was eventful enough.

Only a few days earlier, I'd had a panic attack in the middle of the night – my first bad one in a long time – because Harper had been screaming blue murder. She was hungry. I hear you, girl! I've been there. 'They're empty, hun, I swear to god,' I cried to Ryan, squeezing my boob. I glanced over to Harper, lying on the bed, still screaming.

'Are you sure?' Ryan asked, staring at my broken breasts. 'They don't *look* empty.'

'What are we going to do?' I was starting to panic. 'She needs me. I'm her food!'

Sure enough, Anxiety came thundering into the room, her fists white-knuckled, heading straight for me. *Breathe, Steph, breathe,* I reminded myself, but I wasn't listening. I suddenly felt rough, warm hands sliding up and down my arm, and pressure on my shoulders. It was Ryan, helping bring me back down to earth.

'It's okay, Steph. It's not just you. We're a family of three,' he said. 'We're going to figure this out together.'

I was grateful, but I couldn't help but feeling that I was like another 'baby' for him to look after.

The rest of that night had been filled with tears – both from me and Harper – and a giant pair of useless, empty titties. At least I now had an answer as to why. At this point, it would have made perfect sense to embrace bottle feeding with self-love and gratitude . . . but instead I persisted. It seems my health anxiety had simply taken a new form. My main priority, apart from keeping Harper alive, was giving her the best of the best – so I thought. I pumped relentlessly. I tried medication. I drank gallons of water. I ate enough lactation cookies that past Steph would have had a heart attack. But I would do *anything* for Harper. Sadly it didn't make much of a difference. From everything I'd heard plus what I read online, breastfeeding wasn't as 'natural' as they made it out to be – it could be hard, painful, and anything but intuitive. So I prepared for the worst-case scenario . . . and still felt like I'd failed.

Slowly my day trips out with Harper subsided. I became attached to the pump, trying my hardest to still feed my daughter. And how long did it take for one measly feed? Seven. Hours. Yes, I spent seven hours on the breast pump. I was exhausted. Depleted. And that's when the intrusive thoughts began. Somewhere deep inside me, a tiny voice was whispering, *Bro, this is unhinged. That's a full work shift. Stop being an arsehole to yourself, woman.*

I told her to piss off. I wasn't done yet.

I couldn't fail this.

Fail her.

I had only just started.

Every time Harper cried, I flinched. She was just hungry. But my body told me she was a bear. I didn't think I'd react this way to my beautiful new baby. I didn't realise I was showing the early signs of postnatal depression – I just thought I was failing my child. I should be grateful, right? I *wanted* this baby more than anything. And she was *healthy* – that's all I could have asked for. *Some women would kill to have what you have,* I'd remind myself, as if guilt alone could shake the weight off my chest. *What I would kill for – and here she was. So why the hell was I so miserable?* Soon enough I learnt PND doesn't work like that, and it certainly doesn't mean you're not grateful and love your child like any other parent. That's mental health for you. Sometimes you can't explain it but it's there and it's unrelenting.

At first I kept it a secret from Ryan, until I couldn't hide it anymore. One night, I told him everything. 'I'm scared of her, Ryan. It sounds crazy. I love her and I know she's not scary but I can't explain it. It's just the feeding. I have to keep trying.'

'Steph, remember we can just put her on formula,' he said, level-headedly.

'No. Way.' I was adamant 'breast was best'. 'I'm not going to do it. *We're* not going to do it.'

I never thought of myself as a control freak – that is, until I had a tiny human dictating my life. It's terrifying to think how one person can hold so much power. Most of us don't realise how precious – and exhausting – human life is. Until we become a parent. That's why it can all feel so overwhelming and impossible. This was my first test as a mother and I felt like I was failing. There was an extra layer because I was determined to be a 'good' mother – loving and consistent. Oh, the pressure we put on ourselves.

MY PERFECT PARENTING PLAN VS REALITY

- No Maccas until the kids at least start school.
- Exclusively breastfed until they were one.
- Only organic food I made from scratch.

- Gentle sleep training that I'd nail in one week.
- No dummies. No iPad. No TV.

   . . . Until I actually gave birth and then I'm handing Harper a chicken nugget, throwing on any show she wants, with a pile of ten dummies surrounding her like a fort of comfort (and peace and quiet). I absolutely ate my words . . . and then some. Naïve idiot.

•

Less than a week later, I changed my mind – or rather Ryan changed it for me. When he left for work, I'd been sitting on the couch, pumping, with one hand bouncing Harper in her chair. Several hours later he returned – and I was still there. Pumping and crying.

'That's it, Steph. You can't do this anymore,' he said. 'You're miserable. I can't bear to see you like this. I'm going to buy some formula. I'm putting my foot down.' His features were firm, as though he was ready to go into battle . . . with me.

But instead of protesting I just said, 'Okay.' Before I'd said another word he was out the door. When it closed behind him, I sighed with relief. Permission. A decision made by someone else. It wasn't all me anymore.

'Thank you,' I whispered. The hand that was holding the pump dropped, the plastic suction cup fell onto the couch, and off came the pump – for good. I was free. Ryan didn't feel guilty about this decision, so why should I? I'd learnt my first invaluable lesson as a mother. And no, it wasn't how to make baby food or get milk to the perfect temperature. It was that all Harper wanted was her mum – no matter what that looked like. I had spent hours attached to that pump, measuring milk, labelling it, freezing it – while across the kitchen, my daughter lay on her playmat . . . waiting for the voice she already knew. The smell she recognised. The person she wanted. Me.

We get so caught up in the details – the shoulds, the pressure, the 'rules' – that we lose sight of the only thing that really matters: happy mum = happy baby. If that means you need to go for a walk, get some air, lock yourself in the pantry and blast 'Big Girls Don't Cry' while you cry – do it. Whatever it takes for you to show up as the real version of yourself . . . that's all your kids want. And they will take the imperfect, messy, beautifully *present* version of you over the polished, burnt-out one any day of the week. Looking back, I could have wasted so much more time and energy trying to be the 'perfect' mum . . . When all my daughter needed was one who stayed.

I finally understood that being a good mum doesn't mean doing it all. It means choosing yourself, so you can be there for them. That was the beginning. Of coming back to myself. Of finally putting *me* on the to-do list. Of becoming the mother I needed to be – and the woman I never thought I'd be brave enough to become.

Now I can look back and join the dots: this was the dawn of a new phase. The seeds of inspiration to create a space for mums free of judgement and ridiculous expectations were planted; somewhere we could share our parenting victories but more importantly, the days we felt like we failed, to build a community where no one had to play pretend. Of all the jobs this 'Jack' has done, the seven-hour pump shift was by far the hardest. But it would give me the experience to one day become a voice for others – and offer them the pep talk I couldn't give myself.

This was the beginning of peeling back every layer, every mask, every expectation that had quietly swallowed me since childhood. Bit by bit, a new piece of me was revealed. And along the way I started to believe it was safe to let what was inside – out. To become the woman I never thought I could be – the mother I once needed – all because I finally loosened my grip, handed over the reins, and let what felt right lead the way . . . even when it scared me.

SEVEN SIGNS YOU'RE ACTUALLY DOING BETTER THAN YOU THINK

(Aka evidence you're not a complete shitshow, even if it feels like it.)

Quick check – how many of these can you say yes to?

- You kept a small human (or yourself) alive today.
- You remembered to drink water at least once.
- You felt overwhelmed . . . but still showed up anyway.
- You wanted to give up, but didn't.
- You've grown from the version of you six months ago – even if it's not obvious yet.
- You're still trying.
- You're reading this – which means some part of you still believes in yourself.

Reminder

You're doing better than you think. Keep going.

Chapter 17

Routines for real life

I had always loved the *idea* of being a morning person – you know, the ones who *choose* to wake up before the sun, stretch their arms out and breathe in crisp morning air, while a little birdie sits on their shoulder like a bloody Disney princess. But mornings and I have *never* been friends. For as long as I can remember, my days had begun and ended in chaos – sleeping through twenty alarms, skipping breakfast because I was late for school, work . . . *life*. And our relationship got even rockier postpartum.

While 'Susie from Instagram' had already run 10 kilometres, prepped a month's worth of bone broth, and meditated on a rock for four hours, I was still in bed with dried-up drool on my face, last night's dinner on the bedside, and a rogue boob hanging out of my PJs. How do they *always* find their way out? Escape artist titties. Breakfast usually consisted of cold coffee – or, if I was channelling my inner Gordon Ramsay – cold Vegemite toast shovelled into my mouth between nappy changes. And *that* was my morning routine. What can I say, I was a health icon.

Mornings are brutal when you're struggling with your mental health. But what I *really* hated about mornings was what they represented: the start of another day where I had to keep going, despite feeling like I existed under a storm cloud. And motherhood brought unpredictable weather and no forecast. The warmth of our Kmart sheets held me hostage; wrapped up like a sleepy, human-sized burrito and immersed in a deep, blissful sleep – a rarity these days. Almost as rare as me not wearing yet another Bonds breastfeeding singlet, which, let's be honest, I still wore years after our breastfeeding journey came to an abrupt end.

Until . . . That sound. It started as a faint ringing. Then grew louder. And louder. The creeping realisation hit: I wasn't in a dream starring Thor. I was in our tiny unit, listening to my cute little human alarm clock. No more deciding when my day started. Harper did that for me now.

'Rise and shine, Mum. It's Groundhog Day.'

And groundhog day it was. It had been a few weeks since Ryan had put his foot down and we'd started on formula. Harper was now a few months old and I was on maternity leave from my makeup business. While I missed my clients, I was happy to be having a break from the 3 a.m. wakeups (sparked by brides, not babies). I'd been back on my antidepressants for my anxiety for a few weeks and just like before I could feel Anxiety's grip loosen, but it wasn't an instant fix. Postnatal depression wasn't just a fleeting emotion – it well and truly set up camp in my brain. It didn't help that every time I thought Harper and I had got into some sort of rhythm, BAM, she flipped our schedule on its head. One minute, three naps a day. The next? *None, motherfucker.*

After a while, I began getting a decent amount of sleep – for a new mum at least – but I still woke up feeling drained, low . . . and strangely lost. I had nowhere to be. No job to clock into. No adult banter with co-workers to break up the day. My sole purpose was *Mission: Keep Tiny Human Alive*. Which is amazing – but it can make you lose your fucking mind sometimes. I'd gone from rushing through life to being stuck under a baby all day, staring at the ceiling fan, counting how many times it could spin in a minute. Riveting shit, right? Feed, change, negotiate naptime, repeat. And after hours of this, Ryan would finally walk through the door at 5 p.m. to find a very excited Harper – and an even more desperate-for-adult-conversation me.

One day in the fog of new motherhood, I realised I had to do something about it. It was a Tuesday morning, and I had just finished changing Harper for the fifth time. As I passed the hallway mirror, I caught sight of my reflection. In my peripherals, I saw a mother – a greasy messy bun barely holding on for dear life, dark under-eye circles so deep they deserved their own TED talk, and stretched-out pyjamas from yesterday. I looked exactly how I felt: stuck. This wasn't about vanity – it was about looking after myself again. So what did I do? I wrote a list. Surprise, surprise. My first 'routine'.

Step one: Wake up before the baby – *providing our night hadn't gone to absolute shit*. Waking up on my own terms, not someone else's. Honestly, no wonder we start the day stressed when the first thing we hear is someone else's demands.

Surprisingly, this one stuck. In fact, I'm writing this book right now at 5 a.m. – before anyone else needs me. Back then it felt like an alien concept. Instead of setting my alarm a full hour earlier like Susie (you know the type), I eased in. What I now call the Fifteen-Minute Morning Hack – my way of tricking my brain into waking up earlier without turning into a potato by lunchtime. I started with fifteen minutes. Then another fifteen. And another. Until eventually, I was setting my alarm for 5.00 a.m. – no wedding booking, no work shift. Just me. *Top tip: if your baby isn't sleeping through yet don't be a hero. Sleep, my dear friend.*

Ryan thought I'd lost it. That, or the lactation cookies I no longer needed had gone to my head. But I was willing to try anything. Yes, even getting up early . . . on purpose.

Step two: Daily micro rituals to lift my mood. Growing up, music and light were never part of the furniture – they were special guests that only appeared on rare occasions. But in my new morning routine, they became non-negotiables. At breakfast time, I'd play my favourite playlists which Harper loved. I opened every window to welcome in fresh air and light – and like fairydust suddenly our unit felt larger, open and brighter.

Steph's new morning routine

6.00 a.m.: GET UPPP!

6.05 a.m.: No seriously, remember we said we would do this? H is awake soon, bro.

6.10 a.m.: Okay, now you're just being a little bitch.

6.15 a.m.: Open the blinds, remind yourself you're not a vampire.

6.20 a.m.: Journal time: chill, you won't be sent off to boarding school this time.

6.30 a.m.: Eat prepped overnight oats. Change and feed your human Tamagotchi.

7.30 a.m.: Play music and do a quick tidy so you can sloth later.

I also began adding other habits into other parts of my day.

•

'Where's your lycra leotard and wristbands?' Ryan smirked from the couch.

'Stop laughing. You. Little. Shit,' I puffed between reps.

I'd just been cleared to exercise again at six weeks postpartum and was finally doing something for me. Bodybuilding had turned me off chicken and beans – but not the gym. Throughout pregnancy – and before – I stayed active. That is until I got too swollen and over life and stopped going to the gym and became swimming buddies with the retirees at the local pool. Shoutout to Audrey – hope the grandson is going well. You couldn't pay me to compete again. That chapter taught me how easily the pursuit of health can slip into obsession. Still, knowledge was comfort. I knew my way around a gym, and over time, I learnt nothing helps my anxiety and ADD more than moving. (I went on to get my PT qualification when Harper was six months old . . . because of course I would.)

Although my last attempt at being 'healthy' landed me on stage, starving, shredded and deep in disordered eating, there was one thing I took from that era. The revelation I had on the train ride home from makeup school that day: the *how*. Slow and sustainable. Ironic, I know. But hey, we live, we learn and eventually stop doing dumb shit. So I started working out at home a couple of times a week – just some hand weights, a kettlebell and a $10 yoga mat from Kmart. No pressure. No scales. No judges or judging. I loved this new part of my routine. Harper lying on her playmat, watching me like, *What the fuck is Mum doing?* We were a team – she and I. Like Nan and me. It wasn't pretty. But it was ours. And after everything my body had been through, it felt like a win.

That wasn't the only shift that happened after becoming a mum. As a late-teenager and adult, I'd always been self-conscious about my body – even in front of Ryan. But after pushing a 3 kilo baby out of my hoo-ha? Yeah . . . something changed. I didn't see my body the same way anymore. It wasn't just about how it looked – it was about what it *did*. And suddenly, the things I used to pick apart felt irrelevant. Instead of zooming in on every bump, fold, or stretch of skin, ripping myself apart like I always had, I *zoomed out*. And for the first time, I saw my body in a completely different light. This was the same body that gripped the handlebars of my childhood bike. That healed after every flu, cold and scraped knee. One that navigated a changing teenage frame, ran with my childhood dog, danced on my wedding night, survived comp prep, lost and regained my period, held strong through the chaos of life. And now? It had created, carried and birthed *her*. This tiny, perfect human. And then – somehow – it *kept going*, healing and parenting at the same time.

That shit is incredible.

Why on earth would I be ashamed of that?

Sure, I still had days where I picked myself apart. But I was starting to see my body not as something to fix – but something to thank. And frankly . . . 'bouncing back' can suck it.

MICRO HABITS THAT GOT ME MOVING AGAIN (WITHOUT CRYING)

Start small:
- Put your activewear on – even if you don't work out. It flicks the switch.
- Save your fave shows for treadmill time. I watch true crime and walk (nothing like a serial killer to speed things up).

Still not feeling it?
- Set a five-minute timer. If you still CBF, stop. But 90 per cent of the time, you'll keep going.
- Stack habits: stretch while the kettle boils. Walk the same time each day after drop-off or after work.

Lower the bar:
- That 10,000 step rule? It was made up in a 1960s Japanese ad campaign.
- I swapped it for 8000 and suddenly it felt achievable again. Progress over pressure.

ADHD-friendly:
- Only play your fave playlist or podcast while moving (your brain will know it's time to move).
- Put movement in your calendar: no plan = not happening.
- You don't need to go hard. You just need to *go*.

•

While I couldn't eliminate the normal stresses of parenthood, I could control my micro habits and how I approached my day. Over the next few weeks, I kept tweaking my morning routine, until it felt lighter, brighter and more productive. Even Presence started showing up more. I was onto something . . . I also decided to pick up the pen again and began journalling. Ever since the boarding school showdown I hadn't let what was inside spill out onto paper. But I was a big girl now – well, trying to be – so I made a dramatic main character moment trip to Kmart, grabbed a fresh notebook, and decided to give it another shot. Or at least scribble. I recorded how my new routine was going.

Day 2: Not *that* girl

Woke up feeling like that girl *– you know the one who drinks lemon water and goes for morning walks for fun. Well that was me until Harper decided I shall not be* that girl *today.*

*She randomly decided to wake up at 4.45 a.m. this morning,
so half my pre-planned . . . plan didn't go to . . . plan. Instead
of walking, I found myself in bed, scrolling my phone like me
exactly four days ago. My list, which was supposed to save me,
is now just decoration.*

I'd be lying if I said my new morning routine was flawless.
Motherhood was forcing my routine to be imperfect. No wonder
mums speed-walk through shopping centres like they're contestants
on *The Amazing Race*. You never know what the day will throw at
you. Maybe that was the missing piece to the puzzle. And I was still
a walking contradiction; I thrived on routine, but the second it was
actually in place? I felt suffocated. And with how my brain works
I didn't have the best track record for sticking to new routines.

And suddenly, it clicked.

The routine itself wasn't the problem. The way I built it was.
I was forcing a rigid plan into a life that was anything but rigid.
It was my birth plan all over again – built on best-case scenarios.
Of course it wasn't going to stick. It was like expecting Harper to
follow her exact nap schedule from four weeks ago, when every
stage is different. I can't copy-paste myself into a perfectly for-
matted routine because no two days are the same.

I was doing it all backwards.

That's when I sat down and scribbled out what would become
my 'Routines for Real Life Framework' – the bones I still use today,
and what would later shape my entire brand.

Anchor, don't schedule. Use when-ish triggers, not exact times.
'After school' became my cue for a quick reset.

Start with non-negotiables. Meds. Meals. Movement. Rest. If
I nailed the basics, it was a win.

Make it visible. Checklists, fridge magnets, planners on the bench – if I couldn't see it, I'd forget it.

Build it to break. Life happens. I needed a routine that worked even when I woke up feeling like a different human than the day before.

•

I didn't need a perfect routine – I needed one that could survive real life. I needed options – ones that fit my actual life and my actual energy levels. Some mornings, I'd get out of bed feeling like I had my shit together, ready to smash out a workout. Others? Not even Chris Hemsworth could have dragged me out from under the covers. Okay . . . *debatable*.

And that's when I had my lightbulb moment . . . A menu. I bloody love a good menu, the ones where you can mix and match depending on what you feel like.

- Chicken schnitty with a side of mac and cheese, or a salad?
- Change the sauce? Hell yes.
- Swap the dessert? Done.

Routines should work the same way. Because, let's be real, you're not going to want a *5 a.m. wakeup call* and a *green smoothie* on the mornings your kid was up all night vomiting. No, thanks. On those days, you're ordering the *sleep until I have to get up and then grab a well-deserved coffee*. If you're bloated and just not up for a hectic gym session? Maybe today's choice is the fifteen-minute walk entrée instead. See where I'm going with this? I hope so, or my book reviews are going to say this was a *really* badly written recipe book. How can you expect to show up as 'Energised You' when your body is screaming 'Bare Minimum You'? That's where energy-based routines changed everything. Just like a menu – not one perfect morning routine, but three:

- **Barely functioning:** For when you feel like absolute dog's balls.
- **Average:** For those *meh* days.
- **Annoyingly energetic:** aka Susie.

And this isn't just for the neurodivergent crew, oh no. This is for anyone who wakes up feeling different every single day. Which, the last time I checked, is *all* of us. It might sound overcomplicated having multiple routines on the go, but this brings me to the final piece of nailing a morning routine: it needs to be visible so you can't help but see it.

You know those times when you walk into a room and immediately forget why? You stand there, racking your brain for even a *hint* of why you walked in, and . . . nothing. That's my brain 24/7 – out of sight, out of mind. So naturally, this new menu needed to be in my face. So what did I do? Hyper-fixated for three hours designing the most intricate wall planner known to man. So that the second I stood up from bed – BANG – there it was. No excuses. No forgetting.

For the first time in my life I started working with my brain instead of against it. As my day became more streamlined, it opened up space, which in theory is great but it made the loneliness even louder. While my old friends were out shaking margaritas, I was home shaking formula – and trying to figure out how to do this whole mum thing. Sure, I had Ryan. He was hands-on. But he wasn't a mother, navigating postpartum life. I didn't realise just how lonely I'd become until someone got us a cleaner voucher (side note: best new-mum present ever).

'Busy day? Want a coffee?' I blurted at the poor cleaning lady the second she walked in. I proceeded to follow her around like a needy puppy, blabbing my heart out, probably drooling like one too. Honestly? I think she stayed longer on purpose, out of pity. Let's be real, there is no way it takes two hours to clean a tiny unit.

Some days the loneliness was deafening. I tried the in-person mothers' group thing, but without my usual liquid courage, my social anxiety was off the charts. On days I felt semi-human, after a walk, I'd take Harper and wander around the shops aimlessly – window shopping for things I couldn't afford – just to escape our unit. For some reason, I always ended up in Lorna Jane. The prices were out of my league, but running my hand along the rows of colourful crops and tights felt like I was reaching for a future version of me. One I hadn't seen in a while. It made me feel excited to see her again.

'Steph! How's Miss Harper?' beamed Ash, the store manager. These Lorna Jane visits became my only real social interactions most days. Ash was a mum too and always took an interest in us. Although Ryan had managed to break down my walls all those years ago, I hadn't let many people close – especially not women. But Ash had a consistent warmth about her – one that made my sober, socially anxious arse feel weirdly comfortable. She always remembered things from our last conversation, and it was nice – like, *really* nice. Little did I know, in a few months, she'd ask me to grab a coffee . . . and from that moment, she'd be my person. Best mates ever since.

I definitely didn't walk into Lorna Jane looking for a friend. But sometimes, someone quietly appears in your life behind a clothing rack. No drama. No pressure. No subtitles needed. Just comfort. I was starting to realise . . . I didn't need a whole tribe. I just needed a couple of safe people. My kind of people. Ash would become my safe space – the one I messaged about teething, solids and weird baby rashes. That was all to come. But unfortunately I'd still be lonely for a little while yet.

Since becoming a mum, I had been consuming social media like my life depended on it. To kill time while Harper napped (*when* she napped) I tried to keep myself occupied. And that's how I discovered the world of mummy bloggers and online mothers' groups. Honestly? For all the pros and cons, they saved me. Joining a Facebook mothers' group became a lifeline – and, for a while, my closest circle of friends. Over the next few months, no topic felt off-limits. I wasn't just asking questions anymore – I started sharing what was working for me too. For the first time in ages, I felt useful. Connected. And I was so grateful for this little online community of strangers who just got it.

Then something unexpected happened.

Without makeup as my creative outlet, I found myself thinking about writing again, not just journalling but openly writing. After weeks of scrolling, the same thought kept tapping me on the shoulder: *What if I started my own little corner of the internet?* During my bodybuilding phase, I dabbled in sharing recipes and workouts. But now I was reading mummy blogs – this was the peak mummy blogging era in America, and the wave had reached Australia too. Eye roll or not, when you're feeling alone these blogs become so much more to women in the trenches of a new unknown chaos. But what if I shared *my* journey? Or routines? Or anything I bloody wanted? It felt exciting. But then the self-doubt crept in.

What would people think?

Would my real-life friends think I was a loser?

Worse – would they think I was self-absorbed?

'Oh, here goes Steph again with another idea. Jack's at it again.'

Despite my doubts, I couldn't shake the feeling that I was onto something. I kept thinking back to my traumatic birth and those weeks of desperately trying to breastfeed. I would have loved someone – another mum who'd been through the same – to normalise and validate those experiences; someone to help me embrace the imperfections of motherhood. That online world was still filtered, and I had to look a little harder to find others feeling the same as I did. But could I help other mums like me?

Not preaching.

Not pretending to have it all together.

Just sharing the mess while I was still in it.

This was 2016, and something was missing from the internet – people showing, in real-time, what they were trying, even while still figuring it out. The kind of honesty you'd find in smaller Facebook groups – like the one I was in – but easier for others to stumble across. To feel less alone. To realise they weren't the only ones.

Motherhood didn't just change my routines – it changed how I saw myself. I used to believe I had to 'bounce back' – to get back to the girl I was before pregnancy. But I wasn't meant to go back. I was meant to become, and to evolve. Women are like the moon – some days we're full and beaming, other days just a sliver in the sky. But in every phase, we are still whole. And I was finally starting to believe that too.

Thanks to my new routines, my medication finally doing its job and getting back to the gym, I was beginning to feel like me again. And ready to help others do the same. The question was, would anyone want to read about all my messy mistakes?

A MORNING ROUTINE (FOR WHEN YOU'RE BARELY FUNCTIONING)

Pick one or two things on this list.

- Something for you:
  - Sit in silence with a warm drink.
  - Listen to a comforting playlist while you do the musts.
  - Splash your face with cold water.
- Something for future you:
  - Lay out clothes for later.
  - AM reset (make bed, five-minute tidy).
  - Chuck dinner in the slow cooker (or decide to order in).
- Movement:
  - Five-minute walk outside.
  - Slow yoga (napping in child's pose counts).
- Mindfulness:
  - Journal or think the answer to '*Today I need . . .*'
  - Deep breaths while brushing teeth (don't gag on your toothbrush).
  - Read fiction for ten minutes (bonus points for smut).
- Non-negotiables:
  - School drop-off (in pyjamas is fine . . . you not the kids).
  - Eat *something* – even if it's half a banana.
  - Chuck in one load of laundry (don't fold it yet, that's future you's problem).

And remember you're a human *being* not a human *doing*.

Chapter 18

Just another mummy blog

'What would you think if I started a blog?' I asked Ryan. I might add 'nervously', but, let's be real, by this point in our relationship we had some of our deepest conversations while I was on the toilet. A situation that's only gotten worse now that we have two kids; the second I sit down to poop, it's like a family meeting gets called in the bathroom. But I *was* nervous. Not because I thought I had nothing to write about – I had too much – but because I didn't want to make a fool of myself. In the end, my need for connection was stronger than my fear of looking like a complete douche canoe by putting myself out there.

'I really miss writing,' I went on. 'I need another purpose besides, you know, keeping Harper alive and figuring out what's for dinner every night.'

'Do it, hun. What's the worst that could happen?'

Oh, I don't know. Maybe . . .

A I could become the butt of all jokes (I'm talking from strangers).
B My old school friends might see it and think as Gen Z would say 'cringe'.
C My friends would judge me.
D I might become more of an outcast.
E Insert dramatic ending here.

'I just don't want to embarrass myself or, worse, for people to think I love myself,' I muttered, picking at my nails.

'When did you ever care what people think?'

My head dropped. 'Always. I've just spent my entire life pretending I don't.'

I cared when I was six and the entire class laughed at me because the class clown made a joke at my expense. I cared when I was a teenager, sitting at lunchtime with my friends but feeling like an outsider, scanning their faces for any sign that I was annoying them. I cared when I was twenty, forcing myself to act laid-back and chill, when really I over-analysed every word, every social cue, every look. Well, technically it's human nature. We are programmed to fit in. As cavemen, you must be accepted by the tribe or be eaten by a sabre-tooth tiger. Granted the stakes aren't as high these days – but it seems our body doesn't know the difference. Passive-aggressive doctor receptionists . . . tigers. Same, same.

And now I was a woman, hesitating to start something that mattered to me because for my entire life I'd been convinced not to take untrodden paths. People-pleasing was in my bones. I'd spent years trying to keep others happy, but my brain and body hadn't got the memo that I wasn't in trouble anymore. Little did Ryan know, I had an entire closet of masks I had collected over the years, each one carefully crafted to hide whatever I didn't want the world to see. Those masks were so convincing I even had myself fooled. There was:

- The 'It doesn't bother me'/'I don't care' mask (for when it definitely did).
- The 'sure thing/yes' mask when really I wanted to say 'hell no'.
- The 'perfect daughter' mask (for when I was trying to please others).
- The 'I have my shit together' mask (for when I absolutely did not).
- The 'life of the party' mask (for social situations pre-kids to hide my social anxiety).

I had managed to ditch a few masks along the way, like the 'party girl' mask and the 'my worth is based on my body' mask. But my default was still to hide rather than reveal. Childhood or not I think I would've been an overly empathetic person. But it also made me a prisoner to the approval of others – and I was tired. Little did I know, my blog would help me set fire to every mask I owned.

'Do it, hun,' Ryan said. 'It'll be good for you. And if anyone has something to say, I'll tell them to fuck off.' Charming . . .

Two weeks later . . .

I took a deep breath, opened my laptop . . . and began typing. This was 2016 – the golden era of mummy blogging – a time of chronological Instagram feeds and Valencia filters (I was more of a Paris girl, personally), when you could post a pic of a smashed avo and – BAM – you went viral. At the time, Facebook was where we overshared. We were convinced people cared about what we ate for dinner. If you weren't tagging your friends in 'wine o'clock' or 'checking in' at a nightclub, were you even a real millennial? This was before Boomers began to take over Facebook and wars began to break out in the comments section.

Back in the pre-influencer era, Instagrammers weren't brands – they were just people looking for connection and/or distraction. Some felt the need to pretend to be *that* Pinterest mum who made sourdough and concocted kids' activities out of recycled materials, but most of us were googling 'is toast a suitable dinner for my three year old?' and 'can you die from lack of sleep?'. I wasn't trying to be an influencer (a term that didn't even exist yet). I wasn't even trying to make this blog a 'thing', just a place to let it all out and let others *in*. Socials were either too perfect or too extreme – either baked quinoa cookies and 'mum goals' or train-wrecks that made me wonder if motherhood was just a version of *Squid Game*, maternal division. I didn't see myself in those posts. I was just me, someone who couldn't remember dates and still can't spell the word 'definitely'; a lonely mum, trapped under a sleeping baby, scrolling through curated feeds and wondering if anyone else felt the same. So I went for it and decided to set up a blog and a social media account. But then what? Well, after hours of YouTube tutorials and fifty-seven head tilts, I got a basic WordPress account. But then came the *real* question . . . What the hell do I call this thing? I came up with a few options, which I turned over to my online mums' group.

> *Steph posted: Hey ladies, I'm thinking of starting a blog. Which name do you like best?*

And so *Just Another Mummy Blog* was born.

At the time, I thought the name was hilarious. Unfortunately, I'd end up being stuck with the IG name for years as I eventually earnt a 'blue tick' – before you could pay for them. To change the blog to my actual name, I had to contact Instagram, which is about as easy as men finding the G-spot. As I stared at that first post, my hand trembled as I hovered over the 'enter' button. But I did it. And after sharing it with friends and family, I had a whole twelve followers. Basically a Kardashian.

My first post was an introduction: 'Welcome to my little slice of the internet.' And my writing was a tad rusty but it was honest. 'If I had to sum up my life it would say "she glided through life like a walrus on skates".' I wrote about postnatal depression, anxiety and ADHD. 'Mothers go through this life changing experience when we have a baby. We need to connect with others to realise it's okay you're covered in baby poop and haven't eaten any kale today.'

At the time, I felt like I was behind in the social media scene, but looking back, I got in early. I've been in the industry for a decade now and the amount of content out there is overwhelming. But in 2016, mummy blogging was a 'thing' because I think we were collectively lonely. Too afraid to speak up for fear of looking like a bad mother, or worse: an ungrateful one. As I pressed 'publish', I didn't know what to expect. But I hoped that, maybe, someone out there would read it and say, 'Me too'.

•

'You're on in five . . . four . . .'

I swallowed hard. I could feel the sweat under my dress as the studio lights blinded me. I took a deep breath and adjusted my posture. Standing either side of me, Denise and Ang from *Studio 10*, were chatting in the commercial break. My heart was hammering so loudly, I wondered if the mic would pick it up.

'. . . three . . . two . . .'

'We're here with Steph Pase, from *Just Another Mummy Blog* . . .'

Yep. I was now *live* on national television. I let out a breathy laugh, trying to act like this was a normal thing. Was I nervous? I'd already done twelve anxious poos that morning. It didn't help, I was nearly late – cheers Sydney traffic. I was in and out of hair and makeup in fifteen minutes flat. I wore a beige dress with white polka dots that I was sent at the last minute from a clothing brand I was working with. With Ryan standing behind the cameras for moral support, I had an array of labelled containers in front of me. If you told me I'd end up on national TV showing the citizens of Australia my jars of dry pasta – I'd have told you to seek professional help. But here we were. It was my job to talk them through my organisation hacks – in about six minutes flat. It was over quicker than it started.

As soon as I was done, messages started pouring in. People I had never met, saying they were proud of me. People sent me photos and videos of them standing in front of their TVs, as I did my thing on the screen. They helped me more than they'd ever know.

'Hi Steph, just wanted to say thank you . . . I thought I was the only one who felt like this.'

That right there?

That was my *why*.

It didn't happen overnight – not even close. But over time, the little things started to add up. I posted one blog every Monday, daily stories to Snapchat, and the occasional YouTube video. My online home of choice was/is Instagram – but I didn't have an elaborate content schedule or pre-plan posts. In between cleaning up pumpkin puree off the floor, I'd snap a photo. My favourite part?

Being curled up on the couch post-bedtime chaos, where I would lose myself writing long deep captions or unhinged silly ones.

Being multi-passionate meant I had an endless menu of topics to share – which my community seemed to like. The parts of my mind that I often hated were now providing helpful content for others. I had always thought my brain was 'broken', but, as it turned out, there are a lot of people just like me.

•

'I think my Instagram's shit itself. It says 150,000. That can't be right,' I said to Ryan, as I tapped the 'refresh' button. It had been a couple of years since I first pressed 'publish'. I used to be stoked if even one person felt seen by what I wrote – now there were thousands. A little nervous wee still nearly escapes when I think about it. I wasn't chasing numbers. I didn't overthink it. I'd post in my dressing gown with Vegemite on my sleeve, write from the heart, hit 'publish' and continue with the washing. But as the blog and socials grew, so did the expectations. I soon started second-guessing everything. Suddenly, it wasn't just a post – it was a performance.

I once spent an hour writing a long caption under a photo of me balancing Harper on my hip as she slept. Then I sat there, holding my breath, biting the corner of my lip, waiting – unknowingly – for validation to bubble up in my notifications. I told myself I was past all that, but there I was again, looking for external signs that I was enough. The very thing I thought I'd outgrown when I hung up my stripper heels. I was learning pressure comes with growth. More opinions. More people to judge you. But I kept going. Because my *why* was much stronger than old bad habits and human tendencies.

I kept going because of that deep belly knowing that I just *had* to. Even when I was shit-scared. I'd been muted before – and I wasn't about to be muted again.

I wish I could say I've let go of my Bart Simpson bad habits. But I'm human. The difference now is I catch myself faster when I trip or place my hand on the stove.

•

People seemed to love the free downloads of my routines and schedules. But I still felt like I was waiting for someone to tap me on the shoulder and say, 'Sorry Steph, there's been a mistake – this platform is meant for someone who actually knows what they're doing'. And everyone would disappear.

But they didn't.

I started noticing the same names popping up – the women who always commented on my posts or were in my DMs with love – and some weren't even mums. The support from absolute strangers was mind-blowing. Sadly, I couldn't say the same for some old friends, a few of whom still didn't get it.

'Why don't you just go back to makeup? You're so good at it,' one said.

'Why are you doing this?' another asked.

Years later, when some of those same people started seeing what the world calls 'success' they'd come to me for advice on how to do exactly what they had once questioned. But I tuned out the doubters – because that gut feeling, the one telling me I was onto something special, was louder than any awkward interrogation.

Speaking of special, I'll never forget the day I got my first freebie. The message appeared one morning after I hit 'post': 'We would love to send you a dog subscription box, for you to share with your followers.'

'Ryan, guess what?' I squealed like a teenager, laptop nearly toppling from my lap.

'What?' Ryan jumped at the sound.

'This brand wants to send me a dog subscription box!'

'Huh? What the fuck is that?'

'It's a dog . . . subscription box. You know, it has stuff in it for dogs like treats and shit?'

'No, Steph.'

He was right. Dog treats weren't exactly the vibe I was going for. Still, I couldn't believe it. To my surprise, the offers kept coming, and they kept getting better. Some collaborations – or collabs, as we call them – made perfect sense; there were brands that I already used daily that genuinely fit my life and my values. But then there were some that made me wonder if the company had ever read a single post or just hit 'send' on a mass email. I turned down 99 per cent of them. Because while I'm great at masking, one thing I *cannot* do is bullshit people. I've walked away from more money than I'd like to calculate – not because we didn't need it, but because I never wanted to become a walking ad. Staying true to not only my community, but also myself, has always mattered more. Yeah, yeah, I know it sounds cheesy, like something your mum would hang on her wall next to 'Live, Laugh, Love'. But it's true.

As my platforms grew so did the unexpected admin. I always put being a mum before this venture, but it was becoming harder to juggle everything at once. Suddenly I was spending five hours a day replying to brands, affiliates and my community. I needed help. One thing I hated more than admin was talking about money. I never knew what to charge brands. I started to wonder if being creative now meant I was tied to my laptop. So when my own Kris Jenner called, it felt like fate.

'Hey Steph, I'm Mikhailla. I wanted to reach out to you to see if you had any management representing you?'

'Uh no, I don't,' I replied.

'Oh great. Do you have ten minutes to chat?'

Later that afternoon as Ryan walked in the door after work, I practically bounced on top of him. 'Ryan, guess who has a manager?' I laughed. His face was a spitting image of mine when I first heard the word 'manager'.

Oh, and don't worry, guys. I had friends in the space who were also managed by Mik. No arse-hats this time. She is still my manager to this day.

This new step made it all feel more official, but it was the best decision I ever made. It turns out I was majorly undercutting myself. I once charged a brand less than what I'd spend on a trip to Woollies. I was winging it and still am. We all are – no matter what industry you're in.

•

'OMG! Steph! It's so good to finally meet you!' A well-known influencer I'd been following for years gave me a big hug. We were at a brand event and I wondered if I'd drunk too much free wine – this was a whole new world for me and I felt like a fish out of water. But meeting big names made me realise they were people just like us. What did I expect them to be – aliens? Maybe I wasn't such an outsider, after all.

My daughters know the difference between what they see online and IRL (that's Gen Z for 'in real life'). They saw it first-hand.

Mummy gets dressed up to film a clothing haul for a brand . . . and then gets back into her trackies again. The lesson? Those people with millions of followers have pores, bad days, bloating and breakups just like the rest of us.

'I love your bag!' the influencer said.

'I love your . . . hair clip!' I stuttered. Ryan's way with words seemed to be rubbing off on me. Surrounded by Gucci bags and shoes, for a second I felt like that kid with the bowl cut all over again.

I knew the blog had reached the next level when strangers began coming up to me in public. The first time it happened I questioned if I was dreaming – or high.

'Steph! It's you!' a woman in her twenties said, waving at me in the supermarket. I must have looked baffled because then she added, 'I loooove your blog and how you're so yourself on stories . . . it makes me feel like I'm not the only one.'

'Oh wow,' I stammered, blindsided. 'Thank you, can I give you a hug?'

Too much? I never seemed too much for my community; for the first time my 'too muchness' was just right. I'd found my people, and what a relief it was after a lifetime of feeling separate. Meanwhile, I discovered the antidote to social anxiety was being insanely transparent. It breaks the ice when someone already knows your life story and you don't have to explain who you are/ what you do/why you're having a panic attack in the cereal aisle. Somehow, the things I thought would make me look weak – my struggles with motherhood, my anxiety, my spiralling thoughts, and my tendency to start projects but never finish them – were the very things that resonated the most. The posts where I admitted to failing, to feeling lost, to not having it together were the ones that blew up. It was ironic, really. The messiest parts of me were turning into the most magical.

Hey, maybe what Nan said all those years ago was true – that I'd go on to do big things. By this point, her Alzheimer's had deteriorated and the decision had been made to move her into a care home. My heart broke, but while her memory was still decent she would call me for chats.

New message: 'Steph! You did so well on Studio 10 this morning! I'm actually one of the carers for your nan. I put it on TV for her to watch. And I took a pic for you of her watching you. She is so proud.'

By some twist of fate, one of Nan's carers followed me, and that day, she ensured Nan saw me making my TV debut. The photo shows Nan sitting on the edge of her bed with her hands clasped. The expression on her face is pure pride, her mouth open mid-sentence. I look at this photo often. Nan's carer shared what Nan said as she watched. It still brings me to tears. 'That's my daughter!' Nan exclaimed, beaming like the sun. 'I raised her, you know?' Alzheimer's may have stolen some of her memories, but it never touched her love for me.

Yet even now, as I sit here writing this, imposter syndrome still lurks. Even after all these years, after this book deal – my lifelong dream – I still catch myself defaulting to that little girl who didn't know where she fit, who she was or what she wanted to be when she grew up.

Turns out, I just wanted to be me.

HOW TO START THAT THING, EVEN WHEN YOU'RE SHITTING YOURSELF

Don't wait until you're 'ready' to start. Do it scared, start unsure, just as long as you start.

- Success isn't about doing it all perfectly; it's about showing up consistently and pivoting with purpose.
- Clarity comes from action, not from overthinking.
- Running a business is like juggling a hundred balls – just remember, some are rubber and some are glass. Learn which ones you can drop and which ones need your attention first. The same goes for life.
- My biggest breakthroughs didn't come from grand plans; they came from messy, imperfect action on all the days I felt like giving up – but didn't.
- The best lessons weren't from any degree or online course. They came from my fuck-ups. Always a lesson, never a failure.

Chapter 19

Organisation for the overwhelmed

'Ah, sorry guys, I didn't get a chance to clean my car out. We might have to use the bins.'

I winced as I looked over my shoulder, trying to make space for my friends in the back seat. Except there was one problem: there *was* no space. You see, my car *was* the bin. I was twenty, living out of home with Ryan, juggling uni and work – and a side hustle as a mobile rubbish tip. The car floor was littered with Maccas bags, a questionable sticky cup holder, random receipts and more than a dozen empty water bottles. Apparently, I was also running a Mount Franklin recycling plant. But hey? My tacky hot-pink Playboy bunny car seats at least served as a distraction, just like the old dolphin shower curtain. Turns out teenage rock bottom smells like old Maccas chips and Impulse body spray – a sad, musky attempt at covering the adolescent BO and the despair. Teen spirit, my arse.

My friends' faces said it all: *what a shitshow*. Not just the car – but me.

We ended up filling up *both* of my friends' parents' bins. Yes, plural. I felt terrible. They seemed fine with it, though I bet they weren't thrilled I'd used their prime bin real estate for the week.

But this was nothing out of the ordinary.

The mess had been following me for as long as I could remember.

Fast-forward to now . . . And that same girl? The one whose car should have been condemned by council? She's now a fucking organisation influencer. It's like people taking advice from a human Oscar the Grouch. (Subtract the grouch – more the trashcan lifestyle.)

Oh, the irony.

Back then, Ryan and I were living in a tiny two-bedroom unit with zero storage. The linen closet doubled as a pantry, our laundry was shoved into the garage, and there was no 'just chuck it in the spare room' option – because we didn't have one. Every drawer, shelf and surface had to *work*. I wasn't trying to become an organisation guru – I was just trying to survive and maximise the space we had. The fact I didn't try to cram myself into a box is exactly what helped me think outside of it; especially when it came to hacks.

Although my blog began with health tips and recipes, it was when I started posting 'home + DIY' tips that it really took off. From makeup storage to organising your medicine cabinet and 'my fourteen-day house refresh', to how to not lose your shit when your kid puts jam on the dog, there were a lot of people out there like me who were desperate for realistic answers.

One of the first organisation tips I ever posted was how I made more space in our shoebox of a pantry. It hit a nerve. I clearly wasn't the only one googling 'How to keep my house clean without banishing my entire family'. There were more of us out there – messy, overwhelmed, trying to find answers that didn't mean running ourselves into the ground. We didn't need an elaborate manual – just a label maker and an idea.

That post trickled into more, including a cleaning schedule – a free download that breaks your days into 'cleaning zones' that has now been downloaded over 100,000 times by women in over 149 countries. I'll never forget the day I saw someone tag a post with #stephing as they decluttered their house. I nearly choked on my coffee. *What the fuck?* Guess who found it even funnier than me? Dad.

'So now you're a *verb*, little friend?' He cracked up, throwing his head back.

'Apparently,' I shrugged, just as puzzled as he was.

And that hashtag took off. Every day I was getting tags of people using my hacks and tips, and my 'lazy girl healthy recipes' as I liked to call them. That still blows my mind. How did I go from a former human rubbish bin to helping people organise their homes? Well, not only did being organised and clean and tidy feel foreign, it was something I had to learn from scratch.

At Meadow Lane, we didn't deal with things – we shoved them under the rug where we could pretend they didn't exist. Meadow Lane never really felt like a home. It was dark, loud and tense. Music was a stranger, eggshells metaphorically all over the floor, and I was constantly bracing for impact. When I think of a home, I think of Nan's room. The way she had little trinkets on her dresser, the way she'd open her blinds and let the morning sunlight spill in, her opera music playing softly in the background. A place where I could be held and come undone from holding it together.

For me, home is couches with deep familiar grooves and cosy corners where bedtime stories are read and homework is done. Over by the TV is your favourite Garfield blanket that you've had since you were six. It's a space that holds memories yet to be made. And that's what I wanted my family home to be like, to feel like.

And while I'm not going to buy any grandma doilies and horse statues, I wanted my home to be a place my kids associated with consistency and with safety. Where they return after a long day and completely unravel. I'd be there to catch them, to pick up the pieces of them that had come apart, and then kiss them back together again.

One day I found myself standing in our kitchen, pumpkin puree in one hand, a cloth in the other, looking at Harper who was now orange and resembled *Snooki* circa 2009. I realised I was replaying Meadow Lane – I was hiding the mess. And in doing so, I was failing at giving Harper the home I craved. Home isn't about being perfect. It's about having a safe place to land. Feeling lighter once you walk in the door – not heavier. A stranger might not be able to see the mess. But even when it was hidden, my body still felt it. Yes, I was a new mum so I had a valid excuse to be surrounded by . . . stuff. But my inability to stay organised was a deep cut for me. The chaos I thought I'd left behind had unknowingly jumped into my suitcase and followed me.

I didn't want that for Harper.

Even though our unit was a far cry from my childhood home, the mess still taunted me. Instead of using a shower curtain to magically make it disappear, I used drawers, boxes, cupboards, bins and, obviously, a junk drawer. My childlike logic was simple: out of sight, out of mind. Maybe that's why I struggled to figure out how to keep a home. Because I had never actually lived in one.

Nan, on the other hand, was a domestic goddess. She always knew where my favourite Hedwig shirt was. Each day, she'd 'stage' my toys on my bed, like my teddies and dolls had gone on little adventures while I was at school. Something I do for my kids now. I think that's what made her Alzheimer's diagnosis even harder to accept – she was always so sharp. Quick-witted. She remembered *everything*. Even in high school, when I'd forget my lunch, she'd somehow know exactly where my friends and I sat and hand-deliver it. My friends were always jealous. I had the best Nan/mother figure on the planet. I dreamt of being like her when I grew up; the peacemaker, the calming influence who kept everything clean and serene.

But it didn't come naturally to me.

Ryan was no better. I hate to break it to all the Mr Pase groupies out there but the leading man in this story was just as much a human tornado as me, if not more. The difference was he can live with it. It has never bothered him. But I find mess suffocating. It turns out you can grow up surrounded by mess and never become desensitised to it. I kept thinking of all the things I needed to clean later. Which is also kinda ironic when you're the cause of the mess in the first place, like a dog who has just wiped its arse on your favourite rug and is now giving you their best puppy dog eyes. As Harper became a toddler, my intolerance of the mess grew. Not because I didn't want her to be a kid – they're professional mess makers, after all – I loved watching her when she was playing because she was being all of her, unrestricted.

Up until this point I couldn't figure out why I was struggling to manage it all. Why even the smallest tasks felt like climbing mountains. I had always thought that I was simply too slow in a world that spun too fast. That I was doing something wrong – if I just tried harder I could keep up and juggle it all. I was burning out in my pursuit of 'balance'. Until I heard the saying: 'How you do one thing is how you do everything.'

You know what I say to that?

Bullshit.

Yep, I said it.

Because the way I show up at my kids' school events is *not* the same as how I fold the bloody washing. The way I show up in my business is not the same as the version of me that's three weeks behind on life admin. You're allowed to be amazing in one area and still be a bit of a disaster in another. There is only so much of us. And sometimes something's gotta give. And that something should *never* be your mental health, just to keep up appearances. That's not diligence – that's delusion.

The whole 'consistency equals character' notion ignores the reality of our multifaceted life. You can be a mess in one part and still be magic in another. You don't have to give 100 per cent across everything at the risk of losing yourself. That isn't the one way to be valuable or worthy or successful. Some things will fall through the cracks – and that's okay. You're not broken. You're a whole person.

While I'm on my rant, what our society believes is 'balance' is also bullshit. Not because the intention behind it is bad – but because the expectation is a lie. There are always going to be areas that require more from us, no matter what else is going on. Health, kids, work. You just need to keep moving, day by day. Bit by bit. The goal isn't balance. It's to not drown. Hey, you may even start to float if you stop letting expectations drag you under.

It was time I stopped letting the housework do the same. That's when it hit me. What if I could take the methods I'd used to change my daily routine and apply them to our home? Could I finally crack the cleaning code . . . if I did it *my own way*? I had to break my cleaning schedule down to make it achievable in real life. We're not on a Netflix show where Marie Kondo rocks up and overhauls your entire house in one weekend. After much trial and (mostly) error, I realised my brain didn't vibe with giant tasks like 'clean the house'. Just a touch overwhelming, right? Might as well have written 'just buy one thing from Kmart'; talk about impossible.

So I split it into zones or areas. Suddenly, the shitty tasks I'd been avoiding didn't feel so shitty. Manageable, even. You know what they say: don't think about the whole staircase – just the first step. The same goes for housework. Break it down into micro tasks like 'wipe benches' or 'vacuum lounge'. It's not magic – it's momentum. And because my brain operates like a toddler in need of constant stimulation, I created a dedicated cleaning playlist. One I *only* listened to when cleaning. Weirdly enough, it worked. Gradually, our house started to feel more organised and less chaotic. I was, as the name of this book says, mastering my mess. And yes, it *did* feel like magic.

I'm not saying that ever since that day in my kitchen, my house has been perfect and clean – fuck no. I wish, but not a chance. Homes are meant to be lived in. This was part of the shift: embracing realistic expectations and putting my imperfections on display. If you follow me on social media, you'll have seen my messy laundry, floor-drobe and chaotic office. I'm not someone who only shoots videos in the 'clean corner'. If you can adjust your expectations, everything feels easier. No, you're not failing at adulthood. That's just what happens when multiple human beings all live in one space. And decluttering isn't a one-time thing. Sorry to break it to ya.

I won't go all Tony Robbins on you, but I want you to try something – because we're mates now and you already know entirely too much about me, so it's only fair. Picture this. You wake up and you've got something important to do today – maybe work, maybe life admin, maybe just keeping small humans alive. You walk into the kitchen and *boom* – dishes everywhere, crap all over the lounge, laundry on the floor, bin overflowing. How do you feel? Relaxed? Focused?

Yeah, didn't think so. Suddenly your brain opens twenty-seven tabs: take the bins out, clean up the sticky patch on the floor, find the school note that was due two days ago. That big thing you were meant to focus on? Gone.

Now flip it. You walk into the kitchen and it's clean. Cushions are neatly in place. Bin's out. Dinner's already in the slow cooker. There's even a candle lit. Chris Hemsworth is lying on the couch – oh shit, wrong story. But seriously – how do you feel now? Calmer? More present? Drooling? Thanks to Chris (and let's be honest, probably the clean house too). Actually able to think? Yes. If our external environment is a mess, our mind will be a mess too. Physical clutter = mental clutter. Even the old dudes in lab coats say our brains don't like disorganisation – and you can't argue with science . . . or fancy coats. Every piece of clutter is a reminder of all the things you still have to do, or to be brutally honest, where you feel you're lacking.

My fitness journey helped me crack the cleaning code. Hear me out . . . When you're on a fitness kick you work out a few times a week, eat healthy every day and eventually get fitter. But you can't get fit once, stop working out, stop eating well and expect to stay that way. So why is organising and decluttering our houses any different? Day after day, new junk trickles in from the outside world. Kids' stuff, those bloody Woollies rewards toys, receipts, mail, change . . . You get the picture. If we don't continue to cull and organise, naturally the clutter takes over; the benches fill up with pizza vouchers and hair ties. The junk drawer refills with . . . junk like it's a Coke machine (don't tell Ads), and everything turns to shit. For me, this realisation was just like the health epiphany I had all those years earlier. I needed the same method. And that's exactly what I created . . . and started sharing.

'This is a "wear again" hook!' I beamed at Ryan, dragging him into our bedroom to show off a $3 Command hook. 'So . . . What do you think?' I was bouncing up and down like I'd just painted the Mona Lisa with a toothbrush.

He blinked. 'Um . . . it's a hook.'

'Exactly! For the clothes that are too dirty to go back in the wardrobe but too clean to wash. The . . . wear again hook!' I winked, clicking my tongue, nudging him proudly.

Silence. Tough crowd.

'I mean, yeah,' he patted me gently on the back like I needed to get out more. 'Sure. Hook. Great.'

Men. They just don't know a good hack when they see one.

CULLING CRITERIA: FOR THOSE WHO CAN'T LET GO

Decluttering is like a muscle. The more you use it, the more cut-throat you get with stuff. If you're someone who struggles to say goodbye to objects, here's your go-to criteria!

1. Have I used/worn this in the last six to eight months?
2. If I saw this in a store would I buy it?
3. If I had to pack up my entire life and downsize or go on holidays, would I take this with me?
4. Is this adding to my life or simply adding mess?

•

Six months after I started my blog, I was sitting with Ryan on the couch. The house was quiet. I'd even say peaceful. Harper was in her rocker, making those tiny, blissed-out milk-drunk faces as she slept after her evening feed. Ryan rested one hand on my leg, chuckling at whatever was on TV, probably someone injuring themselves. Humans are weird. I looked around at the scene. It was calm. Still. Everyone was content. The house was organised, thanks to my new cleaning routine. It was the kind of moment you see in movies. And yet, it felt wrong.

Where was the yelling? The slamming doors? The suffocating tension that hung thick in the air, making you hold your breath without even realising it? Where was the walking on eggshells, bracing yourself for what was coming next? Where was the chaos? Suddenly, panic surged through me. My throat constricted, my chest tightened, and before I knew it, tears began to spill down my face.

'Hun, what's wrong?' Ryan turned to me.

I shook my head, unable to put it into words. My mind was trying to make sense of a moment that was meant to be good. But why didn't it feel that way? Why was I so scared? 'Ryan, I know I sound insane, but . . . is everything okay?' My voice was barely audible. 'Are we all okay?'

Confusion flickered across his face. 'Of course. What do you mean?'

I swallowed hard. 'I don't know how to explain this, but where's the yelling? The stress? The loud noise?' I gestured around the room. 'I feel like I'm doing something wrong. Like . . . I don't know. This isn't how families are, right?'

Ryan's expression softened. He placed a hand on my shoulder – the same steady, familiar hand that had grounded me a million times before. 'This is how it's *supposed* to be, Steph.' His voice was gentle but certain. 'This is normal. This is how it *should* have been for you.'

And just like that, it hit me. Maybe my childhood wasn't 'normal' or 'okay'. And maybe – just maybe – it wasn't my fault, after all. This was the first of many moments where I would begin to unravel the truth. When I would start to untangle the mess of memories and realise that the version of 'normal' I had carried with me was anything but. I decided to use my newfound organisation skills to give my own kids the exact opposite.

Eventually, we would move out of our little unit and start building our family home. This coincided with my blog becoming more professional . . . if you squint. By this stage it had evolved into my full-time job, as my sponsored content was earning more than my makeup business. Back then, my Instagram showed images of a 'Pinterest worthy' pantry, complete with perfectly labelled jars and neat tubs of cereal. At face value, you might think I was superficial – greedy even. But beyond the labels was – and still is – a little girl who craves warmth, safety and predictability. It wasn't just a pantry; it was what it represented for my children, and for me. Building the dream home of my childhood, but on my terms.

I dreamt of my kids being able to grab food to eat whenever they wanted, but I also wanted our home to feel magical, something my younger self would have died for. It's funny how childhood shapes you; for me it was the abundant pantry, music in the background and light – lots of light. Our new home had large windows and sliding doors; it was beautiful, airy and inviting. You might be surprised to know we built it a few streets away from Meadow Lane. While that house didn't hold the best memories, the town did and still does.

I know many people who follow my cleaning tips have their own messy memories they're trying to make peace with, and I'm so happy to be able to help. Over time it stopped being about home decor or the perfect laundry, or maybe it was never about that in the first place? Maybe it was about creating a safe space for my children's core memories; and mine too.

A space where I could rewrite my story.

Because now I was the author.

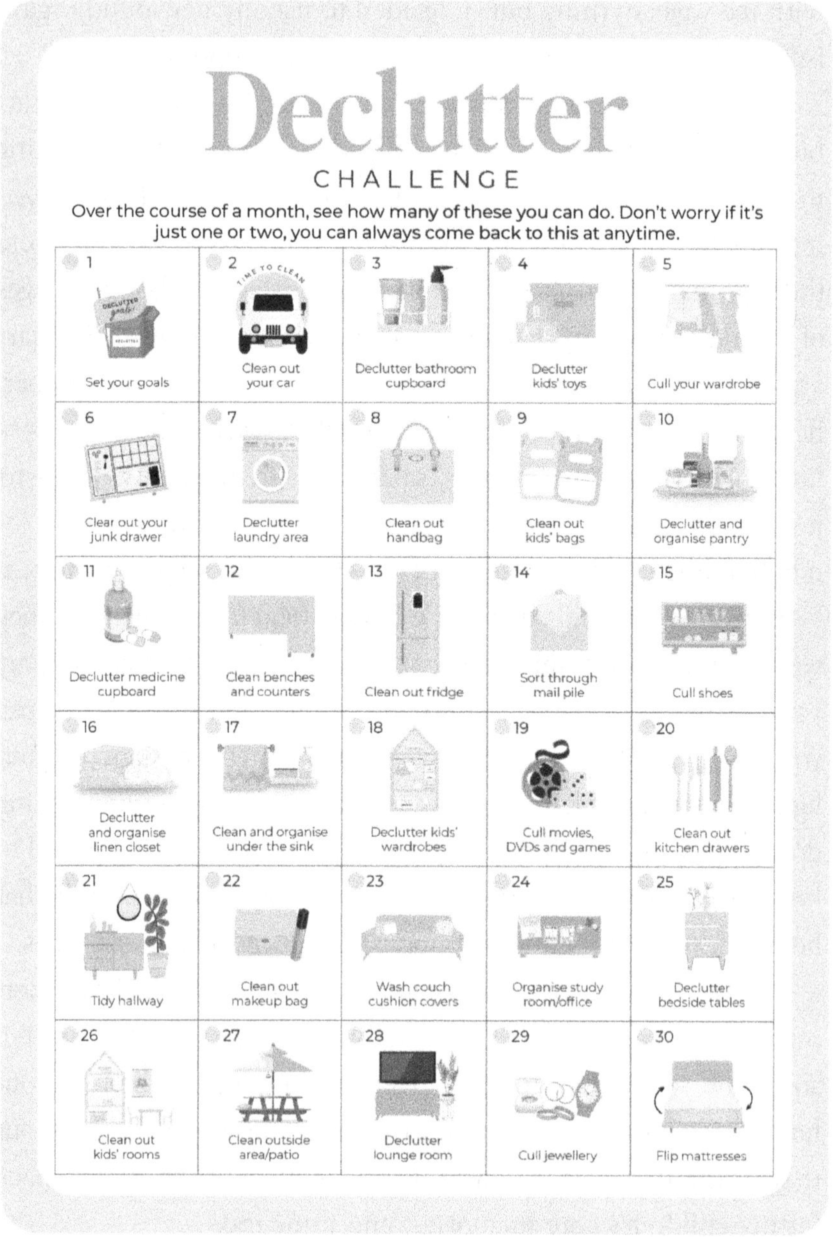

Declutter

CHALLENGE

Over the course of a month, see how many of these you can do. Don't worry if it's just one or two, you can always come back to this at anytime.

1	2	3	4	5
Set your goals	Clean out your car	Declutter bathroom cupboard	Declutter kids' toys	Cull your wardrobe
6	7	8	9	10
Clear out your junk drawer	Declutter laundry area	Clean out handbag	Clean out kids' bags	Declutter and organise pantry
11	12	13	14	15
Declutter medicine cupboard	Clean benches and counters	Clean out fridge	Sort through mail pile	Cull shoes
16	17	18	19	20
Declutter and organise linen closet	Clean and organise under the sink	Declutter kids' wardrobes	Cull movies, DVDs and games	Clean out kitchen drawers
21	22	23	24	25
Tidy hallway	Clean out makeup bag	Wash couch cushion covers	Organise study room/office	Declutter bedside tables
26	27	28	29	30
Clean out kids' rooms	Clean outside area/patio	Declutter lounge room	Cull jewellery	Flip mattresses

Chapter 20

Lessons from aisle four

'Ryan, my waters broke!' I exclaimed.

We were in the middle of Kmart in aisle four and I was holding a pack of containers for our future pantry – in our new house that wasn't even finished yet. It was still three months away, but a girl's gotta dream. I placed my hand between my legs and felt liquid. Pride rippled through me. After being induced with Harper, I was so excited that my body was doing it on its own this time. I'd just hit thirty-seven weeks and I knew second babies could come early. But when I pulled my hand out . . . what I saw wasn't what I expected.

Blood.

I immediately thought, *She's gone.*

It was Wednesday, 6 December 2017.

The week had been a whirlwind – we were building our new house and I was across every single design decision. I'd been in full-blown nesting mode and my latest victim was the pantry, because obviously, that's the most urgent thing to organise before you give birth. This pregnancy had felt lighter than Harper's – well, at least after we got the Harmony test results back. Another healthy girl.

But back in aisle four, everything around me slowed.

I screamed.

Ryan, who'd been pushing twenty-month-old Harper, went white as a ghost – a look I'd never seen before. In hindsight, we should've called an ambulance, but I couldn't wait another second, so we jumped in the car and clipped a crying Harper into the car seat. Ryan grabbed my gym towel to put between my legs.

A few days earlier, I'd been getting what I thought were Braxton Hicks contractions. I assumed they couldn't be real labour – they weren't painful enough – but given Harper had been induced, I didn't know what the start of a 'natural' labour actually felt like. That morning I woke up feeling off and overly emotional – yes, more than normal. I cried for most of the day, grieving the fact that Harper would soon have to share me. Your standard mum guilt on steroids. Between contractions, I squeezed in some cleaning, answered emails, did the groceries and picked up Harper from daycare entirely too early.

On the way home, I called Ryan and asked if we could stop at Kmart for some containers. We decided to eat dinner at the Coffee Club first. One big bowl of pasta later, the contractions were definitely stronger and lasting longer. I started timing them . . . still convinced it wasn't the real thing. Ryan suggested we go home so I could rest but I insisted – I *needed* those fucking Kmart containers. Silly Ryan clearly had his priorities wrong.

Post-aisle four bleed, on the way to hospital, every second felt like I was losing my baby. Oxygen wasn't getting into my body. I called the obstetrician's office and the receptionist told me to head straight to the labour suite. I asked her if this was normal.

'It's not normal,' her voice echoed through the phone. 'Just get to the hospital.'

That's when the anxiety attacks started. I yelled at Ryan to go faster – even though I knew he couldn't. The blood was still coming in gushes. Maybe I wouldn't make it either. Then I realised; my belly was getting smaller.

The outside world began to spin.

I began pinching my leg.

Is this real? Or some sick nightmare?

I rang Mum and Dad and asked them to meet us at the hospital so they could take Harper. When we arrived, they were already there – the look on Mum's face said it all. I gave Harper a rushed, heartbreaking goodbye and was wheeled into the labour suite. I was given a gown, disposable undies and a pad. When I went to the toilet, I felt something come out and hoped it was my mucus plug, but the midwife confirmed it was blood clots. After what felt like a lifetime they hooked me up to the monitor. Squeezing Ryan's hand, we expected the worst.

Until.

Thump, thump.

Thump, thump.

I let out what felt like the first breath in hours. But we weren't in the clear yet. I asked the midwife a million questions, trying to gain some sort of control over an uncontrollable situation.

'It could be a placental abruption,' she said.

I turned to Ryan and burst into tears. I knew what that meant – I'd read the stories. Placental abruptions rarely ended well. After an internal examination, I was 2 cm dilated. The doctor finally arrived and confirmed the baby's heart rate was strong. He was happy for me to keep labouring naturally for the time being.

Throughout the night, I managed the pain of contractions with showers and breathing, but the bleeding didn't stop. The clots were getting bigger – one was the size of a steak (sorry if you like rump). Around 3 a.m., I stood up and more blood splattered across the floor. The nurse looked alarmed and called the doctor. He told her to start the Syntocinon drip to get things moving.

'Whatever you have to do to keep her safe please,' I begged the midwife. An ultrasound showed my baby's head in an awkward position, tilted back, pressing against my pelvis. The doctor said that unless she shifted, I wouldn't dilate.

A little while later, my baby's heart rate started to drop.

'We need to do an emergency C-section!' said the doctor. They administered the epidural and prepped me for surgery. Oddly, it was a relief; they were finally getting her out. But as I was wheeled into theatre, I was still terrified. Ryan meanwhile was taken off to change into scrubs. I'm not particularly religious, but I have never prayed harder in my entire life than in that moment. I knew the baby would be small, being three weeks early, but with everything going wrong, I begged the universe to let her come out okay.

The anaesthetist explained things as they wheeled me in. The theatre was bright, sterile, filled with masked nurses and doctors. A far cry from the natural birth I thought I was having when I first felt liquid flowing in Kmart. They lifted me onto the table and set up a sheet across my chest so we couldn't see anything. I made Ryan put his cheek against mine. As the doctor got to work, Ryan whispered in my ear – telling me I was strong, thanking me for giving him two beautiful daughters. Being positive for the both of us. I began shaking uncontrollably. They told me it was from the medication.

Then I heard the doctor say, 'Okay.'

I felt the first cut. Across my pelvis.

'I CAN FEEL THAT!' I shouted. Was the epidural not working? They kept topping it up until all I could feel was pressure and tugging. The next few moments were a complete out-of-body experience. It was as if I was being hacked apart like a carcass. I could see the bloodbath in the reflection in the lights above me. Then, suddenly, my mind drifted to a beach; my messy mind attempting to distract and protect me.

Then . . . we heard her.

Willow Eve.

Her cry.

At that moment, everything else melted away. Ryan and I looked at each other and burst into tears. They showed her to me for a second and then whisked her off to be checked. I told Ryan to follow them. 'Is she okay?' I called out.

Moments later, out of the corner of my eye, I saw the midwife walking over with our beautiful girl wrapped in a blanket. Her pink little face came into focus. She was *here*. She was safe.

They took her back while the doctors finished with me, but suddenly the energy in the room shifted. I heard murmurs about my vitals and the word 'transfusion'. Ryan and I locked eyes. A heaviness settled over us. Black dots began appearing in my vision.

'I love you,' I told him. 'Look after our girls.'

He sobbed and cradled my head.

It was the most terrifying moment of my life. Saying goodbye to my high school sweetheart. The father of my girls. My home in human form. My girls who I never got to see grow up. Willow, who I never got to hold. Minutes passed and I was still here. I think. Suddenly the doctor appeared again. 'It was a severe placental abruption. The cord was around her neck four times. There's no way a natural birth would have ended well. But everything is stable now.' He placed a hand on my shoulder.

I exhaled.

I was going to be okay.

We were going to be okay.

Ryan dove down and planted a kiss on my lips. As he lifted his head we stared at each other in total disbelief. We made it. *All of us.*

Willow Eve was born 7 December at 11.30 a.m. She weighed 2.4 kgs and was 47.5 cm long. Little bugger. Due to her low weight, she was taken to the nursery. As I lay there in recovery, I was still in shock, blinking hard to make sure I was actually still here. With a small smile, I thanked god, the universe, whoever was up there listening. So fucking grateful.

After a couple of hours they wheeled me into the nursery. As soon as I laid eyes on her, another deep, grateful exhale escaped me. I started crying. Ryan brought her over and told me she didn't even cry during her needles. She was utter perfection. You would never have known this tiny creature had just been through so much. The midwives said her vitals were good. She didn't even need oxygen. Dark brown hair, brown eyes – I was surprised by how different she looked from Harper.

'I'm so proud of you, Steph,' Ryan said. 'You're so strong. I don't know how you got through that.' You could see the gratitude pouring from him. He had his three healthy girls.

Meanwhile, I resembled a soccer-ball ham: swollen, full of fluids and still unable to move my legs. The midwife asked if I was ready to feed her. And I was. I didn't let my struggles in the past take over. I had told Ryan I would see how it went and stop if it didn't work out. No pressure. No expectations. No seven-hour pump shift. I breastfed Willow for the first time and she latched on like the champion she was. My strong little lady. I was so proud of how much she had already accomplished in her short time earthside.

•

Willow's birth was one of the most traumatic experiences of my life – but unlike many placental abruption stories, ours fortunately had a happy ending. We were three months away from moving into our new house and Willow didn't even have a bedroom yet. But that's the thing about life – it doesn't care how prepared you are. Baby bags packed or not, the curveballs still come. You can follow every rule, do everything by the book, and still, things can fall apart. It's obvious by now I've always had a need for control. Until motherhood happened and Willow. As I was healing from her birth I read an inspiring quote: 'Worrying is just making you live through things twice.'

And I knew then . . .

If I had known what was coming, I would've missed it – worry blocking my vision. The ordinary magic of those last months with my first-born. Chasing Harper's laughter through the lounge room. Cracking jokes with Ryan while brushing our teeth. Writing, dreaming, living. It would've been stolen by fear. But that's the quiet mercy of *not* knowing. That's the wild, unpredictable magic of life . . . we don't see what's ahead. Thank fuck, right? No amount of worry, planning or prep could have changed what happened. But not knowing allowed me to *live*. Yes, some moments will rip you in half. Others will feel so incredible you'll wonder if you're dreaming. But if we knew what was coming, we'd never truly *feel* anything for the first time – not really.

Your first wobbly tooth.

That god-awful first kiss.

Your first heartbreak.

Your first job.

The first time you surprise yourself.

Your first deep loss.

Your first real love.

Your first child.

The magic of your 'firsts' would be lost, as though life handed them to you like a scheduled appointment. This is the lesson I return to when I'm gripping the wheel too tightly. Sometimes you need to release the clutch and let life steer, taking you down an unfamiliar road. Because you never know where it might lead. Maybe we're *not* supposed to know the detours and pit-stops ahead. Think about it. The version of you five years ago couldn't have handled what you've faced recently. That's because it wasn't meant for *her* – it was meant for *you*. The one reading this now. The one who's still here. Still standing.

And whatever comes next?

Trust that future you will have it covered.

Wiser. Softer. Stronger.

The paths we crave or fear won't appear until you're the version of you that's ready to walk them.

THE WORRY WORKSHEET

1. **Write down** everything you're worried about. Get it out of your brain and down on paper.
2. **Cross out** anything that's out of your control. (Yes, seriously – *cross it out.*)

3. For everything you *can* control, ask yourself:
   - Is this a 'right now' problem, or a future problem?
   - If it's a 'right now' problem, what are *two small steps* I can take to feel more prepared?
   - If it's a future problem, what are *two actions* I can schedule in to help future me?
4. What's the **worst-case scenario** for my biggest 'problem'?
5. Has this worst-case ever ***actually*** **happened before** – or is my brain spiralling?
6. What's the **best-case** scenario? (Yes, you're allowed to imagine that too.)
7. Now go outside, put on your favourite song, take a deep breath . . . and *let it go*.

Everything will be just fine. I promise.

Chapter 21

Planning with purpose

An array of coloured lights danced across the walls, bouncing off our fancy AF Christmas tree and turning the living room into a jolly little disco. I went a little OTT with the holiday season – decorations went up months early – and the Christmas spirit wasn't just confined to the lounge room; it was everywhere, from reindeer candles in the bathroom to Santa-shaped cookie jars in the kitchen. And in true cringey, vanilla fashion, the whole family in matching PJs.

Mate, my festive bogan life was made.

But the part that made my heart combust? Watching my girls surrounded not just by Christmas spirit – but by each other. Together. Healthy.

We'd made it. All of us.

Willow had entered our lives with a bang and, at just two weeks old, kept us on our toes – back in hospital with a viral infection – while poor Harper had surgery for grommets. That week was the first I felt the tug-of-war of having two kids. But to this day, Willow is the most resilient in our family – the last to get sick, the first to bounce back. Her rough start seems to have given her immune system some balls. Honestly, she could lick a shopping centre floor and be fine.

Besides being a human antibiotic, Willow is what we call a 'Little Nan'. She looks so much like her, which felt strangely comforting as Nan's Alzheimer's worsened. Her fire was still there – and now Willow had some of it too. Willow, Nan, Rosie and my cousin Laure all have the same strawberry patch birthmark on the napes of their necks. Wild, but also rude to leave me out. But back to Christmas. You bet the kids had Santa stockings and sacks. Even Ryan and I had stockings – just took me twenty-seven years to finally get one. I never got a gift from Santa growing up and as superficial as it sounds, it stung – especially when every other kid seemed to. At the time, I thought it meant I'd done something wrong. So filling up their stockings – even my own – felt quietly healing. Like I was rewriting a part of my story through my daughters.

This Christmas was extra special because it was the first in our newly built house as a family of four. We'd invited the whole crew: Ash and her family, my parents, Nan, Ryan's parents, Mum's sisters Aunty Netty and Aunty Rose, Uncle Tony, and my cousins Laure and Sammy. A few more popped in too – the kind of loud, full house I'd always dreamt of.

We were sitting in the lounge room, me next to Laure, my youngest and, debatably, funniest cousin, watching Will Ferrell prancing around like a giant Elf on the telly. I had no clue what part of the movie we were up to; I was too busy thinking about how stressful the past week had been. First, I'd sprinted through the shops like I was being chased by flesh-eating zombies organising things. Then came the panic clean – the *real* Christmas tradition – the frantic, desperate speed-cleaning where every surface is victim to my swearing and swiping. Because, god forbid, anyone realise we *actually* live here – eat, sleep, and (gasp) *poop* in this house. Preposterous.

To help, I whipped up a 'Xmas planner' and of course shared it with my online community. They frothed. The planner had prompts, reminders that broke up one big task, such as bloody Christmas, into smaller tinsel-sized chunks so mums like me didn't end up locking themselves away in the pantry to cry into their rosé.

Cue lightbulb moment.

Why don't I do the same for *life*? A planner to help people 'organise the overwhelm' of their existence. It seemed they only made planners for Type A personalities; the people with an inbuilt timer and calendar in their brains. The ones who buy birthday gifts early and fart reminders. But what about people like me? The ones whose brains make a list in their head, only for their brain to shake it up, flip it over and scramble the letters like a Word Search? The planners I had tried didn't help. For one, they were so *boring*. No colour. No personality. I needed shit to be pretty, inspiring and broken down, so I didn't end up running away to join a cult, churning butter for a living, instead of tackling the never-ending to-do list of the twenty-first century. What I needed was a planner for the 'magical messes' of the world. If it didn't exist, could I be the one to make it?

As these thoughts whirled around my head, I turned to Laure. We have a twelve-year age gap, so she's always a great sounding board, ensuring I don't slip too far into *elder millennial* territory.

'What do you think if I made a planner?'

Laure gave me a point-blank stare. If I didn't know her, my stomach would've sunk straight out of my butt in utter embarrassment. But with Laure that look meant this was serious.

Good serious. And she was never serious. 'Um, yes. You *need* to do it,' she said.

'But do you think people would actually like it or even want one?'

'Are you serious? They would eat that shit up! Even I would buy it.' Which was Gen Z for 'yes'.

Now I'd said it out loud, I could either follow through (the very thought made me want to follow through) or add it to my pile of 'flaky failures'. But no, this was a true tunnel vision moment. *Mission: create planner* was locked and loaded.

And that's the origin story of how Steph Pase Planners was born, or as many people call it now, SPP.

Looking back, it's not surprising that I ended up creating a stationery brand. I've always loved the start of a new year, the feeling of fresh beginnings and endless possibilities when I'd let my mind wander to what the next 365 days might hold. But the thing I loved most was new stationery. Yes, an entrée of notebooks, notepads, highlighters and pens; and the main course? A brand spanking new diary. I loved them all. Roses and chocolate? Pfft, gimme a fresh hardcover A5 notebook any day of the week.

I don't know how old you are, the person (ahem, legend!) who decided to pick up this book, but we all remember the start of a new school year. My favourite thing was walking up and down the aisles of the newsagents ready to make one of the biggest decisions of the year: what contact paper to cover my books in. This was a big commitment. While other girls were sporting Jesse McCartney, Harry Potter always won for me. I don't know if it was the books themselves or what it was beyond the pages. To me, a fresh notebook symbolised the person I wanted to be. Organised. Clear-headed. Someone who was confident, knew what she wanted and had her shit together. I will never forget watching the teen movie *New York Minute* for the first time – the one with Mary-Kate Olsen who reflected more of me (chaotic, messy, doesn't know what day it is), and Ashley who played Jane Ryan aka my hero. I was infatuated with her planner. In fact, it turned me into a planner whore at the ripe old age of fourteen. As soon as I could earn my own money, I bought every planner/diary/notepad under the sun, but it would always go something like this:

1. Buy a new planner.
2. I open it up, smell the pages like it's crack – the smell of a new Steph.
3. I promise myself that I'll use it and write neatly every single day.
4. I write in it.
5. I make mistakes.
6. I get angry at myself.
7. I use the planner for three to six business days.
8. The planner collects dust on the blue shelf behind the dolphin shower curtain.
9. I only pick up the planner when having a mental breakdown.
10. I use it again for two days.
11. It stays behind the shower curtain until it's time for me to stress clean and it gets thrown out.
12. Cycle repeated . . . until I got my first sample of my SPP planner in 2019.

That Christmas couch convo with Laure in 2018 changed everything: it helped take my brand to the next level, and empowered me to sell my own products rather than just recommending other people's. By this stage I'd been blogging for two years. It had become my full-time job. And I'd been flat out between brand collabs. Now we were in our family home I was busy #Stephing it and sharing it online. The original unit helped me uncover many hacks, but now I was going wild. We were busy, but happy, so why not add another addition to Jack's mental load?

I loved promoting brands that I genuinely adored but I wanted something of my own to share with the world too. I'd partnered with brands like Dyson, Disney and my personal fave, Little Label Co. By this stage, everything in our house had a label. If Ryan stood still for too long I'd probably label him too. Organising made my brain go nearly as quiet as my old pal Ally would. Full disclaimer: booze had re-entered my life. Not to the same extremes; from the outside I would appear to be 'highly functioning' but I was still using it a little too often to calm the chatter in my mind. I was still underestimating myself – and the support of my community. From a young age, I had learnt to expect the worst or 'bare minimum'. I figured it was better to just let myself down first – at least I could control it. Nan's positivity was still there, and yet I always assumed I'd fail.

But little by little something shifted. I began to see the ripple effect not only on my life, but on others' too. When I started sharing other small Aussie businesses that I loved, I'd get messages from the owners on how the product sold out or they gained thousands of followers. I was blown away by the feedback. This wasn't just clicks. This was real change, for real people.

What if my 'little slice of the internet' wasn't just for sharing thoughts and hacks? What if I could use all the insights my community had given me, all the tools and templates that had changed my life, and create something that would truly make an impact in a physical sense, not just online? For the first time I wondered – through Nan's rose-coloured glasses – where this could lead.

I'd been sharing my life every single day but at times it felt like you were speaking through your phone into a void. While I saw the numbers, and all the messages, I couldn't physically see my community – it kinda fell into the, 'out of sight out of mind' category. That's what happens when you're a visual person. Turns out this is a positive trait to have when making a product. If I can *see* the system, I can stick to it – that became the heartbeat of every product I would create.

SPP all started with a Word doc . . . Yep, that's it. No business plan or advisory board. Just me sitting on the couch. The journey went like this . . .

Entrepreneur who has no fucking idea what she's doing starter pack

- A sixty-page Word doc filled with word vomit, lists and half-formed ideas outlining a planner that didn't exist yet.
- Days spent searching for a magical course called 'How to make a product' (spoiler: it doesn't exist).
- Late nights doodling templates that only made sense to me.
- A graphic designer (a mum also named Steph) who somehow did make sense of them.
- Hundreds of email threads with manufacturers I found after hours of digging.
- Followed by multiple dead ends, ghostings and 'sorry, we don't do thats'.
- A husband who convinced me I wouldn't lose the money I saved for this venture.
- A cousin named Sammy who'd worked in homewares and reassured me this wasn't a total disaster.
- Too many coffees and crying sessions to count.

So how exactly was I going to make this planner so 'groundbreaking'? Luckily, I had no shortage of content. I knew it would have to include my 'Thirty-day declutter challenge' from page 226 – a gamified template my community loved. There was also my 'Spring Clean Challenge' and 'Healthy Habits Challenge', which looked like a cute bingo card. The idea was to cross off an activity each day to complete the challenge. From there was my 'Christmas Gift Planner', my budgets, meal planners, cute stickers, habit trackers and quote pages; it was going to have it all.

After twelve months of trial and error, designing, a million edits and testing out pages, we finally had a product file. It was close to perfect. Now it was on to the worst part – proofreading – which I did with Dad's help. He had a great eye for detail and it felt nice to be able to do this together.

'Steph, I think one of your samples is here,' Ryan called up the stairs.

It was like I'd just received my acceptance letter into Hogwarts – minus the owl and the magic, that is.

'Coming! Don't open it!' I yelled as I bolted down the stairs.

This wasn't the first sample I had seen. Unfortunately, the other two I'd ordered just weren't 'it'. The quality of the spiral was off, the colour was weird, they just didn't feel luxe . . . or special. I repeated the process again and again. And here was the latest. Which, mind you, was double the price, but I didn't care. I ripped open the box and looked inside. She was perfect. I held up the planner to Ryan, tears streaming down my face, and a smile I couldn't wipe off if I tried. It was like having a third baby.

'This is hectic, Steph. I didn't know you could even make a planner this good!' Ryan said. That was the whole point. At the time, there weren't planners available like this in Australia.

If you're sitting there thinking about 'that thing' you've been wanting to act on forever, but are afraid of failure, listen up. I always thought I was the same. But guess what? You're not actually afraid of failing. You're afraid of *other people's perceptions of you failing*. Bear with me. Let's say you work a nine-to-five job but you dream of starting something of your own; whether that's making products, freelancing or teaching other people a skill online. You save up enough money and quit your job, or you work your normal job on the side. What's the worst that can happen if you do 'fail'? Life goes back to how it was before and you move on. As long as you haven't overcommitted financially, it's just your ego that's hurting. Brutal, but true. Everyone thinks they are afraid of failure but they aren't really. We're afraid of *what people will think and say about our failures*. Let's look at my track record:

- Went to uni. Hated it. Graduated anyway.
- Went to makeup school. Technically 'failed' as a journalist?
- Worked at a gym, planned to be a PT . . . then got distracted by my next thing.
- Built a makeup biz. Loved it. Grew it. Then outgrew it. (Not a failure – just a pivot.)
- Started a blog. People called it a hobby. Turned out to be the launchpad.
- Did a PT course. Ran some online programs for my community. Another 'Jack' qualification that has helped my online space immensely.
- Now writing this book and finally dusting off the ol' journalism degree. Even though I still have to sing the Gwen Stefani song in my head to spell the word 'bananas'.

So, am I someone who failed a lot of ventures, someone who could never find their thing?

No. I realised my 'one thing' was me.

All parts of me.

The more 'failures' the better.

Just like taking a car for a test drive – you need to make sure you're happy with how it runs, feels, if it fits in with your life and what you need – kinda like picking a romantic partner. Our chosen career paths are no different. And just like cars, over time we outgrow them, our lives change and we need to find a new one. Sometimes our old one breaks down and we need to check the mileage and trade it in for something with heated seats and fewer warning lights. (Relax, Ryan, you're still under warranty.)

I would go on to make a lot of mistakes with Steph Pase Planners – many of which I'll spill the tea on soon – but I was sick of letting my self-doubt stop me. Anxiety? You're not on the SPP team. Don't let the door hit you on the way out . . . or do.

•

After much back and forth, I ordered a whopping 1500 units of that first planner. If they didn't sell and I had leftover stock, I figured I could build a planner cubby house. I had to pay a huge deposit which was a massive leap for a business that didn't even exist yet. Ryan and I had agreed that, as long as we broke even, it'd be worth it. All I pictured was my planners in people's hands. That's what mattered. But I was shitting bricks about breaking the news online. What if people didn't like paper planners? Every day a new 'planner app' seemed to launch. Maybe they'd think I was living in the dark ages? But I had to trust my 'why' and the vision behind SPP.

Finally, it was time to spill the beans . . . I created a second Instagram page – because apparently managing one wasn't enough – called @stephpase_comingsoon. My community had no clue what it was, or what I was going to be selling, but seemingly overnight it gained tens of thousands of followers. I was speechless.

'You could be selling your used undies for all they know,' Ryan joked. I do hear there is good money in the industry so if I ever needed some extra cash, maybe? (Kidding . . . I think.)

Finally it was time to post. I paced the living room as the clock neared 7 p.m. Ryan watched me from his spot on the couch. The post was an image of me, sitting cross-legged on one of our arm-chairs, holding up two planners. The expression on my face was pure childlike excitement. Dad's grin.

Posting in five, four, thre— . . . oh fuck, my Instagram is glitching!

What if people are underwhelmed? What if I built up all this hype for nothing?

But just like that, it was up . . . And the comments began rolling in. It seemed people were just as ready as I was to bring these planners into the world.

Maybe I wouldn't have to make a cubby house, after all.

PURPOSE, SMURPOSE . . .

Maybe the goal isn't to be your best self. It's to be the happiest. Not the most perfect, flawless, always-on-top-of-things version of you – but the version that feels energised, fulfilled and at peace with where you are.

Chapter 22

A camp table and a dream

If you'd driven past our house back then, you would've seen a garage packed to the brim, and rows of pallets stacked with towering boxes, spilling out onto the driveway, like a dusty brown game of Tetris. You would've seen a sweaty mum, hair shoved in a messy bun, balancing a toddler on one hip while hunched over a camp table, rolls and rolls of shipping labels, tape and rogue dummies scattered everywhere. The set-up resembled a dodgy daycare centre, waiting for Centrelink to pop by. I'm still convinced Harper stole half my shipping labels to use as stickers – to decorate the dog. Poor Lily. She never stood a chance.

And neither did I. I was packing planners and had my work cut out for me.

•

'Honestly, hun, if I could sell 2000 planners in two to three years, I'd be stoked,' I said to Ryan, hours before the planners officially launched.

'I think you'll surprise yourself, Steph.' Ryan patted me on the shoulder as I stared at the backend of my website for the millionth time. It was go time. Time to find out if all the work and dreaming was worth it. If people were as excited as they seemed. If the world was ready for *not just another planner.* Turns out the world *was* ready. I sold out 1500 planners that night. Yep. Our website couldn't even handle it.

'What? There must be a coding issue!' I said as I watched the order numbers tick over faster than petrol prices.

'Holy shit, Steph. This is incredible. Look at all these people.' Ryan scanned the screen. I opened my mouth to say something, but all I managed was a gurgle and a slow blink. Ryan leant over, kissed my forehead and said, 'I told you.'

Although the online support had been there since I started, it wasn't always there offline. But if the blog had taught me anything, it's if you have a vision, chase it, even if it doesn't make sense to others. Ryan always knew and he supported all my pivots. Not once did he tell me just to stick it out a little longer. Incredible things can happen even if just one person believes in you. And if you don't have that – be it for yourself.

I had officially done it. I'd made it. It worked. So why did I want to throw up?

I wasn't sure what scared me more, that this thing was truly out in the world – and soon to be in people's hands – or the idea that maybe . . . I'd actually built something *real.* Something people genuinely wanted. After years of chasing and never quite feeling enough, now I had to walk the walk. I felt proud. Grateful. But as I began searching 'how to send parcels from home' and comparing shipping labels I caught myself thinking, *Who the hell let me do this?* And more importantly, *Who was I to help other people get their life together, when I was still figuring out mine?*

'Looks like we have enough to pay the rest of the money to the manufacturer now,' Ryan laughed. My shoulders dropped, the stress of that payment no longer lodged in my muscles. But now we had a different problem: we didn't have enough stock to meet the demand.

Over the next two months, I restocked three times. Apparently, people didn't mind waiting weeks for their planner. *Thank god for that*, I thought, glancing around the garage – the once-grey floor now hidden under white packaging. A label printer perched on the table in front of me was hissing – which was concerning. But the thing about being thrown in the deep end is you find a way, fast. You have no choice but to swim.

In between packing orders and preventing the kids from eating paint, I tried to get back to the hundreds of messages and emails I'd received. 'Can you post my planner early?' 'I've moved house, can I change my address?' 'Does the planner come in another colour?' All while apologising to my community for not being able to reply to their DMs, balancing my phone on my ear to my manager, Mik, and sending off brand content between taping boxes. I didn't know how to 'batch print' at the time – when you print a bunch of labels at once – which meant I had to download and print every label separately. Days now looked like this:

- 3 a.m.: Wake up to start printing labels, one by fucking one.
- 5 a.m.: Two hundred labels printed, start packing orders before kids wake up.
- 6 a.m.: Kids get up, give them breakfast and set them up near the garage so I can pack a hundred more.

- 6.30 a.m.: Ryan goes to work or does paperwork from home (the latter means more parcels get packed).
- 7 a.m.: Print more labels . . . one by one.
- 9 a.m.: Pack another 200.
- 4 p.m.: Stand back, feeling proud, looking at the hundreds of packed orders.
- 4:01 p.m.: Glance over at the laptop and realise I hadn't made a dent.
- Repeat until I pass out.

I'd continue that cycle until the kids' bedtime when I'd throw a social post together, reply to more customers, before heading back to the garage until I couldn't keep my eyes open anymore. Then it was back to printing labels at 3 a.m.

•

'If you stop emailing me I'll get your order out faster,' I muttered to myself one morning, eyes burning as I stared at the screen, scrolling through the endless emails that had landed overnight. I couldn't do this alone, Ryan helped as much as he could, but between his work and tag teaming the kids it was impossible. One glance at the number of pending orders was all it took for me to google 'virtual assistant'. I also asked a friend, who lived nearby, to help pack orders.

Despite having the extra pair of hands, it was still a shitshow. Nothing topped the pure adrenaline rush you got with every batch of orders that our postie, Stu, collected. Every time he loaded another box into his van, Harper would start sobbing, 'Mummy, they're taking your books!'

'Baby girl, it's okay. We *want* them to take mummy's books. Mummy only needs one and the rest are to help other people.' After a couple of weeks, she stopped crying and started waving the postman off like a champ.

Oh my ovaries. (At Harper . . . not the postman. Sorry, Stu.)

During this time, most of my routines went out the window. I felt like a fraud but instead of hiding it, I shared it. 'We all go through seasons in life. Some, messier than others.' I didn't know it yet, but this would become my main message and point of difference for my brand. People were receiving their planners and the emails and comments revealed the diverse bunch whose lives were being changed. The mums with PND used it to feel in control again. To tick off 'warm coffee', call it a win, and remember they still mattered. The students used it to survive exam season, to manage social life and timetables. The nine-to-five workers used it to juggle life, work and the in-between. The FIFO families used it to track routines and rosters, to find a rhythm when the house felt half full.

The neurodivergent or messy minded used it to calm the chaos. To create systems that worked for them, not against them. The business owners and side hustlers used it to plan launches from their lounge rooms. The overwhelmed used it to breathe. The empty nesters used it to rediscover themselves. The 'human doings' who wanted to be human beings used it. They all used it their own way. No pressure. Just planners with purpose. And before I knew it came the follows and the orders from media personalities, influencers, celebrities and TV stars. Even Libby Trickett, an actual Olympic swimmer, was a fan!

Meanwhile, I was still swimming in boxes in the garage . . . and somehow *they* were coming to *me* for advice? What alternate universe was this? Well, the same one where a few months earlier I decided to throw a launch event – a party to celebrate the birth of SPP – *before* the full shipment of stock had even arrived. I air-freighted a small batch of planners over and wanted everyone at the event to receive one. While my marketing brain told me the event would help build hype, I really wanted to meet the people behind the screens. The women who had supported me for years. It wasn't only a celebration of SPP – it was a celebration of finding my people.

I've been to plenty of events where the tickets are tiered, influencers have their own section and the whole thing feels a bit . . . divided. And while I don't judge how others run their events, this would be different. No 'us versus them'. Everyone got the same goody bag, the same welcome and stood in the same space. I went against PR 101: send products to influencers early to build hype. It works, but I didn't want that. Not this time. I made everyone wait, influencers included, because I wanted *everyone* to feel special opening their planner; whether they had a million followers or just one. People told me it wasn't a good move. But it felt right. Still does.

To organise the event I called in the professionals – an event planner named Petra, who would become my virtual assistant years later. After scoping out venues, we decided on a bar along the water in Darling Harbour – open space and great vibes. Until I saw the venue capacity: 300 people. You'd think with over 100,000 followers, I'd feel confident. But all I could picture was Ryan and me standing there surrounded by canapes – but no crowds.

'Worst case, we have six months' worth of finger food for dinners,' I said.

Out of pure fear, I made the tickets stupidly cheap – $85 for a five-hour event. Everyone would receive a goody bag worth over $200 *plus* a planner. But I didn't care. I wasn't trying to make money – I wanted to create something people would remember.

In the end, the only thing I'd be eating for the next six months . . . were my words. The tickets sold out in under thirty minutes. I was convinced the website had glitched. Even more surprisingly, a tonne of people said they missed out, so Petra called the venue and somehow managed to wrangle another fifty spots.

The day of the event, my car was stuffed with boxes – goody bags, signage, cables, snacks. I was running around like a headless chook, texting Petra and trying to convince myself this was still a great idea . . . despite having crippling anxiety and a long-standing fear of women. Vaginas are scary. Surely this would be different. Huge white foam letters spelling out *STEPHING* lined the back wall. Music played. Pastel florals wrapped around the white stand. My planner, front and centre. And so were my nerves. A line of 350 women trailed outside, buzzing with excitement.

I spent the entire night meeting people, taking photos, and – for once – not feeling like a Jack. One woman told me she'd driven twelve hours to be there. Someone snapped a photo right as she said it – Ryan and me, eyes bulging, mouths wide open. It was giving *what the actual fuck*, in the best way.

'You helped me during my worst year,' another woman whispered, hugging me like an old friend.

All I could do was say 'thank you', over and over. Some of them cried. So did I. It wasn't just about a planner, or a blog, it went beyond the pages and the posts. It was women – many of us once little girls – who felt left out. Separate. Watching on, trying to work out where we fit. No longer on the outskirts – we found our place, with one another.

Meanwhile, Ryan was being swarmed like some TV heartthrob.

'This is the only time you're allowed to be surrounded by girls buying you shots,' I laughed. 'Enjoy it.'

My family was there – my parents, my cousins, my legendary in-laws, Ash and some friends. But sadly I was missing two of the most important people: Nan and Ady. Nan wasn't well enough to come, and it was too loud for Ady. But even with that, it was perfect.

As the event wrapped up, a woman asked me to sign her planner. Surely I misheard her. 'Are you sure? My handwriting is shocking.' But I signed it anyway. How could I not? Before long, it seemed like everyone wanted me to ruin their beautiful planners with my chicken scratches. As I scribbled my name onto yet another one, I caught sight of Ryan across the room. His eyebrows were raised. We didn't need to say anything. We were both thinking the same thing: *Is this really fucking happening?*

It seemed like all the female attention made one very nervous man an extremely drunk one. He made an early exit.

'You realise you got kicked out of your own wife's launch party?' I told him the next morning.

'Sounds about right,' he mumbled, eating a stale croissant.

While the launch was a success it wasn't all confetti and unicorns. Behind every win . . . there's a fuck-up (or ten). So let me introduce you to:

MY BIGGEST BUSINESS FUCK-UPS
(THE ONES I CAN SAY OUT LOUD ANYWAYS)

- **Dodgy manufacturers.** Lost thousands to a dodgy manufacturer when I branched into lifestyle products. Moral? Vet *everyone*. Pay via PayPal. Get contracts. Be paranoid. And always get external QC before stock lands.

- **Don't assume everyone has good intentions.** A staff member stole from me. Yep – feel the love. And honestly? The heartbreak hit harder than the loss. I loved her. I've always been a bit naïve – assuming the best, even when people do otherwise. So assume the best . . . but don't put all your eggs in one basket. Especially if someone else is gripping the handle.

- **Undercutting myself.** When pricing products, do the maths (or if you don't speak numerals like me, get someone else to). Otherwise you'll lose out.

- **Build processes from the problems.** Serial scammers have mastered the art of getting free products and a refund. No, I'm not telling you how. Don't be that guy.

- **Shit happens . . . floods too.** Our main manufacturer's warehouse flooded and we lost 100,000 pens. They say don't cry over spilt milk – well, I did in fact cry over a ballpoint pen. PS Have insurance.

- **People-pleasing is not leadership.** I learnt the hard way that being a people-pleaser doesn't help the business, the team and it definitely doesn't help you.

- **Sometimes it feels like a pressure cooker.** There's a launch going live, 143 unread emails, a kid mid-meltdown, and dinner's burning. Everything's urgent. Everything's important. And everything's mine. So I did what anyone would do – smiled like a lunatic, got it done and cried in the pantry later.

- **Growth doesn't always feel good.** As the business grows, so do the overheads. Suddenly, breaking even starts to feel a lot like breaking yourself. The goalposts? They don't only move – they reappear ten miles ahead. New level – New Devil.

- **The hardest part?** The stuff no one sees. The 3 a.m. moments where it's just you – exhausted, emotional and doing what needs to be done. No one's clapping when you fix a Shopify glitch that double-charged hundreds of people for shipping. And since my love language is words of affirmation, I had to start giving them to myself: 'You're doing amazing, sweetie.' (Said in Kris Jenner's voice.)

It reminds me of motherhood . . . those quiet, thankless hours when everyone's asleep and you're the one rocking the baby, folding the laundry or googling 'can I die from lack of sleep?' You show up, not because it's easy – but because there's no other choice. Because it matters. You don't achieve success by doing it all perfectly – you get there by showing up consistently, learning from your mistakes and pivoting with purpose.

I've never been one to go by the book. Business start-ups usually begin with a product or idea and *then* slowly and steadily acquire customers, developing their strategies and processes along the way. My brand was built backwards. Kinda like me. I started with customers – but a business that had zero processes, zero staff, and an owner with zero fucking clue. This would come with a lot of issues. The first being space, or lack of it. The garage bloat had returned but now it was bursting at the seams – like my old Supré dress after too many beers. By this point, my product line was growing: first To-Do Lists, then Magnetic Fridge Planners. Soon enough the camp table would buckle under the pressure. I'd never related to a piece of furniture more in my life . . .

One day I realised how much the business had spread into places that I'd sworn were off limits. It was at the end of another long shift at Box City. I dragged my weary feet through the door and froze. SPP hadn't just taken over the garage – it had invaded our house. A house that now resembled my childhood bedroom. Boxes lined the hallway, flattened boxes were piled near the front door, packing tape was stuck to the dog. The calm home I'd envisioned for our family was buried under piles of cardboard and chaos. I had to figure something out – fast – before Lily decided she wanted a new family.

My fingers tapped to the rhythm of Tenacious D playing in the background, a blank expression on my face and an equally blank Word doc staring back at me, filled with exactly zero ideas on how to fix this mess. Until . . .

'How about I work out of a storage unit?' I blurted like I'd nailed a maths question for the first time.

Ryan raised an eyebrow (I think – they're blonde, so it's hard to tell). 'You won't feel comfortable working there alone at night.' He had a point. I'd watched way too many documentaries that involved dead people and storage units – the ones with endless rows of roller doors and serial killer vibes. No thanks. 'What about a small warehouse instead?' he said, grabbing his laptop.

'A warehouse? Are you kidding? What if all this turns to shit? I have no idea how this thing is going to go.'

His brows dropped, at least I assume they did. 'This "thing" isn't just a thing, Steph. Because of you, we have savings and new possibilities for our future. You're literally supporting our family.'

So we started touring warehouses – Ryan, me, and a real estate agent who kept cracking left-field jokes and looked like he worked part-time at Bunnings. My type of person. Each tour was the same. Ryan walked confidently ten steps ahead, like he'd already signed the lease. I dawdled behind. I loved that it was happening . . . but could I take this to the next level? I had three options. One, dive into a warehouse. Two, make a smaller batch of planners each year and piss off a heap of customers. Or three, outsource to a 3PL distribution service where I'd never lay my hands on my own product again. No more ensuring every customer got a love note, products wrapped the way I wanted, to make them feel special.

'I didn't know if I should show you this one,' said the real estate agent. 'A homewares store was using it, but it's technically available.' Located in the next suburb, a street away from my gym, it was a bit of a fixer-upper, but 150 square metres and full of potential . . . oh, and expensive.

As I began to shake my head, Ryan pulled me aside. 'Look, I can also use it for tools and materials, and even have my office here. Does that make you feel better?'

It did. If it would help Ryan too. I was in.

This ended up being the first of three leases we would sign over the next four years. Outgrowing each quicker than the last. A good problem to have, right? Soon after, I hired Sarah, a mum I'd met at the gym. She messaged me out of nowhere offering to help after seeing me drowning in orders on Instagram. Sarah had recently had a baby and wanted an excuse to get out of the house. I hired her on the spot – solely to help pack orders. She's now done nearly every role there is at SPP: assistant (aka therapist), warehouse, customer service, even staff event coordinator. Over the years, she became like family.

I gave that first warehouse a facelift – blush walls, cute frames placed on the desks. We even built a crèche with a cot and a basket of toys so the team could bring their kids to work. Sarah's son would crawl around with my girls, taking turns napping. I loved that SPP was no longer changing customers' lives – but changing my team's lives too.

Mum would bring Nan by most weeks. Nan's Alzheimer's meant she still thought I was a twenty-one-year-old makeup artist but she seemed to love being there, even if she thought every visit was the first. She'd always give me a big cuddle and a kiss, then say, 'What is this establishment?' her eyes jumping from rack to rack.

'This is my business, Nan. See all those boxes? Those are my products. I made them.'

'Oh, Stephy! See, I told you one day you'd make something of yourself!' she beamed, clapping her hands together as though her horse had won the races. I never got sick of that.

I still imagine Dad walking around that warehouse, hands on hips, doing his signature pause before saying, 'This is incredible, Steph.' I can still hear it. I craved that look of pride on his face and think I always had. I started chasing it in places it didn't belong. The question was how far I'd go to keep that feeling.

Like all business owners I wasn't immune to the shitty, dark moments. Even though I share so much online, I kept a lot of the hard stuff private. Not out of shame, but because I didn't want it to sound like I was complaining. *You should be grateful* would run through my head between cooking dinner and writing website copy that was needed four hours ago. Torn between being a present mum, wife, boss and creator, I never felt enough. But no level of success protected me from the blatant sexism I copped. And it wasn't only from men. Women too. All time-travelled straight from the 1800s.

'Oh, *notebooks*? That's cute. Well, as long as it helps your husband pay the bills.'

'It's nice you're letting your wife use your warehouse, Ryan.'

'You're a lucky lady getting to live off all of this. Thank your hubby.'

None of it was true. But god it hurt, like pressing an old bruise, reminding me of a time when people compared the younger Ryan and Steph. I started to wonder if I was ever going to be enough. These strangers didn't know me but they all assumed Ryan was the one with his shit together. The one behind it all. And sure, the comments triggered me – but they also lit a fire: to keep going and prove I was capable. That I'd earnt it. That I was worthy and smarter than the ol' diagnosis I buried long ago as a kid.

When we don't share the hard parts and the fuck-ups, we don't just protect ourselves, we build an illusion. And that illusion convinces everyone else they must be the only ones struggling. You can be 'crushing it' on the outside – and falling apart behind the scenes. The same goes for business. Motherhood. Life. So when people go out and *do the thing* – chase the dream, start the business, raise the kids, and inevitably hit bumps, detours and dead-ends – if all they've ever seen is the polished highlights reel, of course they are going to think *they* are the problem, that they don't have what it takes. If no one opens up, everyone ends up feeling like a failure, quietly, *collectively alone.*

And that's why when people ask me, 'How do you do it all?' I say bluntly, 'I don't'. There's always a part of my life falling apart at any given time. Since that very first launch, it's felt like a sprint. Sometimes I joke that I created a monster – one I love and am so grateful for – but one I struggle to feed. The only thing that's really changed over the years is the bar I've set for myself. And the life-altering truth that every fuck-up and failure taught me something I couldn't have learnt any other way.

A friend once asked me, 'If you could undo any of the things that nearly broke you in business – would you?' And honestly? No. Not one. Because now I know what I want – but more importantly, I know what I *don't* want. And that kind of clarity only comes from discomfort . . . and dickheads. Sure, I'd probably have fewer eye bags and need less retinol, and I certainly wouldn't have said that while I was still in the thick of it, but time gives us the distance to see situations for what they are: lessons. Some days I wish I could go back. I know you've felt it too; whatever role you play. That quiet ache for a time when life was . . . simpler. Not easier. Just lighter. Where your biggest worry was maybe handing in your homework on time. Or heading out for brunch when it didn't require two nappy bags, a stash of baby wipes and a whole lot of silent swear words. Maybe your good ol' days looked like sticky fingers on the walls, laughter echoing down the hallway, bedtime kisses you'd give anything to feel again. People love to say 'be present' and yeah, I try just as much as the next person, but sometimes I catch myself dancing in the past. Twirling in the nostalgic memories of who I used to be . . . how life used to be.

As I write this now – sitting in my third warehouse, surrounded by an amazing team I never thought I'd find – I drift back to the early days. But not dipped in sadness or longing. I head back to that garage. To a mum packing boxes, two little girls running around, a soft glimmer in her eye as she got lost between excitement and fear thinking about what the future might hold. Sure, the stakes are higher now. The pressure's magnified. The goals are bigger. The office is fancier. But at my core, I'm still the girl in the garage, taking a chance on herself.

Maybe it's time you took a chance on you too.

Funny, isn't it?

How it all started with a wonky little camp table.

HOW TO BRAINWASH YOURSELF INTO BELIEVING YOU CAN (PS BECAUSE YOU CAN)

We are biologically programmed to expect the worst. While this trait is there to keep us safe, it can also keep us stuck and stagnant.

Instead of thinking what if things go wrong, start thinking what if it all goes right? What if it turns out *better* than you could ever imagine? This is how you 'brainwash' yourself:

1. **Use your receipts.** Think back to something that you worked up to be terrifying in your head and you were fine – maybe even more than fine. Or all the times that should've broken you . . . but didn't. You made it through that. Proof is power.

2. **Rewrite your what-ifs.** What if it works? What if it works out better than you could ever imagine? What if this reveals the door you were born to open?

3. **Mentally rehearse the good.** Picture it all going right. I have done this for years and especially on the big, scary, important days. Your brain doesn't know the difference between thoughts and real life. This isn't woo-woo – it's science. Mental rehearsal tells your brain what to expect. And the more it sees success, the more you naturally make decisions and act like it.

4. **Write like it's already happened.** Yes, take mental rehearsal a step further (this is part of my journalling practice). Write the day ahead as though it has already happened, including writing your goals every day in the same way!

Chapter 23

Behind the filter

I always thought the worst thing a girl could be called was 'bossy' or 'needy'. Turns out there's way worse. Some schoolyard bullies never grow up. They just move from the playground to anonymous forums, hiding their smirks under a username.

Welcome to the Social Media Schoolyard – where you don't need a blue tick to be enrolled. If you've ever posted a photo or had a Facebook account – congrats, you've been assigned a table! You never graduate, posting and performance is your life now. Let me show you around . . .

First up: 'That Girl' Gang: With their perfect twenty-step morning routines, they are TikTok royalty. Their leaders? A rotating cast of women who made self-development their entire personality. Healing is no longer a journey . . . it's a brand. On Wednesdays, they wear yoga pants, and if you wake up twenty seconds past 4 a.m. you can't sit with them.

Between you and me, they're exhausted. They aren't the problem, the pressure is. Sound familiar? Now they're stuck on the content hamster wheel of 'clean girl aesthetic' . . . because mess isn't marketable. Oh, and don't forget – they have a discount code.

Next: the Keyboard Warriors: They're loud (behind the keyboard), confident (online), and always watching, ready to pick their next victim. Don't make eye contact with them unless you want to end up with twenty passive-aggressive comments that aren't 'bullying' because 'it's their opinion'. They'll ruin your life before breakfast, then post about mental health awareness by lunch. Giggling, they pass notes in class: 'She ignores her kids', 'Her new hair's gross', 'Why is she always so daggy?' Their hobbies include asking for $400 couches on Facebook Marketplace for free, lurking around troll forums for 'fun', and tearing down influencers while their own kids cry in the background. Sorry Billy . . . Mum's got lives to ruin.

Over by the vending machines: the Almosts: They're quiet, not because they don't care, but because they care too much. They scroll in silence, not for 'tea', but for proof they're falling behind. Not pretty enough. Not rich enough. Not successful enough. But maybe . . . one more online course, one more diet, one more hustle . . . then they'll finally be enough. *Almost.* Every day they hit the 3 p.m. self-worth slump. And the worst part? They know it's all filtered – but they keep on scrolling.

Next up: the Doomscrollers: Besties with the Almosts, these guys don't even leave when the bell goes. They only hopped on to check the weather, next minute it's 2 a.m., they've read fifty-two articles, taken twelve quizzes to find out which household appliance they are, and diagnosed themselves with eight diseases and a rare foot condition. Their nervous systems are fried . . . but hey, at least they're informed.

Lastly: the Open Tabs: All scoring an A+ in screentime, they reply to emails while stirring pasta, check messages on the toilet, and fire off Slack replies while putting the kids to bed. Their phones are never on silent – the only notification they ignore is themselves. Their mental health crumbles if they take more than sixty seconds to reply. They don't rest. They refresh. Their wi-fi is their leash that they don't know they can take off.

And that's your online life! Did I mention it's more important than your actual life? Yeah. Even if you're miserable, as long as you look happy on the grid, that's all that matters. I used to think I was in the background. No allocated table. Until one day I looked up and realised I'd been the class joke for years. Welcome to my initiation into the dark side of the internet. Turns out it wasn't the girls from school who did the most damage. It was grown-arse women with a wi-fi connection.

As someone who exists on the internet, I know that nobody is immune to negative comments. Since I started my blog, I've had run-ins with trolls, but their commentary (oh, sorry 'opinions') were usually surface-level shit. An 'ugly' comment on my Kmart haul – they were probably talking about my face, but let's pretend it was the $5 vase, shall we? I learnt to laugh it off and deal with it. Besides, I'd been called much worse.

That was, until, I received a message I wish I could block from my memory.

New Instagram message: 'Have you seen this?'

No context. Only a link.

I should have ignored it. I should have replied with a casual 'thanks, I'll check it later' and gone back to making Harper her hundredth snack for the morning. I wish I could say I never clicked it – but I did. And honestly? If I hadn't it would have found me eventually. Harper's tiny fingers were tugging at my grey, oversized, stained trackie pants, but I barely felt a thing. One hand grasping my phone, the other could have been juggling for all I knew – my mind was somewhere else entirely. You know that deep mystical part of our gut that is 'all knowing'? In this instance my gut already knew what my brain hadn't caught up to yet. That this was going to hurt.

I braced myself, ready to be ripped a new arsehole by some online article talking shit about me. So far the media coverage had been positive, but I'd been waiting for this day. The page began to load . . . painstakingly slowly. Finally, it loaded. I began to scroll and there it was: my Instagram name: *Just Another Mummy Blog*. Or, as I had apparently been rebranded on this forum, 'Just Another Mummy Flog'. Side note: Ryan always joked it should be *Just Another Mummy Bog*, which is way funnier. But we're not trolls, so what would we know? As I continued to scroll, even my sense of humour couldn't stop the slow, sickening drop in my stomach. *What is this place? Why are these people writing about me?* You know that feeling when you're running down the stairs and suddenly miss a step? For a moment, you're hovering in thin air – but not in a fun, I-had-two-wines kinda way. Oh no. This was the moment before the drop.

'*Her house is ugly. So boring, just like her.*'

'*Ryan looks miserable.*'

'*Her voice is so annoying. I can't even listen.*'

As I read the comments, my legs began to feel unsteady, so I plonked on the bottom of the stairs. The phone no longer felt like a lifeline. It felt like a portal. A way for these people to step into my life, pick it apart and leave me with the wreckage. Of course, I should have put the phone down. Instead, I scrolled like

I was possessed; I couldn't control it. Comment after comment. Complete strangers dissecting my life. Over and over again. My home. My face. My voice. My body. My weight.

'*You can just tell she loves one kid more.*'

'*She's ugly.*'

'*Her kids will grow up to hate her.*'

'*She's such a bogan.*' (Well, obvs.)

'*She's obsessed with herself.*' (Bro, have you met me? Oh wait, no, you haven't.)

'*Pfft, Steph Copy-Paste.*' (I actually laughed at that one. I wish my brain that has zero-chill would let me copy-paste shit.)

So I'd been ripped a new one, but not by a big news publication looking for clickbait. From what I could see, these comments were posted by everyday people sitting in their lounge rooms. Everything I had achieved suddenly looked very different. The worst part? Every comment, every assumption was not only false, it was so far from what I was. Who I am. What I stand for. *Did people even like me at all?* Was I someone that people hate-followed? As I tumbled down the rabbit hole into a dark, eerie, digital dungeon, I suddenly felt pulling on my sleeve. When I finally looked up, I saw Harper staring at me with her big, blue eyes. She had no idea her mum had just been ripped apart in the *Mean Girls Burn Book: Pathetic Grown-Arse Women Edition.* This wasn't like the bitchy drama I ignored/was oblivious to at school, because they didn't come with closed captions. These were grown women. Adults. Mothers. People with lives, jobs and families of their own – yet somehow, they had hours to spend dissecting mine. And not just mine. Every second person with a platform. Was this the price you had to pay for being online? For letting people into your life?

I snapped back just long enough to pull Harper into a hug. I needed it more than she did. After a tearful call to Ryan, I turned to Ash and my cousin Sammy. Their words helped, but not enough to scrub off the toxic feeling. That night, I didn't sleep a wink. I tried but every time I closed my eyes, their words lit up behind my eyelids like a neon sign: *She's too much. She's not enough. She's failing. She's fake. She's ugly.* The four walls of my online home came crashing down. I felt like a fool for ever thinking I could just be me and help people. I had felt this way before thanks to arse-wipe Andrew. The man on the phone. Except now it was women on the internet. Just when I thought being myself was the golden ticket to happiness, to belonging, to finding my 'thing', it turned out I was wrong.

•

The only thing that's worse than a troll is letting them know they won. And I'd been there before. Years ago, before SPP, it felt like I couldn't speak out or do anything to change the trollscape. I realised I had two options:

1. Ignore them. They continue writing shit.
2. Reply (which is what they want), fuel it, and they continue writing shit.

The worst part of it was the fact these people faced zero consequences. It was surreal reading comments about yourself that simply weren't true. That forum – which was one of many – only existed to share hate. And there were common 'crimes' they zeroed in on, especially when dissecting females.

- You're either too organised, house too clean, meaning you neglect your kids; or you're too messy, which also means you neglect your kids. It's a win-win, right?
- You're either too health-obsessed, or a phony because, wait a minute . . . was that a Red Bull? (Oh, and you neglect your kids.)
- You're either too career-driven, which means you're a 'bad mum', or you spend too much time with your kids and don't 'contribute financially' – a 'freeloader'.
- You're either too independent, which means you don't love your partner and emasculate him, or you're too needy and reliant.
- You're either too put-together – getting your nails and hair done – which means you're up yourself, or you're a slob – hair in a mum bun, no makeup, leggings again – you've let yourself go.
- You're either too strict – with routines and structure – which means you run your poor family like a bootcamp, or you're too relaxed – gentle parenting, picking your battles – which means you're turning your kids into spoiled brats.
- You clearly love one kid more than the other because you show them more online (maybe because they're a fucking baby and with you 24/7?) But you should also get off your phone and be with your kids constantly.

Again, no wonder Britney shaved her head. Compared to other people with platforms who were getting slammed, my forum posts were quite boring – like me apparently. Because I poke fun at myself, you might think I could laugh it off. But I won't downplay it because online bullying is a huge problem, and it's time we stopped normalising it. 'You should accept it if you put yourself out there.' Nope. I call bullshit.

Instagram message: Why do you sound like a man?

Yes, a charming creature named @dogmom4evaa once sent this to me. I didn't want to be rude, so I hopped on stories and re-introduced myself as Steven. What I didn't realise until years later was that one comment stopped me from starting a podcast. I allowed it to embed itself in my narrative; I couldn't have a podcast because of my voice. That is, until I finally did the damn thing and it hit number two in Australia. Yep, I sat right under Joe Rogan, not physically – on the charts. Awkward. Not bad for an annoying man-voice, right?

Eventually, I learnt to stomach the bogan comments. I could laugh off the odd insult about my voice, the house, my looks. Whatever. But the moment they mentioned Ryan or the girls, or worse, Ady, I was no longer sad, I was raging. Of course I shared moments with my brother online – he's a huge part of my life. I won't repeat the exact comments because I refuse to let the words touch these pages. Rather than driving me forward, that anger only made me . . . smaller.

While this was going on, I kept showing up online. But it wasn't really me anymore. Slowly, I became a watered-down version of myself. Ironically, a 'Steph Copy-Paste' materialised – a Frankenstein the trolls built from the ground up. I started filtering what I really wanted to say to make it sound just like any other post. Throwing out surface-level stuff. I guess I really was *Just Another Mummy Blog* for a while. Growing up, I was so used to keeping Mum happy my body thought I needed to keep everyone happy to feel safe. I had to be liked by all.

Somewhere between clicking that link and sitting at the bottom of my staircase, I'd slipped. Now when I looked in the mirror, I wasn't sure who was looking back at me. It sure wasn't that authentic, fired-up Steph. I had dug up the masks I'd burnt years ago – the ones from my childhood – and had pulled them back on. But now they felt uncomfortable. I had outgrown them. But still, I tried to push through the tight fit.

The internet had rules, and I was learning them in real-time. The social media 'red carpet' could be ripped out at any moment, and I was terrified of tripping. It reminded me of Meadow Lane. Scrutinised. Muted. Waiting for a reaction.

This 'queen' of routines had a new one:

1. Wake up.
2. Hold my breath until I knew.
3. Check the forum.
4. Read what they said about me overnight. Most of the time it was crickets so I would just read over old posts to keep me in check.
5. Mask on. Post something safe.
6. If something good happened that day, search for evidence that I do, in fact, suck.
7. Repeat.

Somewhere along the way, the trolls stopped living on the internet. They lived in my head, rent free, drinking all the milk. Giving Anxiety a run for her money as the 'worst roommate'. But I needed to know what they were saying. And as much as I hated them, I was controlled by them.

You gotta not look at it, Steph.

Just don't look at it.

Why would you even read that, Steph?

You might be reading this thinking the same thing. That was

the response nearly every time I spoke about it – to friends, family, even people in the industry. I'd bite my tongue, force a nod, and say, 'Yeah, you're right.' But really I wanted to say: Imagine this – across the street from your house is a giant billboard with your name on it. But instead of an ad, it's a single sentence about you. And it's nasty. Now, don't look at it. Walk past it every day, head down and pretend it's not there. Could you do it? Could you resist the urge to glance?

If you can – congrats. You're stronger than me and 99 per cent of the population.

•

'So what brings you here today, Steph?'

My new therapist sat, pen at the ready, armed to help me untangle yet another mess I'd dragged into the room. I'd been to my fair share of therapists over the years, each time peeling back another layer, but this time I was tired of taking ten steps forward only to be yanked fifty steps back. I gave her the rundown. By this point, I had launched SPP and was pushing forward despite the trolling – though, of course, the forum had something to say about that too.

'Her planners are just cheap Kmart knock-offs.'

If only they knew the blood, sweat and literal tears that went into every single page.

As I told the therapist about SPP, she smiled. 'This is amazing, Steph. You should be so proud of yourself.' And for a moment, I wanted to believe her. But with everything it had cost me, I wasn't sure if this was what I even wanted anymore.

After I explained the trolling she said something for which I had no legitimate answer. 'For once, I want you to ask yourself, what is the *worst* that can happen?' I must have had a blank expression because she continued, 'What can these people possibly say that can actually harm you? Physically, even your business?' That was the thing my body never understood because it didn't know what safety felt like – not really. So when I saw those words, those lies, those accusations, my nervous system reacted as if I was being hunted.

•

I wish I could say that session with the therapist changed every-thing. It didn't, but it did plant a seed. My healing happened gradually, but I can pinpoint a few milestones.

The first was after I had surgery to fix a condition called ptosis, or drooping eyelid. It had progressed that by the end of each day, I could barely keep that eye open. The headaches were relentless and my vision was suffering, so I finally decided to get surgery. And of course, *they* frothed.

'Surgery didn't even fix it. Looks the same to me – just a lazy eye.'

I read the words as tears leaked through the stitches. I was done. Enough. I was tired of letting faceless strangers dictate how I felt about myself. The day the stitches came out, I looked in the mirror and saw more clearly than I had in years. Not just because my eye was fixed. But because I was starting to see who I was beyond the labels.

The next milestone came a couple months later. It was a typical afternoon when I received a DM on Instagram. I can't recall exactly what this woman said, but I remember it was along the lines of, *'All you do all day is fluff around your house. Your poor kids; get out and be a mother!'*

I replied with kindness. Not because I'm a saint, but because although she was making assumptions, I've never been afraid of people opening up and explaining their side. I wasn't expecting a reply but suddenly, my phone lit up.

'I'm sorry. This wasn't for you to deal with. I lashed out. I've been diagnosed with stage three cancer, and I'm really struggling. I don't know why I said those things. You seem like a beautiful person. I'm really sorry.'

We spent some time messaging back and forth and soon I got it. My heart broke for her. Hurt people hurt people. I had heard this before but now I saw it play out in real life. This person was stuck inside most of the time, wishing she could just get out with her kids. It upset her that it *seemed* that I was always inside, which she acknowledged I wasn't. I share perhaps 2 per cent of my day, which is something that people easily forget.

The third milestone came during an event for the Australian pharmacist, Priceline. I found myself in the same room as Ita Buttrose, the iconic Aussie media personality and, during the Q&A, Ita spoke about how, early in her career, she received endless hate letters – always unsigned. Someone in the crowd asked her how she dealt with negativity and without a second of doubt she said, 'I want to ask you. If you opened your mailbox one day and received a letter with no sender written on the back, would you even bother opening it? No. You'd throw it in the bin where it belongs.'

Mic drop.

Why was I doing the exact *opposite*? Not only was I opening the mail, I was searching other people's mailboxes for it and then nailing it to my front door, scanning it and plastering it over the walls of my home. The internet had already gamified friendships and popularity, and now I was letting it gamify my self-worth.

And the real kicker? One day, my girls will experience this in their own way. So what do I want them to know?

•

It had now been years since I first came across that forum. Years since Ita Buttrose's words of wisdom, and that insightful troll DM who turned out to be a woman hurting. Years of breadcrumbs, lessons and slow realisations. And yet, despite all that, I still found myself checking that forum every now and then, like reopening an old wound. Until one day, in the middle of 2020, I decided I was done. Done with my brand. Done with my blog. Done with being public. Done with all of it.

I was sitting in our lounge room opposite Ryan, the kids bathed and fed, watching a movie. I was clutching my phone, my finger hovered over the 'delete account' button in my Instagram settings. I had done this before – more times than I'd like to admit. But this time, I meant it.

'I can't do it anymore, hun. I'm done. They won.'

Ryan looked up, puzzled. 'What do you mean?'

'I'm deleting it all, my accounts, the blog, SPP. I'll just go back to makeup.'

'What? What about all the people who say that you make their lives better? You're gonna let a few dickheads win?'

My logical brain said the same thing. I knew and I agreed but I just couldn't put it into practice.

'I'm just not built for this. I'm a soft cock. I can't hack it.'

Then something in Ryan's eyes showed me it was on. He walked over. 'Okay . . . so you're not built for this,' he said slowly. 'But look at what you *built*, Steph. All of this was all you.'

I said nothing.

'You have two choices,' he continued. 'One: you quit. Shut it all down. Stop doing what makes you happy. They win. You go back to makeup, and you'll probably be miserable. Or two: you say *fuck it*, people will talk anyway, and you keep going. You focus on the people who love you. The ones you help. The people whose opinions actually *matter.*'

I said nothing. He let that sit.

'It's up to you, Steph. I will support you no matter what but I know you, and I know what makes you happy. If you let them win, you're not just doing yourself a disservice – you're doing a disservice to the hundreds of thousands of people who look up to you. Who feel seen *because* of you.'

Then it clicked. I was *never* going to make *everyone* like me. We weren't meant to process the opinions of millions of strangers. We weren't designed for this type of access. Human beings were built to be part of a *village* – not to be judged by an entire fucking planet. Of course, it was exhausting. Of course, it felt like a lot. But if I loved doing this, I had to do it *for the people like me.*

One day, when my girls are inevitably are faced with something like this – whether it's online, schoolyard bullies or the 'cool girl' in the hallway who decided to stop talking to them – I will cup their faces in my hands and say, 'You don't need to prove yourself to those who have already decided not to see you for who you are. Because no matter what, they never will see you; the true you. They have made up their mind. And that's really sad because you're really fucking awesome.'

None of us is immune to judgement and you don't need a public profile to know what it feels like. Trolls don't just exist online. Some wear corporate lanyards. Some live next door. Some sit at family gatherings, making little back-handed remarks that make people hold in a sob over Christmas ham. Some show up at school drop-off. Some lurk over by the printer at work; you hold your breath as you pass. And now? Kids bring the schoolyard bullies home with them. It's everywhere and it's terrifying. And if we're not careful, it chips away at our courage. But we don't have to let it. We can take a stand against it; we can keep living loudly and proudly, and not let it silence us.

Earlier in this chapter, I said how unfair it was that these people faced zero consequences. But actually they do. They live the consequences every single day. They exist in a cycle of their own making – wasting their lives wishing they had things they don't, doing the things they fear, hating people who *do*. Instead of changing their situation, they spend their time tearing down those who *have*. And where does that get them? Nowhere.

It took me a long time to accept that I don't have the power to change people who *don't want* to change. That if someone doesn't like me, the world actually won't end. The only thing I *can* do is spend the time I have here making the *one* person I *do* have power over – *me* – happy. And hoping that happiness ripples out to the people who choose to be in my world, online and offline, not to hate-follow but to thrive in life with me. In the end, as long as I like me, I'll be just fine.

So when faced with close-minded negativity, don't you dare shrink. Do not stop showing up. And don't you dare open that anonymous letter. Hurt people hurt people, but healed people heal people. And I know which one I'd rather be.

ARE YOU AN ARSEHOLE TO YOURSELF?

We all love a quiz (this one is blunt but it's for the best).

1. You made a mistake. What's your first thought?
    A) I'm human, it happens.
    B) I'm bloody useless.
    C) This is why I shouldn't be trusted with anything, ever.
2. You got through a tough day. Do you:
    A) Acknowledge it was hard and give yourself a pat on the back.
    B) Replay everything you didn't get done or 'failed'.
    C) Negative self-talk loop begins.
3. You finally took a break. What do you tell yourself?
    A) Good. I needed that.
    B) I shouldn't have done that; I have sooo much to do.
    C) I'm so lazy.

If you answered mostly B or C . . . yeah. You're an arsehole . . . to yourself.

How to stop:

- **Switch your view.** Say what you faced that day but talk about yourself as someone else, in the third person. It helps to take a step back and realise you are human. *She was up with the kids all night then had that meeting, no wonder she couldn't keep up. She didn't get that housework done but no wonder* . . . See where I'm going with this?
- **Celebrate crumbs (not actual breadcrumbs).** Brushed your hair? Got out of bed? Ate something green? That's a win. Put it on the board.

- **Forgive the mess.** The emotional kind, the human kind, the house kind, the forgetful kind, the 'I ghosted everyone for three weeks' kind. You're human.
- **Talk to yourself like someone you love.** Because you *are* someone worth loving – even on your worst days.

My motto? Focus on what you *did* get done not what you *didn't*.

Chapter 24

300 days of darkness

'Doctor said Dad has months to live, not years. Don't ring atm.'

That was how I found out my dad was dying. A text from Mum. It was 2022 and I'd just pulled into the osteo carpark, running late as per usual. It took one text message to break my heart, and 300 days to shatter it. After I read it I did what I had been trained to do my whole life – mentally 'unread it' like a robot and went to my appointment.

'Your neck is extremely tight,' said the osteo.

'Oh yes. That's what happens when you hit your thirties, I guess.'

When the hour of torture was over, I walked slowly to the car, sat in the driver's seat and pulled out my iPhone, praying that I'd imagined Mum's message. I tapped the screen . . . and there it was. I don't remember the moment I broke but there in that car park, I was swallowed whole. I don't know how long I sat there, or how I finally worked up the strength to FaceTime Dad. I wanted to appear strong, like I'd been since we learnt he had lymphoma just months earlier. Like he had been for our family, for Ady.

I hate to say this – and I've only ever admitted it to Ryan – but I always had a feeling I was going to lose Dad young. I felt guilty for thinking it, but it sat in my gut. Now I wonder if Dad felt it too. A couple of years before his diagnosis, he'd started suffering from anxiety. Something completely foreign to him. While he knew we all had 'it', he never did. And to be honest, I don't think he really understood it. Dad was a right-brained kinda guy – very logical, very practical. But seemingly overnight, anxiety took hold, especially when it came to the future, or money. In an odd way it brought us closer together. Our relationship past my eighth birthday was minimal. But now I was thirty and my dad – who had never been one for much affection – suddenly wanted hugs. Not as in a quick 'hello hug'. A real one.

'It's okay, Dad,' I said, placing my hand on his. 'I know it feels like something really bad is going to happen, but that's your anxiety. I get it – I really do.'

'Really? Is this what it felt like for you? All your life?'

For the first time, he got it. But I wish he hadn't. I wish he never had to suffer. Whenever he came to our house, he'd always say, 'I feel safe here, Steph.' I knew what he meant. That yearning. A life raft when you're drowning. Waiting for 'it'. The worst-case scenario. In reality the danger is in your own mind. And when *you* are the danger? That's the hardest thing you'll ever battle.

You could see the anxiety had taken its toll. But there was something larger at play. It wasn't just his appetite that changed. Everything did – slowly, then all at once. I may have escaped the bare cupboards of Meadow Lane, but a few weeks before I went to pick up Ady one of his carers began chatting about Dad – his kindness, how he put everyone before himself. Then she said something that broke my heart.

'When he comes to get Adam, he always asks if we can fix him a sandwich.'

Poor Dad. A man who gave everything – and still had to ask for a sandwich.

When he was diagnosed with cancer, I began grieving him although he was still here – 'anticipatory grief', I'd later learn. Over the past few years, he had been more available and affectionate, especially since Ady had moved into full-time care. But too quickly, the cancer ate away at him. He went from looking like he was in his late fifties to his eighties. Up until this point he worked at the tax office and was fairly athletic. Each morning he'd wake up early and head down to the local beach pool. Until he became too weak.

'Why does Pa look like that?' Harper asked one day.

'Pa is sick, bubby. It's okay.'

Remember how I said I'd never seen Dad cry? Well, one Christmas he was sitting on the couch, exhausted. I plonked down next to him to keep him company. His gaze was unmoving from a spot on the floor but then he looked at me, our matching blue eyes full of fear and sadness.

'Steph, you're not gonna let me die, are you? Please don't let me die,' he said. Then it happened. He cried.

'Of course not, Dad. We're going to do everything we can, everything in our power. We won't let this fucking cancer win. I'm not letting you go anywhere, okay?' The worst lie I ever told escaped my lips.

He wanted nothing more than to live. And for the first time in my life, I felt the need to comfort my *other* parent. I held him tightly, while my head rested on his shoulder, my face out of sight as I cried too.

In time, it became harder and harder to hide the grief from the kids. I hated how much they saw me break down. But Harper and Willow saved me. Their innocent little faces made me feel like my world wasn't completely collapsing. I'd been a parent for six years by this stage and there were a few things I believed:

1. Say sorry to your kids when you should – it shows you're human. (Because news flash: you are.)
2. Show them it's okay to feel, as long as they know it's not their fault. Communicate with them how you're feeling and, if you can, why. Growing up, I saw so many emotions – unfiltered when they shouldn't have been, unmedicated when they should have been.
3. Tell your kids you're learning too. I tell mine all the time, 'This is my first time learning how to be a mum. Let's figure it out together.'

So when the girls caught me crying on the pantry floor, I told them why. And if I couldn't, I'd at least say, 'It's not because of you, darling. You're a beautiful girl. Mummy is just sad.' But even with all of that, the amount of times they saw me break was too much. And I felt guilty. In hindsight, I think it was because of Meadow Lane. I wanted our house to be happy and calm. Of course, shit hit the fan. Kids have tantrums – hell, so do I. But I try to make it a nice place to live. More importantly, a place where they feel safe.

The SPP team really stepped up. My cousin Sammy, who had been with SPP since the early days, made a huge difference. Larissa – who I'd pinched from Ryan's business – took charge of planner timelines, which saved my arse, and Sarah was a huge help too.

I'll never forget walking through the hospital hallways. It was the same hospital where I had Willow, but this time I was preparing to say goodbye. Dad's face would light up as soon as I walked in. Every time, he'd ask me the same three questions:

1. How are the girls and Ryan?
2. How's work?
3. How's the house coming along?

Ryan and I had begun building a house on a block of land we'd bought, one big enough for a pool for Ady. When I showed Dad the pictures, he brightened just as much as when I talked about SPP. I brought one of the girls a couple of times, but they got bored quickly. I also brought Sarah – remember my first warehouse staff member turned family?

'I promise I'll look after her for you,' Sarah told Dad, clutching his hand.

We were just post-COVID and although the hospital had strict visiting hours I broke the rules and played dumb so I could stay longer. Still, one of my biggest regrets was not visiting more. That year, I barely changed anything in the planners. Usually, I made big annual updates after listening to our customers' feedback, but that year I just had to get them done as best as I could. There were much more important things going on.

Leaving Dad in hospital after each visit gutted me. But amid all the heartbreak, there was one moment – one conversation – that healed parts of me I never thought I could. I had gone to see him on my own and was asking him about his life. I wanted to get to know *him*, not as Dad, but as a person. Who he was before he became a father, a carer. He didn't hold back. Stories I'd never heard before. Wild, adventurous things he had done. The risks he had taken before children. The man who travelled the world with a backpack and no plan. The man I never got to know. Then he turned to me and said something I will never forget. 'My biggest regret is not giving you more time, Steph.' He gazed down. 'I'm sorry I didn't do more.'

He didn't need to explain. We both knew. The words I'd needed my whole childhood. He was validating my experiences, telling me, in his own way, that my memories were true. This apology wasn't expected, but it held me more than a hug ever could.

A couple of months later, near the end, he wanted to come home. And I wanted him to as well. Not because I lived there anymore but I wanted him to be surrounded by his favourite things: Collingwood posters, photos of his family, his family without visitation limits.

There comes a point where you stop praying for more time and start counting what's left. This was the third time in my life I'd seen what a miracle it is to be here. The first was when I found out Ady defied the odds. The second was when my girls were born. And now – Dad. The week before he passed, we brought Ady to say goodbye. I have it on video. I still haven't been able to watch it. Sadly, Ady didn't know this was it. He just saw Dad – his constant, his safe place, the man who had spent his life caring for him, protecting him, making sure he was okay in a world that often forgot to make space for him. Dad's frail, pale hand reached for Ady, fingers curling, trying to hold on. And Ady, totally unaware, just wanted to play. All Ady would know is that one day, his favourite person – his pea in a pod – would be gone.

I stayed at my parents' house in Ady's old bedroom, just across from Dad's. Each night I lay there, listening. The beep of his morphine machine. His breathing. Every time his stopped, mine stopped. I'd run in. He'd let out another breath. Every second felt like a lifetime.

During the day I was either at the warehouse or at home with Willow, then I'd head straight back to Dad. Ryan was with the kids when I was there; I didn't want them to see what was about to happen. The day before Dad passed, I had a photoshoot to launch our new planners. Our biggest campaign of the year. If I didn't go we'd lose the launch. Now before you judge me, trust me, I hated leaving Dad more than I can put into words. But there was no good option. I had to do it now. Before *it* happened.

I checked on Dad. Told him not to die while I was gone. Dragged concealer under my bloodshot eyes mid-cry, ensured all the pre-launch prep was done. And I showed up. After it was done, I headed straight back. I wiped off my makeup, poured a drink, had a shower and then crawled onto the bed next to my dying father. I stayed there for what felt like hours – playing his favourite songs and talking about the good times from when I was little. I lay with him until he finally seemed to settle. I moved to the couch, opened up my laptop and tried to reply to the emails blowing up my inbox. Which now seemed anything *but* important.

Later that night, Mum and Rosie were in the lounge next to me when Mum suddenly said, 'I might go check on Dad.' She was gone for maybe twenty minutes before I felt it. A gut feeling. *Follow her.* When I walked into Dad's bedroom, I knew. I'd spent the night before listening to his breathing. Now, it was slowing. Not long after, Rosie appeared at the door. 'Is it okay if I come in too?'

We sat beside him, holding his hand. Mum talked about all the amazing things he'd done. The places he'd seen. That was the thing about Mum. She could be hard to read, but she did love him.

She loved us. It was just a hard love – one you couldn't count on. One that couldn't hold you. As she kept listing all the countries he explored, suddenly – he didn't inhale.

Silence.

We waited.

And waited.

Nothing.

'Dad!' I wailed, wrapping my arms around him as tightly as I could. I wasn't ready to let go. Placing my cheek on his, I sobbed. I held on so tight, as if I could hold onto his soul, stop it from leaving. Aunty Rosie wept holding his hand. Mum shot up from the bed, raising her drink in the air and yelled, 'Whooo, go Dave, you're free!' Her grief came out as a celebration. Crying, holding him, leaning over him. But he wasn't there anymore. Dad's body. No longer Dad.

After Ryan and I got home around 1 a.m., I played *Candy Crush* for three hours.

Because humans are weird in difficult circumstances.

Because sometimes, you can't cry anymore.

Instead, you match tiny little cartoon candies while your brain tries to process the fact that the world would keep spinning, and it shouldn't be able to.

•

In the weeks after Dad passed, the world felt backwards. Seeing death up close did nothing to help my phobia. It only made me more confused. How could someone be there one second and gone the next? I didn't know what to believe. All I knew was life would never be the same. My team at SPP stepped up, as I fell apart. But there was only so long that I could step back before the cracks started to show.

Weeks later, a senior team member had to leave – burnt-out. And I got it. I really did. Running SPP is fucking nuts. I had to return before I was ready and take on more roles than ever. When you're the face of the brand, the business doesn't stop just because your world has. You can't just disappear. You have to keep showing up. Ryan in a wig wasn't going to cut it.

I didn't share Dad's passing with my community for some time. When I finally did, it made it feel more final. I know it sounds silly because, yes, I saw him die, but posting it made it feel as real as the death notice in the newspaper. The outpouring of love from my community was instant and it made me grateful for my corner of the internet. Some who'd been through this before truly saw me, while others thanked me for not sugar-coating it.

Despite posting about Dad's death, my emails were still full of business-related shit. People chasing things. Requests to do speaking gigs. I had to bounce back – and quickly. Of course death doesn't just affect business owners. Let's talk about the whole two days of bereavement leave in Australia. Two. Fucking. Days. To process losing someone you love. It's as if the world expects you to just clock back in – like death is a minor inconvenience. As if you're meant to go back to doing life like nothing happened – when in reality, nothing will ever be the same again.

You might be wondering why I named this chapter '300 days of darkness'. Well sometimes, just when you think you've hit rock bottom, life hands you a shovel. Ten months after I lost Dad, Nan died. My mother figure. My home in human form. My dad and 'mum' – both gone. Not years apart. Not decades. Within ten months, 300 days. I barely had time to grieve one before the other was ripped away. Before I could catch my breath, I was drowning all over again. Yet because Nan was 'old' and not my 'actual' mum, it felt like her death, and my grief, wasn't acknowledged in the same way as Dad's. Granted Dad had so much life left to live. But Nan? *She was my fucking person. My everything.*

In the lead-up to her death, Mum and my aunties slept in the nursing home on the floor of her room. Despite her Alzheimer's, she remembered Ryan and me to the end. I don't know what I would have done if she forgot.

'I think you girls should come in now.'

It was 5 a.m. when my cousins Laure and Sammy and I got the text from Aunty Rosie we had been dreading. I had my bag ready. By this stage it felt like a 'your family is dying kit'. In Nan's room, we all took turns to cuddle her. I knew the way the air in the room would shift. I knew the sounds – the slow, laboured breaths that stretched longer. I knew the smell of the moment someone leaves. I crawled into bed beside her, just like I had as a kid every morning, but this time, I wasn't snuggling in for safety or warmth or to play.

I held her as she slipped away, felt her last breath leave her body. Gone. Just like Dad. The cruellest type of déjà vu.

In that moment, I was orphaned in a way that nobody else seemed to see, but I sensed it in my bones. How could I continue to live in a world without the woman who saved me? Who raised me? Who protected me?

Afterwards, Mum turned to me and said, 'You just lost your mum too.'

It felt like the truest thing she'd ever said.

TEN THINGS I'M STILL LEARNING ABOUT GRIEF

- Grief doesn't have a timeline.
- Missing someone and grief does not make you a 'downer' or a burden to others.
- Your grief will look different day to day, hour to hour, minute to minute.
- You can laugh and grieve simultaneously.
- Things you wouldn't expect will remind you of them; let yourself feel it.
- There's no right or wrong way to deal with grief. There's just your way.
- Some people won't get it. That's okay – the ones who do, really do.
- You don't have to be strong all the time, or 'get over it' – ever. This is part of your story and so were they. There is no 'delete' button and you don't want there to be.
- Grief is love with nowhere to go.
- You're doing a good job.

Chapter 25

The cabin on the mountain

Sometimes rock bottom is loud and sudden. For me, it was a school pick-up on a random Tuesday, engine still running, and a world I couldn't seem to face.

I gripped the steering wheel. The leather dashboard blurred as my eyes burnt. The school bell rang and parents bustled past, chatting about how little Johnny finally pooped in the potty and not on the rug. I sat there, wondering, *How the hell do these people keep moving through life?* How did their world continue to spin after mine just fucking exploded.

Here I was once again: separate.

As a functioning adult with offspring, I pulled myself together, collected the kids and made it home. Which told a story all too familiar. My beloved pantry resembled the shelf from my chaotic childhood. The perfectly labelled containers were nearly empty. The dishes were overflowing – like my inbox. Unanswered calls and texts weren't new – but this time, even the delayed replies and polite check-ins never came. Everywhere I looked, 'doom piles' multiplied like the washing that covered the laundry floor. Every day I was leaning more into mess and less into magic.

Like so many people, I didn't get a chance to process, let alone grieve. It was straight back to work. The warehouse that once represented my dream started to feel like a prison of pretend. All the mental rehearsals, heavy-handed swipes of concealer over the eyebags from hours of muffled tears as Ryan slept. Putting on a front for my team, our customers, my community. My job was to inspire and right now, I was about as inspiring as the KFC Colonel giving you a pep talk to go vegetarian. I wasn't only grieving Nan and Dad – I was unknowingly grieving the version of me I fought so hard to become.

At home, I tried to keep up as the mum who left notes in my girls' lunchboxes, who packed their favourite after-school snacks, who staged their toys as if they went on their own adventures. But slowly, those adventures became rare. Either they got tired – or Barbie had too many benders. But really it was me who got tired. Tired of trying to keep up in a world not built for the grieving. I wasn't perfect. Not even close. But the parts of Nan I saw in myself? They were fading just as fast as the memories of her I was terrified to lose.

Motherhood, business, life doesn't stop because of heartache. The show must go on. The curtains get drawn every day whether or not you know your lines or have your costume zipped up. Roles don't pause for grief – they just feel ten times heavier. So there you are, sprinting through the Reject Shop at 9 a.m. after arranging a funeral, grabbing leftover lolly bags for your kid's overpriced birthday party – while apologising to your arsehole boss Richard for being five minutes late to a meeting that could've been an email. They say time heals all wounds, even grief. I say – bullshit.

Every passing day, week, month and milestone only made it more concrete.

They weren't coming back.

My new evening routine was now a mix of whispering desperate 'sorry's' into my girls' ears because Mummy was crying again. Reminding them this wasn't their fault. Mummy was just . . . missing *them*. Just as Dad and Nan slipped away from me, I began to slip away from my girls. Ryan was losing the wife he knew – the one who could talk underwater, the one who always found the silver lining, even through the shit. The mess of my life – one I cleaned up, colour-coded, and turned into a system for people like me – now resembled the car that belonged to my teenage self; sticky, chaotic, and full of things I didn't want to deal with.

Sarah and Ryan started whispering behind my back – not in a bitchy way, in a 'how do we save Steph' kinda way.

'She's getting worse,' Ryan said.

'We need to *do* something,' Sarah replied.

As I heard their whispers echo down the hall, I waited for the usual flicker of resistance. Usually I'd sneak up on them, scare them, joke saying they can't keep anything from me, and say, 'I'm fine. I'm just griefy today.'

But I didn't get up.

Luckily, Ryan had nearly wrapped up his business by then, and was helping more with SPP, which made it easier to disappear. While my antidepressants doubled, the darkness tripled. Panic attacks hit harder, the air thicker. I asked my doctor for Valium and after picking up more meds, I sat in my car thinking about Dad and Nan, how much I'd give for just one final hug. And how exhausted I was from pretending.

Would it just be easier if I wasn't here anymore?

I was scared of dying, but I also didn't want to be here. I needed everything to stop for a moment.

Snap out of it, Steph. How fucking dare you?

But the voice in my head wasn't finished. It piled on guilt, shame and comparisons, all while I plastered on a smile and replied to emails. Until one day . . . I couldn't. I walked up to Ryan and said something I should have said a long time ago. 'I think I need help. I don't think I should be left alone right now.' When I finally said what I needed to say – the words Ryan and Sarah had been waiting for – he got down on his knees like he did the day he proposed. For better or for worse. And he kept his promise. For the first time in a while, instead of silencing my tears with a pillow, I let them flow. Tears soaked his shirt, my face, my neck. They didn't stop until, like every other night, I had no tears left to cry.

I was thinking about checking into a hospital to get full-time care, even though it terrified me. I needed something bigger than medication, bigger than pretending. But before we went down that road, Ryan looked at me and said, 'What if we tried one more thing first?'

•

No Ryan. No alcohol. No sugar. No caffeine. No reception. No internet. No one I knew. No safety net. No numbing out. Sounds like twenty-year-old Steph's worst nightmare, right?

It was actually the Eden Health Retreat in Queensland. A retreat I had bookmarked on Instagram more than once. This time, Ryan and Sarah didn't ask me if I wanted to go; they told me I was going, thank god. And so I packed my bags.

Saying goodbye to Ryan and the kids felt so *final*. Like I wasn't coming back. Well, we hoped I wasn't – not the version of me that was leaving anyway. 'You're going to be okay, bubby,' Ryan whispered in my ear, gripping me tight.

My biggest fear wasn't the inevitable coffee withdrawals. It wasn't even the strangers that Anxiety told me, *might hate my face*, nor was it sleeping alone (but that came a hard second). It was the fact I was raw-dogging adult life for the first time. No distractions, no scrolling, no numbing. It was just Me versus Me. *Fuck.*

'Steph Pase?' a woman holding a clipboard said as I exited the airport into the Queensland humidity.

'Yep,' I said softly, handing her my oversized suitcase.

'Oh . . . I only have you down for three nights?' she said.

'Haha, yeah, sorry. I packed like I'm moving to the forest.'

'You might want to by the end,' she said with a knowing smile.

I glanced at the other people waiting for the bus that would take us to the retreat. A mother and her teenage daughter, a woman in her fifties who had also come alone, and a husband and wife. *I probably won't get to know them. This seems more like a solo thing.*

The smooth asphalt road turned bumpy as the bus climbed into the mountains. A creek ran alongside the road, where families swam. I watched them, feeling something I hadn't in a long time – hope. I sent Ryan a melodramatic text, like I was moving to Hogwarts. Then I scrolled Instagram knowing it wouldn't be long before I was offline. My thumb flicked up and up, and as I waited for a post to load, it didn't . . . I switched to messages, to see if my reception still worked. Nothing . . . I blinked back an odd sensation. Tears welled not out of fear. Relief. For the first time in seven years, I didn't have to keep up appearances.

'Welcome to Eden!' said Blair, our camp leader, or 'Joy' as he was also known. 'We're so excited to have you. Some of the group have already arrived. Let me show you around.' Blair walked us through the grounds, pointing out the gym, the pool, creek, and cabins scattered along the mountainside. I was in awe. It was straight out of a postcard. The grass was so perfect it looked like the fake turf we got from Bunnings. Blair led us into the main building, where we found the change rooms, our lockers, and our welcome packs. Inside the women's change room, I found a locker with my name on it. A tote bag was filled with a map, my cabin number, a name tag, a drink bottle, and a journal. As I turned towards the mirror, ready to walk out and catch up with the others, I saw my reflection. I didn't look like me anymore. Gaunt. Sunken. Sad. Numb eyes that had seen too much. A reflection that took me back, years ago, to a glance in the hallway mirror. A new mum holding a newborn, barely holding it together. Carrying a different pain, but pain nevertheless. That day I made a promise to her for change. That I'd fight for her. And now here I was again. But now she carried death's aftermath – the scraps it left behind. Of *being* left behind. A different pain etched into her skin. This time it was grief – thick, heavy – a coat stitched from every goodbye she never got to say, its fabric laced with fading scents. His worn leather briefcase, her mix of Dove soap mixed with face cream – the exact scent it made mixed with her skin. She clung to its sleeves, grasping onto all she had lost, and was terrified to forget the way their voices sounded. Ones that would never grace her eardrums again. This heavy coat, all that was left behind and one she couldn't take off. But I was ready to change that. I was never much of a fighter – but if I was going to take on any battle, it was this. Because *I* was worth fighting for. And *they* were worth winning for.

'Cabin twenty-seven, hey?' Blair smiled, glancing at my map. 'It's a bit of a walk, but you've got the best view.' The schedule said we had welcome drinks at 5 p.m. I had some time to kill before then, so I decided to trek up to my room, settle in and refresh.

'Oh, and make sure you grab your torch,' Blair called out as I left. 'You'll need it to get back after dinner.' A torch? Maybe I missed the part where we drink kombucha and play a game of murder in the dark.

Two ladies, I guessed in their fifties, walked up the mountain with me. Their cabins were halfway, so we said our goodbyes. I kept walking. And sweating. Blair wasn't kidding about the climb – or the view. My previous 8000-step count goal was the entrée here. I finally reached cabin twenty-seven. It was so high up it felt like I was on top of the world.

After a shower, I stepped out onto the balcony, breathing in the mountain air.

I can do this.

For the first time since the man on the phone, I'd be sleeping somewhere that wasn't a secured hotel with key cards and an elevator. That alone was a huge step, and it was going to be an adjustment. Oh, and did I mention there were no keys to your room? Yep. No locks. Just trust in humanity to not steal your shit. My mate Anxiety? She was losing her fucking shit. But I'd deal with that later. Did I put a chair in front of the door? Ab-so-fucking-lutely.

•

'Sorry, I'm late,' I said to Blair as I sat down at the welcome drinks. You could instantly tell who had been here a while and who was new. The ones who had been here for a few days floated. No rushing. No tension. Simply existing. Then there were the others, like me, powerwalking to meditation like it was a company board meeting – just add crystals.

Dinner was amazing: all organic and tasting like bloody Jamie Oliver on steroids. Susie would have lost her coffee-enema-induced shit. The kitchen had a giant window where you could watch the chefs cook. After dinner, I joined the yoga class, where I met Barry – the eighty-year-old instructor who could fold himself like a pretzel. He broke his back decades ago and healed himself. Meanwhile, I was entering the age where if I slept ten degrees to the left I woke up with a sore neck and a limp. As Barry shared his story, I sat there, mouth agape. He taught me two things. One, I really need to stretch more. And two, people can go through hell and still make it out the other side. A smaller version of me had, once. If others could reset, release and rebuild after everything they'd been through . . . maybe I could too.

That night, after I'd made the trek back up to the cabin, I scanned the room, making sure Ted Bundy hadn't decided to have a bubble bath in my tub. With no TV, no reception, no distractions, I pulled out my journal and began to write.

I won't lie. Being truly alone with myself is terrifying.
I didn't expect to feel this lost and uncomfortable without the distraction of work, people and technology. The past two years have truly broken not only me, but my lens of the world. The one positive thing about being broken is that I can slowly pick up the pieces and build myself back together again. Ridding the pieces that no longer fit, uncovering new ones. Maybe even better than before.

FOUR SCREENTIME HACKS
THAT ACTUALLY WORK

Did you know the average person spends nearly seven hours a day on their phone? This adds up to 17.5 years of your life – and that's only by the time you're sixty. Makes you feel sick, hey? Well . . . good. Because you're about to change that.

1. **Make your phone boring.** Use greyscale/black and white mode. Only keep essential apps on your home screen, which I hate to break it to you are: call, message, calculator, camera and maps. Everything else . . . bye-bye.

2. **Babysit yourself.** Focus modes and screentime limits. My phone blocks all social apps from 5 to 7 p.m. while I'm with the kids. Then it gives me one guilt-free hour of scrolling before locking me out for bedtime. Yes, it's like I'm parenting myself. It works.

3. **Charge your phone away from your bed.** Then you'll actually get up when your alarm goes off. Better yet, wake up to a sunrise alarm clock – more peaceful than dings of doom.

4. **Don't dopamine chase.** For the first hour of the day, do not touch your phone. Not even for a 'quick scroll'. Your brain is like a sponge in the mornings. Using your phone trains it to chase dopamine . . . all day long. Then you wonder why you can't focus.

•

There was banging on the door. 'Morning Steph!' yelled Blair.

Somewhere between writing and waiting to be brutally murdered I must have fallen asleep. It was 5 a.m. and they woke you with a gong. Except if you're up Mount Everest where they knocked to ensure you wouldn't miss out on the day's activities. I rubbed my eyes and pulled open the curtain to the most beautiful scene. A stark contrast to how I felt the night before.

The only place in Eden with internet access was reception. I already made a promise to myself to only go there twice a day to call Ryan and the kids. There was no relaxing that first day: the program was packed with hiking, macramé, painting, yoga, Pilates, gym classes, women and men's circles, and talks on different topics like sleep/manifestation, even sports. You had the choice to pick and choose, even sleep in. But I wanted to do it all. Besides I couldn't rest and be alone – you know, the thing I came here for.

That afternoon we sat around the fireplace and shared what we wanted out of this experience. There were mothers, corporate professionals, students, even a psychologist to the police; all ages, backgrounds, jobs. A few were also grieving. Some were worn out from work. One bloke's wife had upped and left him and he lost his purpose, his direction. A young woman who worked in marketing felt like she couldn't breathe 'out there'. We all had one thing in common: we were burnt-out and had lost ourselves somewhere along the way. The culprit? Life in the twenty-first century which travelled at a speed none of us could keep up with. It took two days for the fog in my mind to clear. Slowly but surely I began learning how to slow down and tap out from the relentless race. For the first time in my life.

·

'Alright, everybody. Put your harnesses on. When it's your turn you'll climb the ladder and soon enough you'll be swinging through the trees!' said Kane, our personal trainer.

This activity was called 'The Swing' and before long, it was my turn. Anxiety crept up beside me, whispering in my ear, *This is reckless, Steph. What if the rope breaks? What if your kids lose their mum? How selfish of you.*

'Ready, Steph?' Barry called out.

No.

But also . . . yes.

Before I knew it the sturdy metal that was beneath my feet vanished and wind whipped my face. I was flying. Camel toe crotch burning. Below me, my new friends stood, staring up, grinning. Then I clocked why. I was laughing. Not typical laughing but head thrown back, cracking up. Like Dad had done and Harper now does too. In that moment, I wasn't simply letting go of the rope. I was letting go of the weight I had carried my whole life; the invisible backpack bursting at the seams with every negative belief, trauma, painful experience and story. And yeah, I knew I'd have to pick it up when my feet hit the ground – because healing isn't a straight line – but for now, in this moment, I was light. I was free. Like those families I had seen playing in the creek.

Maybe that's what life is really about – saying yes to shit we're not ready for. Or saying yes just because. I'd proved to myself before that good things can come from the unknown – even the scary. What if sometimes we need to go through pain to get *just enough* courage to take a leap? Pain being the catalyst for us to make change – do the scary shit that usually turns out to be exactly what we needed. All I had to do was try something new – to see the world from a different perspective. Above the trees.

Trekking back to my cabin on the first night of the retreat I had gripped the torch, flinching at every snap of a twig. But by my last night, the things that scared me the most became the things I loved the most: my treehouse, my walk back in the dark and my nights solo in my room. The dark no longer scared me. It held me. And for the first time in my life, I let it.

Each night, I used the landline to call Ryan and the kids. I loved the nostalgic feeling of playing with the cord as I recounted my day. I missed them but I loved it here; my home away from home. After endless activities; pottery, craft, games . . . it hit me. *When did we stop having fun?* As adults, we rarely do things just for the hell of it. We do things to earn money, to get fit, to clean the house. But fun? That stopped somewhere along the way. It's no wonder life was flashing before our eyes; we never slow down to feel it.

For the closing ceremony on our last night, we were asked to gather random items from nature and share a story. A family shared how they'd lost their dad a year earlier and had come here on the anniversary of his death. After they spoke I went up to the mother, looked her in the eye and said, 'I'm proud of you'. We both cried. Later that evening she came up to me and said, 'I see you'. And see me, she did.

I was now ready to rejoin the world.

•

'Um, I'm sorry, but I'm here to pick up my wife. Who are you?' Ryan said as I squeezed the shit out of him at the airport. 'I don't know what happened at that retreat but I swear you're walking in slow motion.'

He wasn't wrong. I was back in the real world and everyone seemed to be running, bumping into one another, heads down staring at their screens – as I did just days before, but that felt like a lifetime ago now. 'Look, I'm just going to say it: Steph, are you doing weed?' Larissa, my ops manager blurted out during a planner launch meeting. A launch that, before my trip, had me in crippling anxiety. My new business motto was 'we aren't saving lives'. And I was determined to keep up with the promises I made at the retreat just days earlier: to slow down and zoom out. Of course it wasn't all sunshine and rainbows since returning to real life. I felt it as soon as my phone picked up a signal and the alerts started piling in. I had all these plans to keep my body calm. But on the way home, as soon as my phone reconnected, Anxiety barged its way back through the door. After I had looked up for the first time in my adult life, my eyes were forced back down. To the screens, the numbers, the deadlines. From stillness to Slack messages. From meditation to managing a business. From water-falls to wiping bums.

A few days later, I shared my experience online. In the pictures, I looked nothing like the girl who first caught her reflection in that change room mirror. The caption was a list of what I'd learnt, simple things, but hopefully the kind that give others the wakeup call they didn't know they needed. Our world trains us to look down – to not miss a notification, to search for everything we think we lack. But the truth is you never lacked anything. You were just too distracted to see it.

Look up from the screen, beautiful . . . or you might just miss the view.

TRUTH BOMBS FROM THE MOUNTAIN

1. I was existing not living. Only excited for bedtime. So my days consisted of me being excited about being unconscious to my life.
2. I had ridiculously high expectations of myself even when it came to grief.
3. The reason we burn out is because we never switch off. And when we try to switch off we are stressing about not doing anything productive – therefore not actually resting.
4. Other people's urgency isn't your emergency. Emails and messages can wait until you're ready.
5. We stop having fun when we grow up. We forget our hobbies. You are allowed to have fun.
6. I always had to be stimulated by something, even going for a walk.
7. I was always rushing to the next thing. Why was I rushing through my life?
8. It is possible to feel another way – there is always hope.

Chapter 26

Weed and wakeup calls

Remember that time I shat myself at the pub? Well, turns out there's something far worse. Allow me to explain . . .

Back when Dad was sick, I read that CBD with THC in it (the stuff that makes you high) helps cancer patients manage pain. Dad was on it. CBD with THC can also help people with anxiety, insomnia and impending thoughts of death. So off I went to see my lovely doctor, who prescribed me an oil that was *ten times* stronger than Dad's.

I'm not pointing fingers, but Ryan read the dosing directions . . . and the next thing I knew I'd grown dreadlocks and was listening to Bob Marley. A quiet Sunday night at home became a full wakeup call, one I didn't ask for, but maybe one I needed. Santa was probably behind this too. Somewhere between the walls doing the salsa and me shitting my soul out, I saw me – me and all my bullshit. My entire life, I'd been chasing something I was never going to catch. Doing more, being more, achieving more – just to prove I wasn't a failure. That I was worthy. And every time I reached that feeling of 'enoughness' . . . . it never lasted.

And so the goalposts kept moving. And I kept going. Even if it ran me into the ground. I was addicted to the feeling of earning acceptance, earning pride, earning love. My ego needed validation to feel safe – to feel loved. Finally, I saw the goalposts for what they were . . . illusions. And the truth? I was the one moving them.

In that moment, the blinkers came off. I would never feel safe enough to stop. I was never going to achieve enough to feel worthy. Deep down, I wasn't trying to prove it to *them* – I was trying to prove it to *me*. Somewhere along the way it stopped being about multi-passions and became multi-validation to prove I wasn't ungrateful. Or broken. Or 'bad'. And no number of titles, achievements, acknowledgements or followers would ever make a difference. Not while I still believed I had to *earn* love. I wasn't chasing success. I was chasing proof that I was lovable. And the only one who could show me that . . . was me.

Well . . . *fuck.*

Over the next few weeks, I began to notice how this habit played out in real time. During meetings, I'd catch my brain feeding me imaginary benchmarks I needed to hit; ones no one in the room had even considered. And at home with the kids each night, I told myself I hadn't achieved anything. This was a terrible habit, but do you want to know what's more powerful than any ingrained habit? Awareness.

It was time to change shit up. There was no way I had made it through deaths, childbirths and my upbringing that I was willingly going to lose . . . to myself. It was time to flip everything on its head. Starting with my business. I had to create more sustainable processes, stop avoiding the 'gross' stuff like logistics, the numbers, and everything else that scared me. I had to think outside the box. It didn't all need to be on me. I had to hire more highly-skilled staff and create better work-life boundaries. You know, those tiny ripples that in turn make huge waves.

While I was making shit happen in my business, I couldn't shake the underlying feeling that something was still wrong with me. It was as though my brain was still actively working against me, no matter what I did. No matter how much I shifted on the outside or tuned into what was going on in the inside, something deeper was humming.

Growing up, I'd felt the same way. Does 'broken brain' ring any bells? But as the years went on, I was dropping more balls than ever and my sad excuse for a memory was only getting worse. Now that my life involved having multiple important conversations a day, my inability to follow – the constant zoning out – stood out more than ever. Not to mention forgetting the conversations I *did* listen to (which made me feel like an arsehole). And that was just scraping the surface. I could deal with losing my keys, tripping over my own feet or entering my phone number into the microwave. But this was another level. One that wasn't just affecting my work – it was bleeding into my friendships, my home life, everything.

'Why am I like this?' had become the slogan of my life.

'You've got a lot on your plate. Cut yourself some slack,' people would say when I brought up my brain farts. And they had a point – maybe it was stress or burnout. I assumed it was just another downside of overseeing a lot of moving parts. But I couldn't shake the feeling that something deeper was going on . . .

That lightbulb moment? Sure, it lit something up – but not everything. It was like I'd been handed a torch, only to realise the room was bigger than I thought. And unexpectedly, I'd been here before. Briefly. A glimpse, years ago. Into something I didn't understand yet. But I was about to. Thanks to a seven year old.

It was just another humid afternoon at the warehouse. Sarah and I were chatting about her son, who had been newly diagnosed with ADHD. As she began listing his struggles, I felt as though she lodged herself into my memory and recounted my life . . . and me. Everything she was describing about her son was me to a tee. Of course, I'd known that I was neurodivergent for a long time. Remember, I was diagnosed with ADD as a kid. Trust the girl with ADD to forget she had it in the first place. But here's the thing: I was diagnosed with the inattentive type. So I just went on living my life thinking all it did was make it difficult to pay attention. On top of this, Mum and the doctors never made a fuss about it – only the anxiety. That was the focus. But all this other shit? I assumed they were just the many personality traits of Steph the Mess.

So what do you do when you want to deep dive into a medical diagnosis?

Cue opens TikTok.

After typing 'ADHD in women', I hit the search button. And there I discovered the hundreds of not merely videos, but the puzzle pieces that made up . . . well, me. It was as though I had finally seen myself for the first time in a crystal-clear mirror. No filters, no assumptions, no frustrations. Just me and the diagnosis I'd pushed to the side my whole life. Forgetfulness, zoning out, intense emotional reactions, wanting to be tidy but being naturally a mess, sensitivity to rejection, low self-esteem, perfectionism, restlessness, a walking contradiction . . . it was all there.

Yes, I know TikTok gets a bad rap for spreading misinformation, especially when it comes to health, but for me it provided the missing piece of the puzzle. One that didn't make me *who* I am, but helped me see my different edges, why some pieces fit for others but not for me. And why my pieces didn't follow the standard pattern, because the picture I was meant to create was something even more magical. I felt truly seen for the first time in my life.

ADHD isn't a trend like some viral TikTok dance. Women have been misdiagnosed for decades all while being told they were too much, too emotional and needed to get their shit together. The world needs to read a fucking a book about this – one that should have been written a long time ago. Why? Because most of the studies thus far have been on men. So, suck it, Greg, go back to your Reddit dungeon, you don't know shit.

The reason women like me were overlooked was because hyper-activity shows up differently in women. It shows up in our brains. Do racing thoughts, a million thoughts at once for that matter, overthinking and panic ring a bell? This whole time I was being treated for anxiety, not ADHD, the root cause of my anxiety. All along we were treating a symptom, not the cause. So at the age of thirty-two, I went to my doctor and was re-diagnosed.

The results were in. Lock it in, Eddie.

- ADHD: Combined Type (inattentive + hyperactive). Double whammy.
- Generalised Anxiety Disorder. (If you mean I generally feel like I'm gonna die all the time. Then yes.)
- Health anxiety. No shit.
- PTSD? Checks out.
- Pending: Autism. Explains why girls are scary and I don't get drama.

I was prescribed ADHD meds and will never forget the first time I took them. It was just after I dropped the kids off at school and was getting ready to tackle my offensively long to-do list.

Until I noticed it. Silence.

My brain was quiet. The background noise I'd learnt to live with – the fifty strains of thoughts and internal monologues – were gone. My mind had always been like a bar you used to love – before you realised the music's too loud, the floor's sticky, and everyone's twenty-two and yelling. Suddenly it was as if everyone had packed up and gone home. I was able to think one thought at a time. It was beautiful and heartbreaking all at once.

'Is this what it's like for everyone else?' I asked Ryan.

'I've always told you, Steph, you have a brilliant brain. I'm just relieved that it's finally clear enough so you can see it too.'

Despite this, it was hard not to feel a bit ripped off. No wonder I struggled to concentrate, remember things, and was overstimulated 99 per cent of the time. The exhaustion I'd grown so used to, from all the noise . . . was gone. Replying to an email was no longer like writing a thesis. Remember at the start of the book I said I felt like I was in a race, but tied to a tree? Well, now it made sense. No wonder Ryan was so calm; his brain didn't have all these thoughts, ideas and worries bouncing around it like a pinball machine.

'Yes, Stephanie, all the symptoms you mention are very common for those with ADHD,' said my psychiatrist.

It all made so much fucking sense now: the dependence on alcohol, the Jack of all trades, my closet of masks; even the feelings of dread the week before my period. Having ADHD is like throwing glitter into a fan and wondering why it's such a mess. But guess what? It's a *beautiful* mess, one that you have to clean up from time to time, hyper-focus on a single piece of glitter, or figure out where you got the glitter from in the first place. I wasn't distracted. I was seeing a million possibilities all at once. Each piece of glitter, an idea, a creation, a part of me and my wonderful, limitless brain. Mic drop.

As I write this, I'm still on my ADHD medication journey. There are pros and cons and I'm not sure what the future holds. Although this might make it seem like it was an easy fix, it wasn't. It's been rocky to say the least. A lot of trial and error. But the biggest change is that I began to meet my brain with not only compassion, but understanding.

Because you don't understand what you don't know.

And now I knew.

No matter what labels you wear – anxiety, ADHD, depression, body image struggles, single, divorced, confused, binge-drinking or -eating, self-harm – they are not *who* you are. You are a separate entity to all of those things. ADHD is not who I am. It's simply one of the switchboards on my control panel – but now that I knew how it worked it was easier for me to steer. Now I could build the ship that was worth captaining.

Rejection sensitivity? Okay, I'm not the person to reply to customer service emails for SPP. Struggle to sit down and focus for long periods? Set a timer and take breaks. PMDD? I try to group work tasks around my cycle. The week before my period, I avoid filming and throat-punching people and instead work on admin, approvals and lighter tasks. If I'm in my follicular phase, I realise the world isn't so bad and I'm ready to film, get creative and meetings aren't so painful. Don't sleep on your hyper-focus – utilise it. That intense focus and obsession is your superpower. Starting tasks feels like pulling teeth? Body double! The very thing that allowed me to write this book – the concept where you're able to be productive with others working in the room with you.

I'm Steph Pase. I love hard, get big ideas and I'm a good person. My worth isn't tied to how well I did at work today, how many diagnoses I have or whether or not I was productive today – full fucking stop. And just like that, I placed the last piece in my imperfect, worn, colourful, vast, multi-passionate puzzle that makes me . . . me. I stood up, took a step back and saw the whole picture for the first time. The chaos. The family. The generational trauma. My messy mind. How although sometimes it held me back and made life trickier than I'd like, without it I wouldn't have built something incredible. Something worth fighting for. Without it, I sure as hell would not be here.

I turned to my old friend Anxiety, the one who'd been running the show since day one. With a knowing smile she said, *We've created some magic together, haven't we?* She then met my eyes, placed her hand under my chin and said something that would change everything, *I was ADHD all along.*

TURNING MY ADHD TRAITS INTO SUPERPOWERS

The MESS = My MAGIC
- Can't sit still = momentum to act on what I'm passionate about.
- Overthinks everything = has empathy + thinks outside the box + solves problems others can't.
- Talks too much = helps me lead (and be a natural story-teller and brand builder).

- Hyper-fixates then burns out = achieves things mere mortals couldn't.
- Distracted = mind canvassing a million possibilities.
- Emotionally intense = connects deeply with people.
- Starts twenty things, finishes one = learns what I want in life.
- My mess = showing up authentically.
- Always 'too much' or 'not enough' = 'just right' for the people who needed to feel seen.

Stephing up

Yep, I've been turned into a verb again. It's cringe, it's nostalgic and it's giving 'I just Stephed my pantry' vibes. Fun fact: *Stephing Up* is the name of my podcast, a project I paused to write this book. See, the Queen of Yes is now the Queen of Boundaries. Look at me go. *Obnoxiously flicks hair.*

Now, I know why we are all gathered here today:

1. You bought my book because you're a legend and clearly know a good read when you see one.
2. You had no clue who I am and by now think I'm slightly insane – that's okay, I still have time to win you over.
3. You are literally finishing a book . . . duh.
4. Oh right? How did it all turn out? Did I ever reach 'enoughness'?

Over the next year, Jack didn't just survive – she changed the game. With my new imaginary friend, ADHD (who I thought was Anxiety all along), I started seeing things more clearly. As for SPP – my blush business baby – she's still a beast, but now there are more hands to feed her, love her, and help care for her. I transformed my business so much, you wouldn't even recognise it now.

This is where my hyper-focus and obsessive tendencies came in handy. I went all in. And this time, I didn't need Ryan to tell me I could do it. I backed myself because I knew I had this. I knew I'd find a way, because in hindsight I always had. Except this time, it wasn't a pile of old sheets and textas I was using to make a Pokémon – it was something much bigger.

Over the next few months, I rebuilt SPP from the ground up. I became Steve Jobs – minus the receding hairline and the turtleneck. I threw myself into all the things I used to avoid – the stuff that terrified me: processes, numbers, systems. I finally looked at the financials I'd been too scared to touch, worried I'd uncover a mess I couldn't fix. But I did it anyway – I stopped hiding so I could show up. I hired incredible people – unicorns who had done this before and knew how to help.

And the biggest shift? I stopped being a people-pleaser. I stopped re-doing other people's work. I stopped putting everyone else's needs before mine. If people didn't follow the new way I gently called them on it (after apologising a million times – what? Baby steps). I learnt I could be firm but fair. And more importantly, I finally hired someone to manage the team so I could stick to the hat that suits me best: the *good cop creative*. Because let's be real – *bad cop* never suited me.

In interviews I was transparent in explaining that SPP can be a busy mess but that we were getting our shit together, and I wanted them to be part of the solution. This is a message I have always shared with my community and customers. We aren't planners for perfect people, we're planners for real people. For the messy minds of the world. Over the next few months, I hired six full-timers, knowing I could barely afford them, but betting it all on saving SPP, my family and me.

Sometimes you don't realise how heavy something is until you put it down. My backpack had well and truly fallen apart a long time ago, just like my Temu map which I threw in the bin where it belonged. I spent years trying to patch it together with threads and no needles, with the little resources and energy I had left. But I will never forget the moment I realised things didn't have to feel so hard, so heavy – that I didn't have to carry so much all the time, all on my own. And all it took was a simple Post-it note. It was a few weeks after Katie, our head of design, started. I had asked her for a selection of new fonts, which we could potentially use in our products. Barely thirty minutes later, I walked back to my desk to see a pile of neatly stacked papers. A Post-it note was stuck to the top that said 'ready for you' signed with a heart.

I stood there staring at it, as if a magic lamp had suddenly materialised. It sounds small but from where I came from and all I had done, I had to push back tears. Yes, I could ask for help, and help would come. I didn't have to do this – life, parenthood or business – alone. Slowly but surely, instead of being Steph who wore all the hats and did the roles of fourteen full-timers, I could just be me. I could do the role I was made for – create cool shit and connect with my community. Granted, when you're a boss you're still across it all, but I didn't have to do all the heavy lifting anymore. Or work out all the little details that add up to big wins or losses.

Honestly? The only reason I could write this book is because I have an amazing team and processes in place. This meant I could pass the stick-things they use in relays (again, we've established

I don't do sports), and pour my energy into writing. We mothers carry such a heavy mental load and not having to micro-manage my business felt like taking a bra off after a long day at the airport, filled with delays and screaming kids. It gave me more space to be the mum and wife I am meant to be. I want my girls to grow up, after watching their mum, believing they can do things differently. I want them to know their mum followed her heart. And although I had to dig us out of some sticky situations, I want them to know they never have to force themselves into a box that was never meant for them.

•

I'd dreamt of writing a book ever since I was six years old working on *The Dolphin Daily*. Before Dad passed, during a hospital visit, I told him so.

'What's it going to be about?' he asked.

Up until that point I didn't know. But in a moment of clarity, I said without a shadow of doubt, 'Me.'

'I bet it's going to be incredible, little friend.'

A part of me finally believed my story was worth telling, and that I was worth telling it. Although Dad and Nan are no longer in this world, I'm glad they got to see the beginning of the life I was unknowingly building. At times I was distracted by the cracks and the faults, but they got to see it all. See me. I will forever hold onto the memories of Dad walking through the warehouse, hands on hips, in awe of what his daughter had built; his face when he first saw Harper and became 'Pa'; and Nan's hands clapping whenever she visited or saw her great-granddaughters dance. I don't know what happens after we die, but I do know

Dad and Nan are the ones who gave me the strength to write this book. They are part of these pages, the book's inner heartbeat.

It's bittersweet achieving things and reaching new milestones without some of the people you love most to celebrate them with. Not being able to see their smiles; the way I know Dad's eyes would have crinkled with his childlike grin that matches mine, or how Nan would have yelled, 'You beauty!' when they found out their Steph was now an author. The best part is, I didn't chase this. I was offered a book deal for just being . . . me. Swear words, terrible jokes, being gravitationally challenged, my different take on the world, and most of all my messy mind in its entirety – that was enough for Penguin to get in touch. My dream publisher saw the purpose behind the perfect pantry, the magic buried beneath the mess. And through my journey, my soul scribbles, twenty tangents and way too many references to Chris Hemsworth . . . they saw that I could help people. My goal all along.

Writing this book has been one of the most heartbreaking, healing, exhausting and toughest things I've ever done. And I've been through some shit (some self-inflicted – whatevs, I'm human). Immersing myself anew in every heartache and trauma, then editing it all down to a respectable 93,000 words (from nearly 250,000) was one hell of a trip. One that came with a massive Uber Eats bill. I'm now approximately 80 per cent Indian food. But in true contradictory form, writing this book was also one giant exhale. A full-body sigh after years of holding it all in. Years of people-pleasing. Of shrinking. Of letting trolls win. Of saying 'yes' when I should have said 'no'. Of rushing through life, thinking I'd be worthy if I just reached another goal, did one more thing. Unknowingly turning my life into a race I never even entered.

But when you stop running, stop performing, and slow down so you can finally not just show up as you, but get to know you and understand you – that's when the magic appears out of the mess. This book forced me to sit still long enough (which is hard for me . . . #ADHDthings) to actually acknowledge all of me – every contradiction, every chapter. To see the full journey. And to bask in the magic I've created by being the mess that is Steph.

When we think of success, we often see dollar signs. I see the stability, the health, the freedom, and being able to be all of me and provide for my family all because of my crazy ideas. Now I get to support Ryan, as he has always supported me. And because my business is now sustainable, it doesn't come at the cost of my wellbeing.

I recently reread a journal entry from when I was at the health retreat in Queensland:

> *Slow mornings, dinners by the fire, playing with my girls without the nagging dread in the back of my mind that I need to be doing X, Y, Z.*
> *I want to be living, not just existing.*

Have I achieved that? I'll let you decide . . .

Right now there's a guitar leaning against the wall, one I started learning to play months ago. Next to me is an iPad with a half-finished sketch. The laundry's not folded, and the emails can wait until tomorrow – and I'm okay with that. And so is SPP. The girls are about to watch *Clueless*. I'm about to join them. There's music playing – not for a reel, not for content – just because it makes us happy. And somewhere on the kitchen bench is the planner that started it all, that helped me hold it together. It's open, worn, messy and lived-in. Just like me.

I often get messages from people who've bought my planners, but who are 'scared to write in them'. Why? Because they think their handwriting is too messy and they don't want to 'ruin them'. They're so ashamed of their 'mess', they won't even let themselves use the tool that's meant to help.

I get it. That used to be me.

But not anymore.

My family and I are living in the house Dad and Nan never got to see – our dream home. It's incredible, yet incredibly unfinished, cabinet handles pending. Some corners are chaotic, some are calm, some are a mess and some are pure magic and everything in between – it's a work in progress. Just like you and me. After I finish this book we'll continue to make this unfinished house a home, where the kids want to bring their friends over. Where we have sleepovers, and jump on the couches singing Taylor Swift as loud as we can. A place we recount our days as we giggle at bedtime. And you bet, we have huge windows that let the light in. While I'm not 'healed' from my PTSD, every joyful moment in this house, every moment I see my kids feeling safe, happy and most of all heard, helps me get closer.

At the time of writing, Harper and Willow are seven and nine, and I can be a present parent most of the time. I still scroll on my phone, lose my shit and, yes, they get fed chicken nuggets. We're not Susie with her homemade organic water (is that even a thing?) But I'm always working on myself, without turning it into obsession. I'm always showing my girls that adults are just giant kids with bigger bills, crow's feet and sore necks. In my girls, I see parts of me that were suppressed; their craziness, their untamed energy, their voices which are absolutely *not* inside voices. I'm going to continue using Nan as my guide. Slowly but surely my brain is learning that yelling and rage aren't part of the furniture.

The girls now go to my old school. Each day I send them off in the same uniform I wore, just a classroom away from the one I was in – with my friend Jenna. A full-circle moment. Except there is no history repeating itself; my girls are safe to be themselves, all parts of them. They aren't too much, they aren't ungrateful and they *do* deserve things. They certainly aren't bad people; they're humans with feelings and feelings that are safe with me. As long as I'm breathing I will listen to all they have to say and show them Mum isn't perfect, but she will do whatever it takes to make them feel safe, loved and heard.

As for our leading man, Ryan Pase – my golden retriever husband and teenage sweetheart/shithead – he still wakes up next to me as we have done since we were seventeen. The teenage boy who saved me, taking over the reins from Nan, has given me stability ever since. He's the ultimate 'girl dad', makeup smeared on his face, letting Harper and Willow put his hair in tiny ponytails. It has been incredible to watch the transformation from teenager to a father who has dreams of building a care home for people with disabilities. While our journey together has been far from perfect, I know the universe delivered him to me for a reason. He held me and I held him right back.

Ady's now thirty-six. He certainly showed those doctors a thing or two about not making it past the age of two. He still beats everyone at skolling a beer and refuses to get out of the pool; every Sunday he comes to our place for a swim. The girls adore their Uncle Ady and still share their toys with him . . . until he tries to keep them. It seems wrong to see Ady without Dad, and

I'm not sure that feeling will ever go away, but I feel closer to Dad when Ady's around.

My relationship with Mum remains difficult. There is little I have been able to say and share about this. At a certain point I realised I couldn't carry her anymore, her words or her actions. In some ways losing her was harder than losing Nan and Dad because physically she's still here. Becoming a mother made it impossible to keep justifying what I'd once accepted as a daughter. You realise a wound can't heal if it keeps being reopened. And so, I choose to heal. To release the labels given to me, long before I understood them. I don't know what the future holds but I have to find a version of peace with our relationship, and our story. But if there's one thing I've learnt, it's this: sometimes you have to love yourself enough to walk away. Even when it hurts. Even when it feels unnatural. Because you deserve peace. And you deserve love that doesn't come with conditions or eggshells stuck to the soles of your shoes.

So here I am, typing these final words, sitting at my desk in our unfinished home, sipping an iced coffee Ryan made me. I glance across my desk and, in my mind, Nan and Dad sit – smiling at me like they always did. Dad's soft hand reaches for mine and gives it a light squeeze. Nan gives me that knowing look, the one I know so well, wearing the watch of hers I wear when I need her most. 'I told you, Stephy,' she says with a wink. 'You were always going to do big things. You did well, kid. You showed 'em.'

I glance over at Dad, who looks just like he did before he got sick. 'This is incredible, Steph. I'm so proud of you, little friend.' Then he pauses and his stare deepens. 'Do you want to know why I always called you "The Steph?" Because only you could build this from nothing . . . only you, with that brain full of big ideas and a drive like I've never seen before. You always had that spark inside of you.'

I used to think other kids grew up effortlessly. That everyone else had a clear path. That women with perfect bodies had foolproof meal plans that didn't lead to depression. That mothers were handed an instruction manual on how to raise humans without messing them up. That my parents knew everything, and bosses had some secret uni degree I didn't know about.

But none of that exists.

All along, my *mess* was the *map*.

The path is you.

Before you close this book, there's something you should know. The day before this manuscript was due, I had a panic attack. One of many, to be honest. That's what happens when you speak up about things – and people – you once protected, and pour your heart out and prepare to let the world 'rate' your life. I was supposed to be uploading final files but instead, I was on the floor, still in my PJs. I pressed 'play' on one of my favourite songs, 'Vienna' by Billy Joel. I'd sung those lyrics a hundred times, especially when Dad got sick. As I sat there, I realised something: everything I'd written – the lessons, the healing, the wakeup calls – I was still learning. Still fumbling. Still feeling. And maybe that was the point. No more hiding in shame behind the shower curtain.

The world needs delusional dreamers. Doers. Distracted girls looking out the window in class, who grew into strong women who don't put up with shit – because their nan taught them better. We need women who create magic and communities out of their forgetfulness, their silliness and their vulnerability. We need women who make others feel seen, even when they're told to stay quiet, not step off the path, and not share their story. We need women who refuse to keep what happens behind closed doors and continue sharing anyway – because the biggest tragedy isn't saying too much . . . it's saying nothing at all.

This is a story of how you can turn a life of chaos into clarity. But it wasn't written *after* the mess – it was written right in the middle of it. Mid-panic attack. Mid-laundry pile. Mid-figuring-it-out. And more people need to see that. So no, I didn't write this book from a mountaintop, healed and perfect. I still give my all to my business, and my heart to my community. But now, when Harper and Willow run into my study and ask, 'Mum, can you play with us?' instead of saying, 'Just fifteen more minutes, Mummy needs to finish these emails,' I close my laptop, smile and say, 'Wanna watch me smash your father in *Mario Kart*?'

Signing off,

Steph the Mess (and fucking proud of it) xx

P.S. Slow down . . . you're doing fine. You always were.

P.P.S. Oh, and ADHD and me? We're friends now. It's your turn to make peace with all parts of you. Without them, you'd be someone else. And that, my beautiful soul, would be a tragedy.

Acknowledgements

Well, shitballs (always the lady, aren't I?), after writing 240,000 words this is one of the hardest parts to write. Crafting a book is no small feat and it truly takes an incredible army (and an offensive amount of carbs and caffeine) to pull it all together.

A huge thank you to Penguin Random House Australia for seeing the message behind my mess, the purpose beyond the labels and pantry. And of course to Ashwin, my legendary publisher, thank you for believing in me and being the incredible human that you are. Your patience and understanding are unmatched.

To Amy, thank you for holding me through this wild ride. Without your guidance (and masterful pruning of my original 240,000-word monster), this book wouldn't be what it is today. I wouldn't have made it through with my sanity (partly) intact. You are a gift to messy-minded writers.

To Rod, my editor, thank you for somehow trimming my outrageous word count without trimming my terrible jokes. Your comments made me laugh at 2 a.m. and made me trust the process . . . even when it was painful.

To my SPP team, without you feeding and caring for the beautiful blush beast that is Steph Pase Planners – and having the same passion and love for SPP as me – I wouldn't have been able to finish this book (or survive in general). Sarah, thank you for being my person. Your support off the page made all the difference. Lorren, thank you for being my work mum and for being one of the first to read my book and stop me spiralling. Katie, thank you for your beautiful words, which now live on this cover and in these pages; your heart is all over this project. And to the rest of my bloody amazing team, I adore you.

Mikhailia, my Kris Jenner, thank you for being my biggest hype-girl and seeing something in me even when I see a potato. You truly are the best momager with the biggest heart I could ask for.

To Aunty Rosie, thank you for always being there to answer the questions I probably should've remembered myself. Whether it was my struggles with PND, life, grief or just navigating this wild ride, thank you for always picking up the phone.

To my cousins Sammy, Laure and Katie, you're not just family . . . you're my sisters. Thank you for loving me through all seasons.

To my family and my beautiful in-laws, Tom and Carol, my earth parents, thank you for grounding me with your love and support. I adore you more than you'll ever know.

To my friends, Ash, Liv, Nick and the rest – you know who you are – thank you for sticking with me through my most boring era ever. And rooting for me anyways.

To Ady, my silent angel. You have inspired more of this book than you could ever know. You have the purest heart. Thank you for no longer ripping up my homework or clothing.

To Nan, my mother. My first home in human form. Without you I wouldn't be here today. Thank you for teaching me to see the silver lining, that you are as only as old as you feel (in this case I'm eighty), and that you can go through terrible things and still see the world as a good place.

To Dad, the most selfless man I knew. I did it! Told you I was going to write that book. I just wish you and Nan were here to see it. Thank you for all you did for Ady and our family.

To Ryan, my anchor, my constant. The teenage boy who took over from Nan and has kept me safe and feeling safe ever since. Thank you for staying up in sympathy until 3 a.m. while I wrote this book (couch naps aside, you're a legend) and literally peeling me off the floor after writing entirely too many words for one day. You proved to me from a young age that messy people *can* do magical things if they just back themselves. Thanks for walking unknown paths with me, even when it got scary. I love you.

To my girls, Harper and Willow. Thank you for being so patient while Mummy wrote her book to help people like her. I won't mention how every single day you came into my office asking, 'Am I born yet in the book?' But I *will* mention how proud of me you were when I finally finished writing (well, the first draft). You are the reason I fight so hard to pause, heal, grow and, more importantly, try again, even when it's far from perfect. I hope one day you read this (flick fast through how I met your father) and see how much of you lives in these pages – your untamed fire, laughter, curiosity, your mess, your magic.

And a huge thank you to *you*, my beautiful community. Whether you've been here since the pantry labels or joined somewhere along the way, I appreciate you more than words can say. If it weren't for you, I wouldn't be able to write this book. I hope my mess, my fuck-ups and my dark humour might help even one of you through. I'm so grateful to have found my people. In a world that keeps trying to sell us perfection, you chose real. Here's to the ones who colour outside the lines (on purpose), live life on their own terms and keep showing up – mess and all.

I wrote this for us.

Powered by Penguin

Looking for more great reads, exclusive content and book giveaways?

Subscribe to our weekly newsletter.

Scan the QR code or visit penguin.com.au/signup